Human-Computer Interaction Series

HCI is a multidisciplinary field focused on human aspects of the development of computer technology. As computer-based technology becomes increasingly pervasive—not just in developed countries, but worldwide—the need to take a human-centered approach in the design and development of this technology becomes ever more important. For roughly 30 years now, researchers and practitioners in computational and behavioral sciences have worked to identify theory and practice that influences the direction of these technologies, and this diverse work makes up the field of human-computer interaction. Broadly speaking it includes the study of what technology might be able to do for people and how people might interact with the technology. The HCI series publishes books that advance the science and technology of developing systems which are both effective and satisfying for people in a wide variety of contexts. Titles focus on theoretical perspectives (such as formal approaches drawn from a variety of behavioral sciences), practical approaches (such as the techniques for effectively integrating user needs in system development), and social issues (such as the determinants of utility, usability and acceptability).

Titles published within the Human-Computer Interaction Series are included in Thomson Reuters' Book Citation Index, The DBLP Computer Science Bibliography and The HCI Bibliography.

For further volumes:
http://www.springer.com/series/6033

William Sims Bainbridge

Personality Capture and Emulation

William Sims Bainbridge
Arlington, VA
USA

ISBN 978-1-4471-7075-4   ISBN 978-1-4471-5604-8 (eBook)
DOI 10.1007/978-1-4471-5604-8
Springer London Heidelberg New York Dordrecht

Contents

Chapter 1
Background

As people make greater and greater use of computers at work and in their daily lives, fragments of each person's identity infiltrate the global information system with potentially revolutionary consequences. Visionaries like Ray Kurzweil, Frank Kempelmann, and Robin Hanson have suggested that some time during this century people may become immortal by being computerized [1–4]. This may happen through uploading to the net, emulated as avatars in a world that has become largely virtual. Of course science fiction writers like Arthur C. Clarke, William Gibson, and John Brunner have long suggested this possibility, and it may be a false hope, given how limited our ability to simulate human cognition is after more than half a century of progress in artificial intelligence [5]. However, even very limited personality capture and emulation could have profound implications.

Personality capture is the process of entering substantial information about a person's mental and emotional functioning into a computer or information system, in principle sufficiently detailed to permit a somewhat realistic simulation. This term draws an analogy with the widely used technique called *motion capture*, in which the movements of a human being are entered into a computer, usually by some kind of machine vision system, so they can be used to program realistic images of people in movies and videogames. If motion capture records the motions of a person, personality capture records the emotions, attitudes, opinions, beliefs, values, habits, perceptions and preferences of a person.

The Leiden Institute of Advanced Computer Science once used *personality capture* in exactly the sense intended here, but the term has not yet become firmly rooted in the lexicons of either computer science or social science, and it's not currently used on the institute's website [6]. Altiris, a software company, used the term to refer to the process of migrating a person's files and software preference settings from one computer to another, and after Symantec acquired Altiris, this usage appeared on many pages of the Symantec website [7]. The abstract of a computer science journal article about modeling a person's interpretations of images begins: "Personalizing web search engines, a crucial issue nowadays, would obviously benefit from the system's ability to capture such an important aspect of a user's personality as

W. S. Bainbridge, *Personality Capture and Emulation,* Human-Computer Interaction Series,   1
DOI 10.1007/978-1-4471-5604-8_1, © Springer-Verlag London 2014

visual impressions and their communication." [8] Clearly, computer science is on the verge of adopting the term *personality capture*, and I suggest that social science consider doing so as well.

Some research connects personality capture to motion capture. For example, researchers have developed computer vision systems that can scan a person's facial expressions into a software system that performs *emotion extraction* to duplicate these expressions graphically in an electronic "clone." [9, 10] Several kinds of conventional software already perform limited forms of personality capture. For example, a person who wants his or her word processor to handle speech to text dictation must train the speech recognition software by reading long samples of text aloud, thereby capturing the parameters of his or her own unique voice. Whenever we set the preferences on complex software, we personalize it to some extent. Some recommender systems construct computer models of the individual's preferences, in order to target advertising more effectively, but incidentally preserving and emulating an aspect of the person.

Recognizing that human personality can express itself in many different modalities, and people are a collection of fragments as much as they are a unity, this book will explore many distinct technologies. It will show conclusively that some of them really do achieve personality capture and emulation, in a limited but significant manner. The full meaning of these technologies becomes apparent only when we imagine integrating them, to capture and emulate an entire personality. That not only presents huge scientific and engineering challenges, but also takes us some distance into the realms of fantasy.

1.1 A Question of Immortality

In the year 2001, which astronomers consider the first year of the twenty-first century and when the influential 1968 movie, *2001: A Space Odyssey* wrongly imagined that computers would be able to duplicate human intelligence, *Communications of the ACM* published a special issue on the next thousand years of computing. The first article, "Digital Immortality," was written not by a science fiction author, nor by a crazy pseudoscientist, but by two of the acknowledged leaders of the computer science profession, Gordon Bell and Jim Gray. They begin by noting that immortality is a spectrum of kinds and degrees of preservation, emulation, and activation of a human personality:

> Digital immortality, like ordinary immortality, is a continuum from enduring fame at one end to endless experience and learning at the other, stopping just short of endless life. Preserving your ideas is one-way immortality—allowing communication with the future. Endless experience and learning is two-way immortality—allowing you, or at least part of you, to communicate with the future in the sense that the artifact continues to learn and evolve. Current technology can extend corporal life for a few decades. Both one-way and two-way immortality require part of a person to be converted to information (cyberized) and stored

in a more durable media. We believe that two-way immortality, where one's experiences are digitally preserved and which then take on a life of their own, will be possible within this century. [11]

Gordon Bell's Wikipedia page summarizes his stunning but apparently conventional career: "An early employee of Digital Equipment Corporation (DEC) 1960–1966, Bell designed several of their PDP machines and later became Vice President of Engineering 1972–1983, overseeing the development of the VAX. Bell's later career includes entrepreneur, investor, founding Assistant Director of NSF's Computing and Information Science and Engineering Directorate 1986–1987, and researcher at Microsoft Research, 1995-present." [12]

Since co-authoring the article on cyberimmortality, Bell has worked on a project at Microsoft called MyLifeBits: "Gordon Bell has captured a lifetime's worth of articles, books, cards, CDs, letters, memos, papers, photos, pictures, presentations, home movies, videotaped lectures, and voice recordings and stored them digitally. He is now paperless, and is beginning to capture phone calls, IM transcripts, television, and radio." [13] At lunch one day I asked him if the goal of the project was to develop tools that would help ordinary people capture their life's experiences, and he replied that Microsoft did not intend to produce software of this kind. On a different occasion, a colleague with extensive expertise in the area of digital preservation called MyLifeBits an example of "write-only memory"—a joke implying that nobody would ever access all the data Bell was saving about his life. However, as inspiration and a demonstration project, MyLifeBits is a significant contribution to the development of cyberimmortality.

According to his own Wikipedia page, Jim Gray was "an American computer scientist who received the Turing Award in 1998 'for seminal contributions to database and transaction processing research and technical leadership in system implementation.'" [14] The barriers to a technological response to human mortality are reflected in the mystery of Gray's disappearance in the Pacific Ocean early in 2007. He had sailed in his yacht to scatter his mother's ashes, then vanished, and extreme computer-assisted attempts to find his boat failed utterly.

A fundamental question in talking about immortality is what you actually consider your own personal identity to be. Are you your body? Or are you your unique attitudes, opinions and beliefs? Your memories? Your deeds, reputation, and legal status as a citizen, or the social roles you play? Are you a unique locus of transcendental consciousness, or an already immortal soul? Technological preservation can be more successful with some of these than with others, and you will have to decide which are most important to you personally.

From one perspective, even a perfect duplicate of you, capable of self-awareness and of impersonating you in public, is not really you. William F. Temple's 1951 novel, *Four-Sided Triangle*, concerns the duplication of a woman so that the two men who love her will each have a copy, leading of course to tragic results [15]. If the woman had put her copy into cryonic suspension, we would still be reluctant to say she had found a way to preserve herself—her very own unique self.

We already possess technology that can allow aspects of your personality to influence the world in a dynamic manner, even after you are no longer living in it. This falls short of true immortality, because you (as conventionally defined) will not be conscious of it. Your evaluation of the possibilities for future cybernetic immortality will depend, therefore, not merely upon your estimate of the technical possibilities but also upon your personal conception of yourself. In their book, *Infinite Reality*, avatar researchers Jim Blascovich and Jeremy Bailenson report that people do identify with their computerized representations, the more so the more realistic they are. A chapter titled "Eternal Life" lays out some of the future possibilities, and their book also devotes a page to one of my own efforts, described here in the following chapter [16].

Already, it is possible to place a deceased person's record in a computer database that can participate in social life by advising living people and serving as a virtual friend. In time, it might be possible to incorporate a recorded personality in a robot—for example, a space probe or a cyborg astronaut helping to colonize the galaxy. Eventually, it may be possible to resurrect the personality in a cloned body that is identical to the original, whether on this world or on a distant planet that has been terraformed to make it livable.

However, it is crucial to understand that personality capture research can be tremendously valuable even if it never fulfills these grand visions, and a few general principles can focus our near-term efforts in this direction. A good starting point is to realize that human-centered computing has connections to the social and cognitive sciences, but has not drawn upon them nearly as vigorously as would be needed. At many points, this book will highlight connections that others have already made, but also suggest new connections.

Roughly twenty years ago, when cognitive science achieved liberation from psychology, it became obvious that personality psychology and cognitive science were equally important fields, that must be combined to understand an individual. But it was also clear that they must work in partnership with social psychology and sociology, because every individual lives within a society and cannot be fully understood in isolation from it. Thus, this book will draw upon a wide variety of existing research, to make the necessary connections between schools of thought and methodological approaches, yet will also introduce many new studies—many brief pilot studies but also a few more extensive research projects. We will consider many principles of analysis and design, which may be combined in many ways, but one set of four desiderata for emulations provides a basis for developing capture methodologies:

Fidelity: The emulation must be true to the essence of the original person, but there are multiple ways of defining that essence.

Integrity: Not only must the parts of the person be unified, but the person must also be integrated into a community.

Utility: The emulation must serve valuable purposes for other people, not only to justify its existence but also as a criterion to evaluate its quality.

Durability: The information captured about the person must be preserved indefinitely, but emulated flexibly so that it can harmonize with changing world conditions.

Before we introduce more principles, or consider such ideas in any depth, we need some form of empirical background to provide an intellectual context. The two following sections will achieve this by looking backward in time, at two major scientific approaches to personality capture that were developed to some degree separately decades ago, although they did not explicitly set capture and emulation as their goals. The first can be called *depth psychology*, including but not limited to Psychoanalysis, and exemplified by a team of eminent researchers at Harvard University in the 1940s and 1950s. The second is *questionnaire research*, exemplified by the General Social Survey that has surveyed American adults periodically, beginning in 1972. Many of the other approaches described in this book stand between these two pillars of social and behavioral science, for example psychological tests designed to measure surface manifestations of depth psychology, but administered through questionnaires.

1.2   Depth Psychology

Whatever we may think of Psychoanalysis, it placed a great emphasis on the early life history of its clients, and the implications of those early days for today. Sigmund Freud and his disciples conducted what amounted to free-flowing interpretive interviews with their clients, as the central activity in a treatment course intended to resolve neurotic conflicts. Thus, most people who were psychoanalyzed were patients seeking help with mental or emotional problems, but Freud hoped that he was learning truths about humanity in general, and that his techniques were applicable to everyone. Indeed, each aspiring psychoanalyst was expected to undergo a didactic analysis with a senior colleague, even with Freud himself. It is entirely possible that for some people Psychoanalysis was an effective treatment, but its discoveries might have been spurious, because indoctrination into a philosophy of life can provide meaning for clients who previously lacked a framework for organizing their feelings [17].

Freud's theories, his claimed research findings, and even the reliability of the interview procedures came into question from critics, especially from therapists belonging to the behaviorist school of thought, which discounted the significance of a client's early life experiences, and placed its emphasis on recent conditioning of the individual by contingencies in the environment [18–20]. An especially useful example for personality capture is the case of Little Hans, sometimes called Little John in English translations, a five-year-old boy whose father was one of Freud's associates. Freud examined the case in some depth in a 1909 paper, then provided the following summary in his book *Totem and Taboo*:

> I reported the "Analysis of the Phobia of a five-year-old Boy" which the father of the patient had put at my disposal. It was a fear of horses as a result of which the boy refused to go on the street. He expressed his apprehension that the horse would come into the room and bite him. It proved that this was meant to be the punishment for his wish that the horse should fall over (die). After assurances had relieved the boy of his fear of his father,

it proved that he was fighting against wishes whose content was the absence (departure or death) of the father. He indicated only too plainly that he felt the father to be his rival for the favor of the mother, upon whom his budding sexual wishes were by dark premonitions directed. He therefore has the typical attitude of the male child to its parents which we call the "Oedipus complex" in which we recognize the central complex of the neuroses in general. Through the analysis of "Little John" we have learnt a fact which is very valuable in relation to totemism, namely, that under such conditions the child displaces a part of its feelings from the father upon some animal. [21]

First, note that Freud is not so much interested in the unique personality characteristics of Little Hans, but in how he illustrates the *Oedipus complex*, which Freud argued was a universal condition of varying severity among human males, because of the natural structure of the family. The son is the rival with his father for the sexual affections of his mother, leading to a desire to remove the father from the competition, even killing him. However the father is powerful, and the conflict may thus lead to castration anxieties in the son. Such feelings cause inner conflict, so sons repress them, in consequence causing even more psychological tensions, which Psychoanalysis is designed to cure by bringing the repressed feelings to conscious awareness. Thus, the case of Little Hans is first and foremost an advertisement for Psychoanalysis, asserting its fundamental diagnosis of neurosis and suggesting that even only a little bit of treatment, if administered in a timely manner, can be beneficial.

Second, the paragraph quoted above was part of a book that sought to understand much about early human history, including the totemism and taboo of the title. Bronislaw Malinowski, one of the leading cultural anthropologists of Freud's period, disputed Freud's fundamental assumption that patriarchal family structures are universal. In *Sex and Repression in Savage Society* and other publications, Malinowski focused on matrilineal societies, in which fathers were less important in the family structure, the mother's brother was more important, and sexual repression was less of a factor [22]. In modern societies, where divorce is common and family dynamics vary greatly from household to household, we might argue that many different complexes may exist, and one cannot assume how significant each one is for a particular individual, until that person has been studied very closely.

Third, as Freud's behaviorist opponents argued strenuously, Freud had not in fact studied Little Hans closely, and thus was in no position to judge which of many factors might have caused the boy's phobia of horses. Joseph Wolpe and Stanley Rachman thought it was more likely the boy had been traumatized by objectively frightening episodes involving horses he had experienced, including one in which a horse pulling a cart had fallen down and was killed [23]. These particular behaviorists were selling their own kind of treatment, behavior therapy, so we cannot place any special credence in their interpretations either. The fact that today we know the real identity of Little Hans—or Herbert Graf (1904–1973)—means we can place this legendary character in a realistic context. He even has his own Wikipedia page, because he rose to prominence in adulthood. That page explains:

This was one of just a few case studies which Freud published. In his introduction to the case, he had in the years prior to the case been encouraging his friends and associates, including the parents of Little Hans, to collect observations on the sexual life of children in order to help him develop his theory of infantile sexuality. Thus Hans' father had been sending notes about the child's development to Freud before Little Hans developed his fear of horses. At the age of five Herbert became a patient of Sigmund Freud (1856–1939), who identified him in his writings as "Little Hans". He was the subject of Freud's early but extensive study of castration anxiety and the Oedipus complex. Freud saw Herbert only once and did not analyze the child himself, but rather supervised the child's father (Max Graf) who carried out the analysis and sent extensive notes to Freud. In the published version, Hans' father's account is abridged and punctuated by Freud's own comments. [24]

Apparently, in adulthood, Graf had no memory of having been psychoanalyzed, and many other episodes of different kinds shaped his personality. The son of an author and musicologist, Little Herbert—if we may thus edit his pseudonym—became a leading producer of grand operas, first in his native Austria and then in the United States. So one way in which his relationship with his father influenced his personality was in the field of music, where he gained skills and interests rather than neuroses. Wider events in the world outside the family also had an effect, as his move to America was stimulated by Nazi anti-Semitism, which not only threatened his life in a way that conflict with his father never did, but as a simple practical matter cost him his job. Freud is certainly right in general that early childhood experiences are important, and the behaviorists may be right that recent circumstances are important, but so are all the other experiences from birth to now, as well as innate characteristics of the person's brain. Personality capture must be done in full awareness that humans do not fit into a few narrowly defined categories, but on occasion the theory of one or another psychologist may fit an individual—naturally, rather than being imposed by a therapist who benefits from having a salable ideology.

1.3   A Wider Depth Psychology

Despite the failings of Psychoanalysis, there are several reasons to see merit in the general approach. First of all, Freud's disciples quickly dissented from a number of his assumptions, competing with each other to establish their own brands of therapy, which had the effect of generalizing the method so that it need not be practiced in a biased manner [25, 26]. Second, several potentially productive lines of research were opened up, beginning with the controversial but intriguing analysis of dreams, the free association technique that sought to trace the conceptual connections in a person's mind, and the documentation of specific episodes in the person's life that may have been formative [27]. Third, in their chaotic competition to define the new field, Freud's disciples generated many alternative theories, for example arguing that hunger for power, rather than repressed sexual desires, was the prime motivator for some people [28].

By the middle of the twentieth century a number of research projects had been devised, built upon the diverse history of Psychoanalysis but incorporating a variety of other kinds of data and methodology, that had the potential to render it more objective, or at the very least using it to explore a number of directions that psychological research might take.

One such approach was employing psychoanalytic methods to understand the personality of an historical individual, on the basis of written records without the opportunity to conduct interviews with the person. Perhaps the most respected example was the book *Young Man Luther* by Erik Erikson, which argued that Martin Luther's form of Protestantism was a resolution of his personal identity crisis, a theory having implications for personality capture because it concerns how psychological stresses can trigger rapid personality change [29, 30]. A more controversial example was *The Mind of Adolf Hitler* by Walter C. Langer, written under contract to the Office of Strategic Services during the Second World War, which advised the American government about the mentality of its chief enemy, and thus might have provided bad advice, given that it contained many factual errors [31]. One virtue of these *psychohistories*, as Erikson called them, is precisely that their subjects are public figures, and thus other scholars have access to the same information and can verify or dispute their findings.

When Psychoanalysis arrived at Harvard University at the beginning of the 1930s, it separated itself from Freud's authority and sought to incorporate new insights and other perspectives [32]. Renamed *personology* and often using *psychobiography* as a central method of research, it sought to establish a new paradigm for personality psychology, more scientific and influential than the somewhat haphazard explorations that had gone before [33]. Central to this effort was Henry Murray, who established a tradition of trying to understand specific individuals through a comprehensive approach, among many other things guiding Langer in his project. Murray is commemorated at Harvard by The Henry A. Murray Research Archive, which today has over 100 terabytes of diverse social science data. Originally hosted at Radcliffe College, the women's institution historically associated with Harvard and which merged with it in stages ending in 1999, the archive features psychological data about women's lives in its core, called A Center for the Study of Lives:

> Raw and computer-accessible data from over 270 studies including some small, in-depth case studies, larger studies with open- and closed-ended interviews, and national surveys emphasizing panel (longitudinal) data on changing life experiences of American women. Original protocols may include interview transcripts, open-ended questionnaire items, personality tests, and psychological projective tests. Data sets also include publications based on the original data collections, blank copies of the measures, computer-accessible data with accompanying codebooks. Major subject areas include life patterns of educated women, including work situations and career aspirations, women in blue-collar occupations, family structure, physical and mental health, satisfaction and personal values, self-esteem, attitudes and orientations, aging and retirement, decision-making, role conflict, sex role socialization, and social networks and support systems. Collections include data from mostly female subjects from age three to the elderly. The center also has two specialty archives focusing on mental health, one of which includes over 25 data sets drawing from samples that include ethnic and racial minorities. [34]

One of Murray's studies of a specific individual concerned a very shy man who fantasized about flying and whom Murray surmised suffered from an *Icarus complex* [35]. Many ambitious psychoanalysts sought to discover their own alternatives to or variants of the Oedipus complex, in hopes of achieving fame in their profession. Icarus, of course, was the mythological son of Daedalus who was given artificial wings made by his genius father, but told not to fly too close to the sun. Icarus ignored this advice, perhaps wishing to prove himself superior to his father, and fell to his death in consequence.

Murray himself is a controversial figure, who like Freud may have used his theories and methods to dominate other people, rather than learn the truth about them. In recent years, well after Murray's death, a bizarre controversy arose when it was revealed that the "Unibomber" terrorist, Theodore Kaczynski, had been one of Murray's research subjects in a study that imposed severe psychological stress on the research subjects—far more intense that would be permitted under today's rules for treatment of human research subjects—conceivably causing the psychopathology that led Kaczynski to murder three people and injure two dozen others [36, 37]. Whatever the truth of these claims, Harvard has sealed the records for Kaczynski, and researchers no longer have access to them [38].

The history of Psychoanalysis is replete with examples in which the analyst behaved in a self-serving fashion, or even displayed symptoms of his own neurosis in treating the neuroses of his clients, yet that superficially discrediting fact really provides more evidence for the importance of depth psychology. The challenge becomes how to do it in a controlled, ethical manner, maximizing the probability that results will be valid and minimizing the potential for harm. The way Harvard implicitly achieved this in the late 1930s was by bringing together many psychologists, most of whom seem to have been free of character flaws like those Murray possessed in abundance. Together, they assembled a toolkit of methods and theories that had the effect of preventing any of them from imposing one rigid interpretation on the people they studied. Functioning as a community of scholars, they seem to have implicitly developed an ethic that constrained their treatment of their research subjects.

The one ethical issue we might today see in their publications concerns privacy. They often published extensive reports about single individuals, always applying a pseudonym to their subject but providing so much information that the real names might have been deduced by friends and family members of the subject. Furthermore, the reports often contained rather intimate criticisms of the subject, who might have become severely embarrassed by reading, given they would always recognize themselves beneath the pseudonyms.

After Murray himself, one of the most prominent members of the Harvard personality group was Robert W. White, whose influential 1952 book *Lives in Progress* used reports on only two men and one woman to illustrate the general principles of human personality [39]. These were not neurotics given supposedly curative treatments, as in Freud's work, but presumably normal people who experienced considerable psychological change—perhaps naturally from environmental events and personal maturation—and White stressed the dynamic nature of personality. His preface identifies four main principles of his approach:

1. He focused on a small number of individuals because it is necessary to go into great depth in a case study, and to understand the life of the individual in its totality.
2. He studied these individuals on his own initiative, rather than studying people who came to him for help during periods of unusual difficulty, and studied each at two points in time to observe natural evolution of personality.

3. He favored "a broadly inclusive approach to the understanding of lives" (p. iv), on the reasonable assumption that lives and personalities are complex and seldom can be understood in only one way or explained in terms of a single factor.
4. He stressed the natural growth of a human personality, considering the person to be an active agent in a dynamic environment, and thus normally capable of significant change rather than being the prisoner of subconscious conflicts acquired during childhood.

These points all seem quite reasonable, but they do raise a serious question about the goals of the research. Earlier in its history, the purpose of depth psychology was to identify complexes or subconscious conflicts, and giving them fancy names like Oedipus and Icarus, thereby claiming significant scientific discoveries. But if each personality was the unique result of many complicated factors operating in different ways over time, what general discoveries could be made? Of course, for us here the goal is different, to capture personalities in all their complexity. But the path Harvard personology took in the 1950s seemed to be a rush toward an abyss of ambiguity.

One study that stood out above others, *Opinions and Personality*, was co-authored by White along with M. Brewster Smith and Jerome S. Bruner [40]. Ten men were studied not only to understand their personalities, but to see how personality might shape opinions toward Russia, or the Soviet Union as it then called itself. Most of the data were collected during 1947, when the wartime alliance between the US and Russia was turning decidedly sour. In 1950, a team headed by Theodor W. Adorno published *The Authoritarian Personality*, based on an amalgam of Psychoanalysis and neo-Marxist thinking that was to become quite popular for years afterward, explaining the appeal of Fascism in terms of the psychopathology of its followers [41]. The Adorno team had suffered from the European holocaust, and thus had an understandable motivation to find a clear explanation for it that might prevent a recurrence, but its scientific rigor is questionable and it has been misused for decades to accuse political conservatives of psychopathology. Smith, Bruner, and White did not take an ideologically strict position in their study of opinions about Russia, and their rather careful and far less spectacular book was not published until 1956, nearly a decade after they began their research.

The data about the ten men have been archived at the Murray Center, along with comparable data from 46 other people studied in other research projects White was involved in:

Data collected from some or all of these participants include a written autobiography; extensive interviews covering family, parents' personalities, early memories, school and college history, social relationships, health, sex, religious beliefs, emotions, abilities and talents, current interests, ethical values, opinions and attitudes, and general outlook on life; standardized tests such as the Wechsler-Bellevue Adult Intelligence Test, the Vygotsky Concept Formation Values, Rorschach, Thematic Apperception Test (TAT), a sentence completion test, and a free association hour. In addition, for older participants and in follow-up studies, extensive interviews concerning relationships with parents and siblings, marriage and family, childbearing, occupational satisfactions and frustrations, social life, and personal values and ideals were conducted. [42]

The use of standardized tests, along with interviews, forms a bridge from the purely qualitative explorations of depth psychology through the personality questionnaires of social psychology to the survey research methods of sociology. The reason for using this range of methods is not merely to capture a variety of aspects of the individual, but to place the individual in the social and cultural context that shaped the individual and will be the environment for emulating his or her personality.

1.4   Questionnaire Research

Public opinion polls and scientific questionnaire surveys produce data describing large numbers of people, but the fundamental unit of analysis is the individual respondent. Anyone who has responded to a major scientific survey can be confident that his or her data will be preserved for decades—perhaps for centuries—in well-maintained archives, providing insights and even advice to future generations. Here we will introduce some fundamental concepts about questionnaire immortality, using the General Social Survey (GSS) as our primary example [43]. As it happens, I managed federal funding for this enduring research project throughout much of the 1990s, and have used the data myself in many studies, but this does not give me any advantage over the reader, because anyone may access the data online, and an absolutely vast scientific literature exists, documenting the methodology and findings [44].

Every year or two since 1972, well designed GSS questionnaires have been administered to reasonably representative samples of American adults, repeating many questions to chart changes over time, but also adding many temporary modules this year or that, focusing on special topics. To begin here, I have drilled into the 1972 data to find the oldest man and oldest woman who responded to the questionnaire. I do not know their names or identities, and will perhaps disrespectfully here call them Geezer and Crone. The names of questionnaire respondents are typically held confidential, and sometimes erased from the database altogether. I use these names merely to suggest that in future a person's name could be reassociated with questionnaire data after death, just as the real names in the US census become part of the public record after 72 years.

Indeed, of the 1,613 GSS respondents in 1972, only one man and one woman fell in the most senior age category, "89 or above." Thus they were probably born at the beginning of the 1880s. If they were alive today, they would be around 130 years old, so we can reasonably deduce that both of them have passed away. Coincidentally, both of them lived in the South Atlantic region of the United States, he in a rural town of only about 2,000 population, and she in a suburb of 46,000. He was a member of the Methodist church, while she was a Unitarian. Their responses to some of the other questions are shown in Table 1.1.

Table 1.1 is intended not merely to show that much personal information about Geezer and Crone has been preserved, but that the different pieces of information belong to very different categories or dimensions of each person's life and personality. Of course, the facts given are just the slimmest of hints. Crone married at age 17, was divorced or separated at some point in her married life, and now considers herself to be a widow. Clearly, we would need a vast amount of additional information to gain real insights into her experience of married life, but at least these facts would be a starting point if she were alive today and we could interview her or give her a much more extensive questionnaire. The questions about marriage remind us that people are not isolated phenomena, like comets floating in outer space, but belong to communities of people, and social relations are among a person's most formative experiences.

Geezer had four children, and Crone had just one. The experience of "having" a child is, of course, different for men and women, and we could imagine many more questions we might ask about how each individual experienced the reproductive process. He, also, came from a slightly larger family, one of eight children—himself plus seven brothers or sisters—while she was one of five. Yet both have come to the view that two children is the ideal number. These simple facts should remind us that people are not just repositories of experience, but judge their experiences in different ways. In effect, he is saying that he had too many children, while she implies she had too few. Or perhaps both of them mean that they had too many siblings, and just one sibling would have been ideal. Or, perhaps they are talking about the number of children that other people in their community should have, about the right number to sustain the population at its current level.

One GSS question asked: "If you were asked to use one of four names for your social class, which would you say you belong in: the lower class, the working class, the middle class, or the upper class?" Geezer said he was working class—and people tend to avoid the lower class option—while Crone said she was middle class. Subjective social class has potential ideological as well as factual aspects. For example, a wealthy Marxist might claim to be a member of the working class, while even poor ordinary Americans may like to think of themselves as middle class. Therefore, the GSS researchers used a second way to measure social class, asking the respondents to name their primary occupation, and then recoding that name as a coefficient from a table of the typical social prestige of people having various occupations. The procedures for developing occupational prestige scores are extremely demanding, and lifetimes of social science effort have going into that work [45, 46]. Here we see that indeed Crone has a higher occupational prestige score than Geezer, in line with her claim of membership in the middle class.

Seven attitudinal questions follow, showing a good deal of disagreement between Geezer and Crone, but they agree the courts should be more harsh, and that a wife should not work if her husband can support her. On the other issues, Crone seems much more liberal than Geezer, although the question about school segregation may not be as salient today as it was back in 1972. Indeed, all opinion items must be understood in terms of the conditions of the period in which the questions were asked, and within a larger ideological context. The GSS included a complex

Table 1.1 Illustrative responses of the two oldest GSS respondents in 1972

Question	Geezer	Crone
Sex	Male	Female
Race	White	White
Labor force status	Retired	Retired
Marital status	Widowed	Widowed
Age when first married	21	17
Ever been divorced or separated	No	Yes
Number of children	4	1
Number of brothers and sisters	7	4
Ideal number of children	2	2
Subjective class identification	Working class	Middle class
Occupational prestige	14.5	23.5
In general, do you think the courts in this area deal too harshly or not harshly enough with criminals?	Not harsh enough	Not harsh enough
Do you think most people would try to take advantage of you if they got a chance, or would they try to be fair?	Take advantage	Fair
Would you say that most of the time people try to be helpful, or that they are mostly just looking out for themselves?	Looking out for themselves	Helpful
If your party nominated a woman for President, would you vote for her if she were qualified for the job?	No	Yes
Do you approve or disapprove of a married woman earning money in business or industry if she has a husband capable of supporting her?	Disapprove	Disapprove
Do you think white students and (negro/black) students should go to the same schools or to separate schools?	Separate schools	Same schools
Should a book against churches and religion be removed from your public library?	Remove	Not remove
In 1968 presidential election...	Voted for Nixon	Did not vote
Generally speaking, do you usually think of yourself as a Republican, Democrat, Independent, or what?	Republican, and strong	Republican, but not strong
How often do you read the newspaper—every day, a few times a week, once a week, less than once a week, or never?	Never	Every day
Educational attainment	Not high school grad	Not high school grad
Highest year of school completed	0	11
Highest year of school completed by mother	9	8
Highest year of school completed by father	9	No answer
In general, what was the respondent's attitude toward the interview?	Friendly and eager	Cooperative but not particularly interested

battery of items about tolerance of "radical" viewpoints, of which one was: "There are always some people whose ideas are considered bad or dangerous by other people. For instance, somebody who is against churches and religion... If some people in your community suggested a book he wrote against churches and religion should be taken out of your public library, would you favor removing this book or not?" This battery specifically references the views of the surrounding community, rather than focusing exclusively on the opinion of the individual respondent.

Despite his opposition to school integration, and his residence on the South Atlantic region of the country, Geezer did not vote for George Wallace in the 1968 presidential election, but for Richard Nixon. Despite her apparently more liberal views, Crone did not vote for Herbert Humphrey, and indeed did not vote at all. Of course, our views of Nixon take into account his resignation, and all the revelations that precipitated it, which had not yet taken place in 1972. Thus, only with care and historical awareness can we place the responses of these two people in an appropriate context of meaning. Both considered themselves to be Republicans, but he a stronger one than she. She read a newspaper every day, while he never read newspapers. Of course already by 1972, many people got their news from television, and today many get their news from the Internet, but we can infer that she was better informed than he.

The pair's responses to four questions about educational attainment raise questions we wish we could ask them. Neither graduated from high school, although her 11 years of school would have brought her to the threshold of graduation. He claimed zero years of schooling yet said both his parents completed grade school. This was not impossible, for a boy growing up in the 1880s and 1890s, and is consistent with his never reading newspapers. Did he answer the questions incorrectly, or did he have an extremely deprived childhood? We shall never know. When I saw that she had failed to answer the question about her father's education, I checked a question about the family they were living with at age 16. Geezer had lived with both parents, while Crone lived just with her mother, implying she may not have known much about her father, and had no answer to give about his education.

The final row of Table 1.1 is a question answered by the interviewer, who came to the respondent's home and usually spent ninety minutes administering the questionnaire verbally. Geezer gave the most positive impression, and Crone's was the second-most favorable of four standard responses. The other two available to the interviewer on the questionnaire were "impatient and restless" and "hostile." This item illustrates two facts. First, people's answers to questions are at least partly an expression of their mood at the moment, and they might have given a different answer in a different mood. Second, surveys can observe behavior, as well as relying entirely upon self-report judgments from the person under examination. Both of the points place the question-answer process in a social context, as does the fact that questionnaire data are generally analyzed in the aggregate, rather than focusing on single respondents as we have done here.

1.5   Subcultures of Survival

Having compared two individuals, we can now use items from the General Social Survey to compare what amount to two subcultures, in a way that properly illustrates how complex, and indeed ambitious, questionnaire survey research can become. A battery of ten questions included in the GSS in the 1983–1984 period concerned conceptualizations of the afterlife, and thus are highly relevant for this book. What do people hope—or fear—existence after death would be like? At the beginning of the afterlife battery, the interviewer would read these words to the respondent: "Of course, no one knows exactly what life after death would be like, but here are some ideas people have had. How likely do you feel each possibility is? Would you say very likely, somewhat likely, not too likely, or not likely at all?" Table 1.2 gives the percentage of at least 2,374 GSS respondents saying each one was very likely, along with data from a questionnaire based on the GSS I administered to 1,025 members of an unusual religious group.

Table 1.2 arranges the 10 conceptions of the afterlife in descending order of how many GSS respondents considered each description to be likely. Technological immortality, if indeed the term comes to have real meaning in coming years, cannot promise union with God. However it could offer some semblance of each of the next four benefits, at least in some metaphoric sense. A minimal definition of union with loved ones would be having one's data preserved in the same archive as data from those loved ones. Words like *peace, tranquility, intellectual* and *spiritual* suggest not only subjective feelings—which may or may not be achievable—but also transcendence of material conditions which information to some degree possesses. In any case, we might take this list of 10 conceptions of the afterlife as a preliminary list of goals for personality capture and emulation, at least some of which might be plausible.

The other data in the table come from a questionnaire study I carried out with a very unusual religious group that calls itself The Family but journalists and others often called the Children of God (CoG). The second paragraph of my book about them offers enough perspective to indicate they were a very distinctive subculture, that logically would have different views of the afterlife from the people polled in the General Social Survey:

> The Family, or Children of God, is among the most vilified religious movements to arise in twentieth-century America. It is also among the most innovative, and it has attracted great interest among journalists and scholars alike. Born in California in the late 1960s, the movement burst out of the United States to send missionaries across the entire world. For a decade, it experimented with a sexual ministry and still today practices sexual sharing among committed adult members. They believe they are in contact with the spirit world, and the majority of them think they have channeled messages from the beyond. Surviving without regular jobs, educating their children outside of schools, they live in hundreds of small communes in dozens of nations. [47]

A total of 1,025 members filled out a long questionnaire that drew most of its items from the General Social Survey, to permit comparison of this group with the general public. As social scientists might expect, the result showed a mixture of similarities and differences, rather than placing the group beyond the pale. It is a functioning subculture, many of whose members live satisfying lives—as I observed during extensive field ethnography of the group—while belonging to a subculture with distinctive beliefs and practices.

The first thing to note about Table 1.2 is that on average members of the Children of God considered the ten descriptions of the afterlife to be 54.1 % "very likely,"

Table 1.2 Beliefs about the afterlife among GSS respondents and the Children of God (CoG)

	Very likely		CoG factor loadings		
	GSS	CoG	Factor 1	Factor 2	Factor 3
Union with God	79.2%	93.1%	0.64		
Reunion with loved ones	71.0%	97.7%	0.58		
A life of peace and tranquility	64.9%	65.4%			0.49
A place of loving intellectual communion	52.2%	72.7%	0.56		
A spiritual life, involving our mind but not our body	46.3%	7.2%		0.71	
A paradise of pleasure and delights	35.6%	86.5%	0.67		
A life like the one here on earth only better	28.9%	72.0%			0.65
A life without many things which make our present life enjoyable	20.9%	4.6%		0.62	
A life of intense action	11.8%	41.7%			0.71
A pale, shadowy form of life, hardly life at all	5.2%	0.1%		0.52	
Mean across all 10	41.6%	54.1%			

compared with 41.6% for members of the American public surveys by the GSS. This might just reflect greater religious faith, but if we scan the ten pairs of percentages were see that a couple of differences stand out. The Children of God are more than twice as likely as the GSS respondents to believe the afterlife is a paradise of pleasure and delights and a life like the one here on earth only better. They are a millenarian group that anticipate Christ will soon return to the Earth to preside over a terrestrial paradise, and they consider consensual sex to be a spiritual experience. This is a major doctrinal difference with the majority, as well as expressing a more sensual definition of spirituality.

However, people in all cultures and subcultures possess a degree of individuality. For example, when Robert B. Edgerton surveyed members of four traditional east African societies about their views on mental illness, he found not only four somewhat different indigenous theories of psychology, but also significant variation within each society, plus differences in how homogeneous the viewpoints tended to be in each society [48]. In my field research inside the Children of God, I observed a good deal of individual variation, but not a clear split between factions, although one apparently existed earlier in the group's history when some Latin American communes asserted a degree of independence. The three columns on the right side of Table 1.2 use a method called *factor analysis* to explore the possibility that the ten items represent three dimensions of disagreement among the CoG respondents.

Many statistical methods exist for clustering questionnaire items on the basis of similar patterns of response, but factor analysis is the oldest method still in use, familiar to practitioners in the social and psychological sciences, and convenient for the uses I will put it to in this book. It is not necessary to understand the computational or mathematical details, and indeed there are many options within factors analysis. The basic idea is this. The computer calculates the correlation coefficients between all possible pairs of the variables, then goes through procedures to see how well it can identify dimensions of variation running through all the responses that can reduce the data and the correlation matrix to a simpler model. In technical terms, I told the computer to use the principle components method and use the varimax rotation method for the number of factors having eigenvalues greater than 1. More simply put, this was an exploratory analysis that discovered three dimensions of variation that mapped the data pretty well.

The development of factor analysis goes way back well over a century to Charles Spearman's research to determine whether human intelligence had a single dimension of variation, and was later used to chart multiple dimensions of personality variation [49]. If it had been invented much more recently it would be described as a kind of machine learning within the wider field of artificial intelligence. Thus one reason for occasionally presenting a factor analysis here is to point out that computers are capable of abstracting deeper meaning from raw data, something artificial intelligence must be able to accomplish if it is to emulate human beings. Alone, factor analysis can accomplish only part of that task, so now we must use the human mind to achieve a degree of understanding.

The results of this factor analysis are quite nice. It divides the 10 items into three nearly equal groups of 4, 3, and 3 items. Clustering methods differ in terms of whether they conceptualize their results as dimensions, the typical way with factor analysis, or as groups of items, but for present purposes we can think both ways. The numbers in the columns are factor loadings, analogous to a correlation coefficient between an item and the underlying dimension represented by the factor. Each item gets a loading on each factor, but the table shows only the highest one for each item. The item with the strongest second-place loading was "a life of peace and tranquility" which got 0.36 on Factor 1, 0.02 on Factor 2, and 0.49 on Factor 3, so it is here assigned to Factor 3. The only other case in which even moderately weak loadings showed up on more than one factor was "reunion with loved ones" which got 0.58 on Factor 1, −0.29 on Factor 2, and −0.24 on Factor 3. A negative loading can mean that the opposite of the idea is associated with the factor, which in this case might mean estrangement from loved ones.

So, what do the three factors mean? Throughout this book we will explore many methods for interpreting meaning, so here at the beginning we do not need to be very rigorous. Here is how it looks to me. Factor 1 primarily represents faith in the belief system of the Children of God. The other two factors represent reservations that some members may feel, even as they are primarily committed to the shared belief system and there is no faction of disbelievers in the group. Factor 2 seems to reflect a worry that some things a person values may be absent from the afterlife. Superficially, Factor 3 seems contradictory, including both tranquility and intense action. To me this factor looks like relatively abstract ideas that lack the specific optimism of the first factor and the worry expressed in the second factor. A factor analysis such as this one can serve various functions, including these:

1. It finds deeper meaning in a set of measures by combining in a sophisticated manner the responses of many people.
2. It is one of many methods for finding underlying patterns of response that can potentially predict a person's behavior in response to other, similar items.

3. It provides a framework for connecting the individuality of a single person with the shared culture of the wider community.

By comparing responses by members of the Children of God to those of the general public, we illustrate an important principle that is more generally true, and that we already saw in the finding of the *Opinions and Personality* study: Individuals fit into the human matrix in a variety of ways, and can neither be understood in isolation, nor treated merely as members of a homogeneous group.

Full emulation requires deep understanding of a person, for two reasons. First, and most obviously, understanding achieves greater accuracy in simulating behavior, not only because it can refine a predictive algorithm, but also because it can provide guidance for selecting which algorithm to use in a given situation. Second, understanding is important because emulation has other human beings as its primary audience, and they can appreciate the simulated person more deeply, the better they understand the person's point of view. Understanding is expressed through words and numbers, both of which are cultural products, and emulation ideally increases the contribution the individual can make to society.

1.6 Five Scenarios

Personality capture and emulation is a new field, and we will not know for some years how radical versus incremental its innovations will be. Competent but visionary leaders—Bell, Gray, Kurzweil, Blascovich and Bailenson among others—have suggested that a really profound revolution in the conditions of human life may be achieved. They may be totally wrong, but in that case we can still expect greater personalization of our technologies through methods like those described in this book. Given the wide range of possibilities, we neither should become committed prematurely to wild dreams, nor should we reject them categorically. For now, a roster of five conceivable outcomes can provide a framework for thinking about specific technologies.

1. *Transmigration.* The most extreme conceptualization of personality emulation is the transfer of a human personality to a new home, at such a high level of precision and comprehensiveness that it can be said the person has moved but not changed. Philosophers and mystics might debate whether the original consciousness of the person also moved, and it must be noted that human consciousness is already discontinuous, because our lives are punctuated with thousands of periods of sleep or other unconsciousness. As a practical matter, we may guess that this is the most unlikely of the scenarios actually to be achieved, because all the technologies we can currently imagine are rather imprecise. Yet as a benchmark it can help us think about the issues.

To this point in history, popular notions of transmigration have concerned religious debates. The Christian and Islamic traditions imagine that at death the souls of a person is completely liberated from the physical world, to dwell in an entirely supernatural environment—Heaven, Hell, or Paradise. Hinduism, in contrast, believed that souls could return to live again in this world. The religious expression *transmigration of souls* is often used as a synonym for reincarnation, but it actually has a slightly wider meaning. *Reincarnation* means being born again into the conventional biological form, whereas *transubstantiation* means transference into a different medium, and *transmigration* leaves open the question of the soul's new home. Thus we may prefer to use *transmigration* as the name for this scenario, because, for example, it leaves open whether a captured personality will be emulated inside a genetically engineered biological duplicate of the person, or in a non-biological robot.

For something over two centuries, some tension has existed between science and religion, with respect to what aspect of a person could possibly be immortal, given that brain injury or disease can rob a person of memories, skills, and even fundamental personality traits [50, 51]. The Christian word *soul*, or the equivalent Hindu word *atman*, assumes there is some irreducible, immortal center to a human personality, something psychology and cognitive science have yet to discover [52, 53]. Like the English word *spirit*, *atman* is derived from the word for breath—the breath of life—and thus is a metaphor for something that passes understanding. The transmigration goal for personality capture and emulation is frankly more ambitious, postulating lossless transfer of all relevant information constituting the person to a new substrate.

2. *Apotheosis*. This scenario is ambitious in a different way from transmigration, accepting some inaccuracy in personality capture and emulation because the goal is to create an idealized version of the person, not necessarily a technically accurate copy. In ancient Egypt and the classical civilization of Greece and Rome, it was conceivable for an exceptional person to become elevated to the status of a minor god, something that makes sense within a polytheistic religious tradition. Thus, apotheosis has a certain elitist quality, and may not be available for everyone.

This raises one of the most difficult problems for both transmigration and apotheosis: Where shall we put all the emulated personalities? Christians put them in the afterlife, Hindus put them into the bodies of babies, but the world would fill up if we put them in new bodies on Earth, even as babies continued to be born and add to the number of persons in the world. An appealing but technically very difficult alternative is to outlaw full forms of emulation on the Earth, but encourage placement of emulated personalities on other planets, eventually colonizing the galaxy and merging the two traditional meanings of *heaven*. This idea has a certain attraction, because it could provide the motivation required to colonize the solar system and beyond, yet the required investments and innovations are staggering.

The alternative, that apotheosis would be available only for a small minority of human beings is distasteful but, perhaps sadly, traditional. In his novel *Watch the North Wind Rise*, Robert Graves postulated a society in which only a tiny minority of poems were allowed to be printed after the deaths of their poets, and only a tiny fraction of the real people of the past have engraved their names boldly in history [54]. Personality capture may be laborious, so only a small fraction of the world's population may be willing to invest the time and money that may be required to capture their own personalities. Still, the troubling elitist quality of apotheosis must be kept in mind.

The apotheosis scenario requires some technical terms to describe its components. Already the Hindu word *avatar* has become common in computer games and virtual worlds, to designate the virtual representation of the user, who operates it in realtime. In other work, where I have explored the possibility of playing the role of a specific deceased person in one of these electronic environments, I have suggested that the Hindu-Buddhist term *sattva* be used for the model on which the avatar is based [55, 56]. I did not call the basis for the avatar its *atman*, because that would imply that the original spirit of the person was operating the avatar. Adjusting the meaning of *sattva* somewhat, as was earlier done with the word *avatar*, I suggested it designate a purified essence of the person, a meaning not a spirit, thus appropriate for apotheosis.

3. *Progeny*. Near the middle of the spectrum from radical to conventional is the option to create multiple simplified representations of oneself that may act as our agents during our lifetimes as well as afterward. Hans Moravec called these *mind children*, perhaps too evocative a term, but here we can use the more abstract and general term, *virtual progeny* [57]. The Hindu gods, notably Vishnu, had many avatars, each representing a different aspect of the deity's transcendental essence, and so the notion of partial representations is quite ancient in that tradition. Yet the concept need not be at all mystical, because some people already possess semi-autonomous computerized agents that act on their behalf, at least to some degree adjusted the reflect the person's values and preferences.

A concrete example is *trading agents*, automatic systems that act on behalf of a person in the marketplace, and the National Science Foundation has sponsored students to program increasingly sophisticated agents that battle each other in competitions [58]. The simplest version is a stop-loss order that automatically initiates a trade if a security drops to a price designated by the owner, potentially expressed as a single line of programming code or a number in a data field. A person might buy a stock at $100 per share, hoping it will rise, but tell the trading system to sell if the market price drops to $90. By having a stop-loss order at all, and by setting the particular price that triggers a sale, the person is expressing a personal attitude toward risk.

Artificial intelligence agents already exist in a wide variety of forms, and in future we must imagine that many people will possess a complex team of specialized agents, some of which may operate even beyond the individual's zone of control. Another example of a minimal agent is the thermostat in a home heating system, where the owner may set preferred daytime and nighttime temperatures, and the hours to switch from one to another. Now, smart homes are coming into existence, that operate all the complex systems in a domestic environment according to the owner's preferences, perhaps even using machine learning methods to adjust to the resident's behavior, rather than requiring the user to give detailed formal instructions [59]. Considerable progress has been achieved in recent years developing AI control systems for automobiles, and it is conceivable that in a few years we shall speak to our cars, rather than driving them, telling them which of our accustomed destinations we wish to go to [60].

Exactly how these artificial intelligence progeny might function after the death of the owner is open to debate, and most would be expected either to die as well, or be reprogrammed for new owners. Conceivably, a form of agent will be developed to function as an intelligent last will and testament. A trading agent could continue to function following the deceased's instructions until the assets had been officially transferred to the control of an heir, and this might take many years in cases where the deceased left trust funds that did not come under the direct control of the heir until the heir reach a specified age. Already, in many contexts beneficiaries are specific under various contingencies—if this heir dies before inheriting, then the bequest goes to that heir—and one could imagine sophisticated wills that distributed an inheritance in a complex manner, depending upon events.

4. *Incorporation*. One reason that agents might continue to operate after the death of their original owner is that they serve valuable functions for other people. Therefore, in varying degrees across many societies, people continue to live after death through the contributions they made to the community that survives them. One can see this in a secularized version in the writings of sociologist Emile Durkheim, who argued that God was really just a metaphor for society [61]. One's legacy is one's eternal life, whether it been manifested in children, good deeds, or works of art or literature. Thus, incorporation in a community provides a kind of immortality.

Already, we have seen several examples of the incorporation approach. The elderly people we called Crone and Geezer contributed to social science, and even to some government policy decisions based on information about the social conditions in America, through inclusion of their data in the archive of the General Social Survey. When I completed my book on the Children of God, I placed the data in an archive—the Association of Religion Data Archives—and anyone who visits thearda.com online can download the responses of all 1,025 members. The archiving process required me to provide a *codebook* that both preserved the questionnaire and provided information about the responses to ensure that any future user would understand how the data could be used properly. With luck, those data will be useful long after all the respondents, and even the scientist who enlisted them, have passed away.

One of the later chapters of this book, focused on recommender systems, builds on the fact that literally millions of people have expressed their preferences for movies or books, either by answering a questionnaire item for each one or simply by paying to obtain it, and their data now serve to advise other people what to watch or read. Indeed, one can conceptualize a recommender system as a *community artificial social intelligence* system, that combines reflections from many people to illuminate the possible choices for others [62]. Through oral legends and written records, the people of the past already serve as advisors for us, but advanced information technology will enable us to be more dynamic advisors for the people of the future.

5. *Personalization*. If we strip away all the grand hopes, and consider the most modest possibilities, we have the solid fact that people may personalize information systems to serve their individual needs better. All the formatting options in a word processor or spreadsheet can be set in different ways, and indeed one of the flaws of

spreadsheets is that often one person sets idiosyncratic preferences then passes the spreadsheet to another person who has trouble managing it because of very different assumptions of how the options should be set. We may wind up, after extensive effort doing research on personality capture and emulation, merely with a larger array of methods for personalizing tools, rather than anything so grand as immortality.

However, personalization has a deeper meaning, when the person reflects upon the implications of the process of personality capture. If users learn about themselves from the process, then they effectively personalize themselves. Thus, many of the studies described in this book provided some form of feedback to the user, from the raw data, to summaries of the data, to simple analyses. That is to say, computer-based personality capture may be the twenty-first century successor to Psychoanalysis, hopefully more accurate and less dogmatic. Indeed, to the extent that personality capture is under the control of the person, then capture itself is personalized, and could allow individuals to develop perspectives on themselves that harmonized with their fundamental values and beliefs, while having a degree of objectivity. This may enable people to emulate their own personality ideals, even as they discover their psychological natures as unique individuals and members of communities.

1.7 Chapters

The seven chapters that follow report results from many pilot studies and a few deeper explorations, organized in seven somewhat different areas of technical opportunity and challenge. Chap. 2 builds upon traditional survey methods, through computer-administered massive questionnaires that ask an unusually large number and variety of questions of the individual. Chap. 3 continues that theme, but takes it out into the field, through personality capture by means of mobile and ubiquitous computing. Chap. 4 focuses on one already successful if narrow form of capture and emulation, the recommender systems that have already proved their value in commerce. Chap. 5 considers how human short-term memory and classification can be measured computationally and imitated by artificial intelligence, then explores expert systems as a way of going far beyond traditional aptitude tests. Chap. 6 documents autobiographical memories and suggests how the lives of many members of a community could be preserved through oral histories and digital libraries. Chap. 7 touches upon the methods and perplexities of text analysis, including treating written documents as if they were respondents to questionnaires, and using translation between languages to raise fundamental philosophical issues about meaning. The final chapter offers virtual worlds, such as massively multiplayer role-playing games, as a nearly ideal environment for capturing human behavior, and as a laboratory for developing many forms of emulation.

References

1. Kurzweil, R. (1999). *The age of spiritual machines: When computers exceed human intelligence.* New York: Viking.
2. Kurzweil, R. (2005). *The singularity is near: When humans transcend biology.* New York: Viking.
3. Kempelmann, F. (2000). *Unsterblich durch Selbstüberlieferung.* Hamburg: Libri Books on Demand.
4. Hanson, R. (1994). If uploads come first: The crack of a future dawn. *Extropy, 6,* 2. hanson.gmu.edu/uploads.html. Accessed 13 July 2013.
5. Bainbridge, W. S. (2004). "Literary Representations" and "Personality Capture". In W. S. Bainbridge (Ed.), *Berkshire encyclopedia of human-computer interaction* (pp. 431–439, 546–551). Great Barrington: Berkshire.
6. http://www.liacs.nl/home-en/. Accessed 13 July 2013.
7. http://www.symantec.com/configuration-management. Accessed 13 July 2013.
8. Bianchi-Berthouze, N. (2002). Mining multimedia subjective feedback. *Journal of Intelligent Information Systems, 19*(1), 43.
9. Magnenat-Thalmann, N., Kalra, P., & Escher, M. (1998). Face to virtual face. *Proceedings of the IEEE, 86*(5), 870–883.
10. Magnenat-Thalmann, N., & Thalmann, D. (Eds.). (2004). *Handbook of virtual humans.* Hoboken: Wiley.
11. Bell, G., & Gray, J. (2001). Digital immortality. *Communications of the ACM, 44*(3), 29.
12. http://en.wikipedia.org/wiki/Gordon_Bell. Accessed 15 July 2013.
13. http://research.microsoft.com/en-us/projects/mylifebits/. Accessed 15 July 2013.
14. http://en.wikipedia.org/wiki/Jim_Gray_(computer_scientist). Accessed 15 July 2013.
15. Temple, W. F. (1951). *Four-sided triangle.* New York: Fell.
16. Blascovich, J., & Bailenson, J. (2011). *Infinite reality* (p. 261). New York: William Morrow.
17. Bainbridge, W. S. (2012). The psychoanalytic movement. In W. S. Bainbridge (Ed.), *Leadership in science and technology* (pp. 520–528). Los Angeles: Sage.
18. Rachman, S. (1971). *The effects of psychotherapy.* Oxford: Pergamon.
19. Bandura, A. (1969). *Principles of behavior modification.* New York: Holt, Rinehart and Winston.
20. Eysenck, H. J. (1985). *Decline and fall of the freudian empire.* New York: Viking.
21. Freud, S. (1918). *Totem and taboo* (pp. 212–213). New York: Moffat, Yard.
22. Malinowski B. (1927). *Sex and repression in savage society.* New York: Harcourt, Brace.
23. Wolpe, J., & Rachman, S. (1960). Psychoanalytic "evidence": A critique based on Freud's case of Little Hans. *Journal of Nervous and Mental Disease, 131,* 135–148.
24. http://en.wikipedia.org/wiki/Herbert_Graf. Accessed 10 Feb 2013.
25. Brown, J. A. C. (1967). *Freud and the post-freudians.* Baltimore: Penguin.
26. Finkel, N. J. (1976). *Mental illness and health.* New York: Macmillan.
27. Freud, S. (1913). *The interpretation of dreams.* London: G. Allen.
28. Adler, A. (1927). *Individual psychology.* New York: Greenberg.
29. Erikson, E. H. (1958). *Young man luther: A study in psychoanalysis and history.* New York: Norton.
30. Erikson, E. H. (1968). *Identity, youth, and crisis.* New York: Norton.
31. Langer, W. C. (1972). *The mind of Adolf Hitler.* New York: Basic Books.
32. Bainbridge, W. S. (2012). The Harvard Department of social relations. In W. S. Bainbridge (Ed.), *Leadership in science and technology* (pp. 496–503). Los Angeles: Sage.
33. Wiggins, J. S. (2003). *Paradigms of personality assessment* (pp. 93–122). New York: Gilford.
34. http://portalcs.hul.harvard.edu/archives/0036.html. Accessed 28 May 2013.
35. Murray, H. A. (1955). American Icarus. In A. Burton & R. E. Harris (Eds.), *Clinical Studies of Personality* (pp. 615–641). New York: Harper.

36. Chase, A. (2000). Harvard and the making of the unabomber. *The Atlantic monthly, 285*(6), 41–65.
37. Oleson, J. C. (2000). Book review of Harvard and the unabomber: The education of an American terrorist. *Western Criminology Review, 5*(1), 70–74.
38. Studlien, K. G. (2000). Murray center seals Kaczynski data. *Harvard Crimson*, July 14. http://www.thecrimson.com/article/2000/7/14/murray-center-seals-kaczynski-data-plondon-buried/. Accessed 28 May 2013.
39. White, R. W. (1952). *Lives in progress*. New York: Dryden.
40. Smith, M. B., Bruner, J. S., & White, R. W. (1956). *Opinions and personality*. New York: Wiley.
41. Adorno, T. W. (1950). Else Frenkel-Brunswik, Daniel Levinson, and Nevitt Sanford, The Authoritarian Personality. New York: Harper.
42. *http://dvn.iq.harvard.edu/dvn/dv/mra/faces/study/StudyPage.xhtml?globalId=hdl:1902.1/00614* & studyListingIndex=0_16cb6898777b927dd869a4d0de83. Accessed 28 May 2013.
43. http://www3.norc.org/gss+website/. Accessed 28 May 2013.
44. http://sda.berkeley.edu/archive.htm. Accessed 28 May 2013.
45. Siegel, P., Hodge, R., & Rossi, P. (1964). Occupational prestige in the United States, 1925–1963. *American Journal of Sociology, 70*, 286–302.
46. Temme, L. (1975). *Occupation: Meanings and measures*. Washington: Bureau of Social Science Research.
47. Bainbridge, W. S. (2002). *The endtime family* (p. xi). Albany: State University of New York Press.
48. Edgerton, R. B. (1966). Conceptions of psychosis in Four East Africa Societies. *American Anthropologist, 68*(2), 408–425.
49. Spearman, C. (1904). 'General Intelligence,' Objectively determined and measured. *The American Journal of Psychology, 15*, 201–293.
50. Ray, I. (1871). *A treatise on the medical jurisprudence of insanity*. Boston: Little Brown, and company.
51. Descartes, R. (2008). *Meditations on first philosophy*. Oxford: Oxford University Press.
52. Bloom, P. (2004). *Descartes' baby*. New York: Basic Books.
53. Bainbridge, W. S. (2010). Cognitive science and the new atheism. In A. Amarasingam (Ed.), *Religion and the New Atheism* (pp. 79–96). Leiden: Brill.
54. Graves, R. (1949). *Watch the north wind rise*. New York: Creative Age Press.
55. Bainbridge, W. S. (2013). Ancestor veneration avatars. In R. Luppicini (Ed.), *Handbook of research on technoself: Identity in a technological society* (pp. 308–321). Hershey, Pennsylvania: IGI Global.
56. Bainbridge, W. S. (2013). Perspectives on virtual veneration. *The Information Society, 29*(3), 196–202.
57. Moravec, H. P. (1988). *Mind children: The future of robot and human intelligence*. Cambridge: Harvard University Press.
58. Stone, P., & Greenwald, A. (2005). The first international trading agent competition: Autonomous bidding agents. *Electronic Commerce Research, 5*(2), 229–226.
59. Rashidi, P., Cook, D. J., Holder, L. B., & Schmitter-Edgecombe, M. (2011). Discovering activities to recognize and track in a smart environment. *IEEE Transactions on Knowledge and Data Engineering, 23*(4), 527–539, 2011.
60. Thrun, S., & Stanford University (2010). Toward robotic cars. *Communications of the ACM, 53*(4), 99–106.
61. Durkheim, El. (1915). *The elementary forms of the religious life*. London: G. Allen and Unwin.
62. Bainbridge W. S., Brent, E. E., Carley, K., Heise, D. R., Macy, M. W., Markovsky, B., & Skvoretz, J. (1994). Artificial social intelligence. *Annual Review of Sociology, 20*, 407–436.

Chapter 2
Massive Questionnaires

Traditionally, questionnaires designed by personality and social psychologists consisted of a few short batteries of related items. There were two reasons for this. First, using the old-fashioned pencil-and-paper technology, it was inconvenient to administer the questionnaires, and costly to enter the data into a computer by hand, so short questionnaires were especially desirable. Today, administering via computer eliminates the data entry task, and the respondents themselves may find answering more comfortable and thus be willing to answer more questions. Second, the goal of the research was to discover and verify one or two theoretical principles per study, each requiring more than one item to achieve reliable data, but best measured by a small number of items that had been laboriously pretested. We shall continue to value such well-designed measurement scales, but our purpose is very different, to capture the complex characteristics of a particular individual, which will require many new items as well as many well-established measurement scales.

During the 1980s, like many other sociologists I explored the possibilities for computer administration of questionnaires, but doing more of the programming myself than many of my colleagues chose to do, even publishing software that would allow students to construct their own questionnaires, administer them via computer, and then analyze the results using increasingly complex statistical analysis procedures [1]. Starting in 1997, I worked with other researchers to explore the potential not only for administering questionnaires online, but using the Internet to develop large numbers of questions that reflected the full range of popular opinions, rather than the theoretical predilections of scholars.

A transitional project was a series of studies carried out from 1974 until 1986 on public perceptions of space exploration, initially as a side study connected to my doctoral dissertation, *The Spaceflight Revolution*, that was a social history of the space program, and resulting in *Goals in Space*, a book about the diversity of viewpoints held by knowledgeable people about the potential benefits [2, 3]. The fundamental methodology was in two parts. First, I would include in one questionnaire a few open-ended questions asking respondents to write in their own words what they personally felt was a legitimate reason for supporting the

W. S. Bainbridge, *Personality Capture and Emulation,* Human-Computer Interaction Series,   25
DOI 10.1007/978-1-4471-5604-8_2, © Springer-Verlag London 2014

space program. Second, fixed-choice items for a second questionnaire would be distilled from all the text derived in the first questionnaire, this time asking respondents to rate the values of a range of well-defined ideas on a standard quantitative scale.

During the 1974–1986 period, it often proved necessary to write my own analysis software from scratch, for example writing a block-model clustering program as an alternative to the relatively limited factor analysis software then available, each run taking about 36 hours on an Apple II. This is extremely slow by today's standards, but quite convenient given that I could be doing work on a different computer while that one dutifully processed data without the need for my supervision. The following chapter will bring that multitasking principle up to the present day, by considering how mobile and ubiquitous computing and communications can contribute to personality capture. The challenge here will be to build upon the introductory material in the previous chapter, about personality theory and questionnaire methods.

Tens of thousands of questions will be required to measure the full complexity of any individual's personality, and the salience of any particular question will vary from person to person. Many competing personality theories exist, and our null hypothesis must be that all of them are true, but each applies only under certain conditions for certain people. Thus we need to develop flexible systems for gathering and collating information, using statistical tools like correlations and factor analysis, but not by any means limited to them. Indeed, one of the ways in which a person can be emulated is for another person to understand him or her, developing a mental model that represents that other person. Theory is not only a tool for organizing data and making decisions about what data to collect, but itself is a mode of emulation. To clarify these and many related issues, we shall begin with one of the classic measurement instruments, the MACH scale based on the personality of a single historical individual, Niccolò Machiavelli.

2.1 Machiavellianism

Niccolò Machiavelli (1469–1527) was among many things a very influential political theorist, and social science college students even today read his pair of short books, *The Prince* and *The Discourses* [4]. Machiavelli's Wikipedia page suggests how his ideas are generally remembered: "He asserted that social benefits of stability and security could be achieved in the face of moral corruption. Aside from that, Machiavelli believed that public and private morality had to be understood as two different things in order to rule well. As a result, a ruler must be concerned not only with reputation, but also positively willing to act immorally at the right times. As a political scientist, Machiavelli emphasizes the occasional need for the methodical exercise of brute force, deceit, and so on." [5]

Machiavelli's works became very widely known; his memory was often reviled, and *Machiavellianism* came to be a term of opprobrium, signifying a pattern of deceitful behavior. The 1970 book by Richard Christie and Florence Geis, *Studies in Machiavellianism*, reported the very promising results of a study to develop a questionnaire measurement scale, in which many items were based directly on Machiavelli's own words [6]. Subsequent research confirmed that this scale predicted some real-world duplicitous behavior, although it correlated to some degree with other measurement scales, and thus may not be an entirely distinctive characteristic. Perhaps it merely reflects honesty versus dishonesty. Imagine this simple, one-item measurement scale:

> Think for a moment about your everyday interactions with other people. In general, how honest versus dishonest are you? Circle the one number below that best describes your typical degree of honesty:
> Dishonest 0–1–2–3–4–5–6 Honest

Clearly, this question has problems. Perhaps an honest person will brood over it for many minutes, trying to remember various recent social interactions in which honesty was an issue, then finally circling the number 4, which represents modesty more than honesty. A dishonest person may answer quickly, circling the number 6, which claims to represent complete honesty, despite the fact the respondent was lying. This example illustrates more than just the thorny problem of how to elicit correct responses, because researchers in the heyday of traditional questionnaires developed a number of principles of scale construction that required multiple items to measure any important variable. Right away we see two: (1) the mind of an honest respondent is often better able to handle several questions about aspects of an issue, than a single question that lumps everything together, and (2) it is cognitively easier for the respondent to lie in response to one simple item than to a battery of items arranged in such a way as to elicit a complex pattern of responses. Both of these points recognize that question-answering is a cognitive task, that may be affected by the respondent's mental skills as well as the respondent's intentions. Often, such issues were discussed in terms of reliability and validity.

Reliability is the quality of an item or index that gives consistent results. A reliable item tends to get the same response from a respondent if administered twice, so long as the relevant circumstances have not changed. While some frequently-used measurement scales are single items, many are multi-item indexes because each response may include some random error, and combining several items tends to reduce their combined random error. Many statistical methods were developed to estimate the reliability of an index composed of several items, such as splitting the list of questions into two halves during the analysis, for example comparing the scores of the odd-numbered versus even-numbered items, or applying a summary statistic like Chronbach's alpha that is effectively the average of all possible split-half comparisons [7].

Validity is the quality of an item or index that measures the phenomenon it purports to measure. A valid item accurately reflects the desired aspect of the respondent's thoughts, behavior, or characteristics. A reliable index may be invalid, for example if it measures something different from what we assume it does. An unreliable index is probably not valid either. The validity of an item may vary depending upon the characteristics of the respondent, as the example of our honesty question illustrates. We may use the term *conditional validity* to refer to situations in which the item itself is well-designed to be valid, but some respondents under some circumstances fail to understand it or otherwise fail to respond properly. This is why many of the questions in major public opinion polls are very simple, avoiding the use of words that some respondents will not recognize, and topics many people are not familiar with.

One way social psychologists attempted to deal with dishonesty was to develop special measurement instruments focusing on it directly but cleverly. Often this was conceptualized in terms of *yea-saying bias*, a tendency to agree with statements in a questionnaire quite apart from what they said, or *social desirability bias*, the tendency of a respondent to give socially acceptable answers to questions [8, 9]. Much effort was invested by several researchers to develop separate indexes of items to measure these forms of bias, but they encountered the problem that some people really did agree with the set of items in a yea-saying index, or so completely conform to social expectations that their natural responses were always nice and acceptable.

The historical period in which personology was developed, was one in which many psychologists believed that people were not fully conscious of their own thoughts and feelings, under the influence of the Psychoanalytic Movement. This may or may not be true, but it justified the arrogant belief on the part of some researchers that their respondents would naively answer all the questions in a questionnaire, blissfully ignorant of what the researcher was trying to accomplish. Much questionnaire research seems to find that educated people have very different attitudes from those of uneducated people, yet I always wonder when I see such a study whether the results came just from the fact that the more educated respondents could "psych out the study" and give socially desirable responses to the stupid researcher. With our focus on personality capture, we can hope that respondents will self-consciously develop a commitment to honest responding, and that with a very large number and wide diversity of measures we can capture the truth.

Reliability was not the only reason Christie and Geis developed Machiavellianism indexes composed of many items; they began with the goal to capture Machiavelli's thinking more generally, and only later in a long research process distill its essence. The first step was to go through Machiavelli's writings, in English translation, and copy out statements about human nature. Many had to be edited slightly to turn them into straightforward statements suitable for use in a questionnaire. At this point, the researchers felt they understood Machiavelli's perspective, and of course he had written long ago in a different language, so they felt it was reasonable to add a few more similar items from their own experience of modern life.

Given that the work was being done before personal computers, the researchers used a typewriter to put each example on a separate 3×5 file card. These were shown to colleagues, each of whom went through the set twice, first expressing personal agreement or disagreement with each statement, then explaining how they interpreted each one. Some statements proved to be ambiguous and were removed, leaving a set of 71 statements. These were assembled into a questionnaire administered to 1,196 college students. Each student was scored in terms of the 71 responses as high Machiavellian, medium, or low Machiavellian, and the two extremes were compared. The 50 items that best distinguished respondents at the extremes became one major MACH scale, and then a subset of 20 became the most frequently used index, called MACH-IV. To control for the yea-saying bias, half were written so that Machiavelli would agree with them, half were rewritten so that he would disagree, and the sum of one group minus the other gave a single number as the Machiavellianism score.

A student of mine, Lyn Jacobson Hoefer, found this work very interesting, as did I, so we carried out a study to boil MACH-IV down further [10]. We administered a questionnaire containing the 20 items of the index to 810 college students, and then performed statistical analysis to see how the items related to each other. If MACH-IV were a perfect measurement instrument, we would expect the positively-phrased MACH items to correlate positively with each other, the negative-phrased one to correlate positively with each other, and items in different groups to correlate negatively. This proved mostly to be true, but some statements did not correlate strongly, and the strengths of the correlations varied even among the ones that did seem connected.

For example, one of the original statements extracted from Machiavelli's writings was, "Most men are cowards." I have some trouble seeing how that relates to being honest versus dishonest. Does a dishonest person lie to cover their cowardice? Or does dishonesty require a special kind of courage to brave the possibility of being unmasked? Perhaps cowardice and dishonesty are different facets of Machiavelli's negative view of humanity, but not closely related other than in their negativity. Christie and Geis actually reversed this item, to produce one of the 10 that Machiavelli would have disagreed with: "Most men are brave." That revision took the item one step further from Machiavelli's thinking, in an attempt to correct for yea-saying by the respondent. But the item has a different problem, namely that it refers to "men" rather than to "women" or to "people." To the male and female respondents of a decade later than when MACH-IV was created, this item may seem sexist, or just unclear. It did not correlate well in our data, so we dropped it out when we created a short form of the MACH scale.

Another item that did not work well had not come from Machiavelli's writings at all, but from popular American culture of the period before 1970: "Barnum was probably right when he said there's a sucker born every minute." This item might not make sense to respondents in later decades or outside the United States. "Barnum" refers to American circus entrepreneur Phineas T. Barnum (1810–1891) who frequently perpetrated hoaxes. Searching for the word "sucker" in Wikipedia takes one to the page titled "Gullibility," which defines that term as "a failure of social intelligence in which a person is easily tricked or manipulated into an ill-advised course of action." [11] This sucker item came from a different person and a different culture from the genuine Machiavelli items, but seemingly harmonized with his thinking because a sucker is the perfect victim for a liar. It did not correlate well with other items, for our respondents, so we dropped it out.

The result was a short-form 10-item MACH scale with an equal number of positively and negatively phrased items, which turned out to have two slightly different but mutually reinforcing subscales within it:

High MACH
Tactics:
Never tell anyone the real reason you did something unless it is useful to do so.
It is safest to assume that all people have a vicious streak and it will come out when they
  are given a chance.
It is wise to flatter important people.

Perspective:
Generally, people won't work hard unless they're forced to do so.
The biggest difference between most criminals and other people is that criminals are stupid
  enough to get caught.

Low MACH
Tactics:
Honesty is the best policy in all cases.
There is no excuse for lying to someone else.
One should take action only when sure it is morally right.

Perspective:
Most people are basically good and kind.
Most people who get ahead in the world lead clean, moral lives.

Machiavellians tend to agree with the High MACH items, and disagree with the
Low Mach items. The tactics items advise a person about how to behave, while the
perspective items describe the world the respondent inhabits. Thus an honest person
living among dishonest people might score Low MACH on tactics but High MACH
on perspective. For our respondents, the subscales correlated with each other at the
0.21 level, statistically significant but individual items tended to correlate higher
within each subscale than across them.

After Hoefer and I derived this short-form MACH index, I used it in a software-
textbook educational package on questionnaire survey research, as part of a dataset
students could analyze for practice. Respondents were 200 business executives, and
the main focus was on popular management philosophies. Items were derived from
management science publications, in the same way Christie and Geis derived items
from Machiavelli's writings, and many of them functioned like extensions of the
MACH scale. In some cases, the only clear connection to Machiavelli was the extent to which workers could be trusted to perform well, versus needing to be under
strict control. For example, Table 2.1 shows 14 items derived from the pair of management philosophies contrasted in Douglas McGregor's classic writings [12, 13].

Douglas McGregor (1906–1964) was a professor of management, who proposed
an influential framework that contrasted two different leadership theories, which he
called X and Y. Theory X was more authoritarian and superficially looked somewhat Machiavellian, while theory Y was more trusting of subordinates and tried
to motivate them through helping them achieve their own goals. Many readers assume, perhaps correctly, that McGregor himself believed in Theory Y and used
Theory X merely to provide contrast and better advocate his own values. McGregor
said that different managers out in the real world followed one or the other theory,
although Theory X may have been in fashion early in the twentieth century, and
Theory Y was more fashionable later on. This raises a general point that any person's conceptualization of a major issue will include alternative ways of thinking

Table 2.1 Correlations between Machiavellianism scales and McGregorism items ($N=200$)

	Agree (%)	MACH	Tactics	Perspective
Theory X:				
X1. People are fundamentally lazy, irresponsible, and need constantly to be watched	5.5	0.18*	0.10	0.22*
X2. Most people must be coerced, controlled, directed, and threatened with punishment to get them to work hard for goals set by their employer	2.5	0.24*	0.14	0.29*
X3. The average human being prefers to be directed, wishes to avoid responsibility, has relatively little ambition, and wants security above all	17.0	0.24*	0.16	0.26*
X4. The average human being has an inherent dislike of work and will avoid it if he can	5.0	0.34*	0.17	0.44*
X5. To motivate his subordinates, a good manager will use the economic incentive of wage rises more than the intangible rewards of honor and respect	15.5	0.25*	0.18	0.24*
X6. The most important things a good manager does are to direct people's efforts, motivate them, control their actions, and modify their behavior to fit the needs of the organization	69.0	0.21*	0.17	0.16
X7. A good leader should give detailed and complete instructions to his subordinates, rather than merely giving them general directions and depending upon their initiative to work out details	31.0	0.00	0.02	−0.03
Theory Y:				
Y1. Under proper conditions, the average human being learns not only to accept but to seek responsibility	74.0	−0.03	0.08	−0.21*
Y2. People are fundamentally hardworking, responsible, and need only to be supported and encouraged	72.0	−0.32*	−0.19*	−0.37*
Y3. People can exercise much self-direction and self-control when their work satisfies their needs for personal achievement and social respect	96.5	−0.12	−0.04	−0.19*
Y4. Group goal-setting offers advantages that cannot be obtained by individual goal-setting	58.0	0.05	0.06	0.01
Y5. The most important thing a good manager does is to create a work environment in which people achieve their own personal goals best by working for the goals of the organization	89.5	−0.11	−0.07	−0.10
Y6. To motivate his subordinates, a good manager will use the intangible rewards of honor and respect more than the economic incentive of wage raises	51.5	−0.09	−0.02	−0.17
Y7. Most people have untapped resources of imagination, ingenuity, creativity, and other intellectual potentialities	86.0	−0.10	−0.01	−0.21*

*Statistically significant beyond the 0.01 level

that the individual understands but rejects. This implies that personality capture must deal with both, documenting not only the person's favorite perspective, but also the competing perspectives the individual is able to conceptualize.

Thus, the 14 statements in Table 2.1 express McGregorism, just as the 10 items listed earlier express Machiavellianism, but the two subscales of McGregorism contradict rather than support each other. The 200 modern business executives seem to favor Theory Y over Theory X, with fewer than 20% agreeing with 5 of the 7 Theory X items, and majorities agreeing with all of the Theory Y items. However, they tend to agree with both X6 and Y5, which are central expressions of the two competing theories' management philosophies, or perhaps there is a grain of truth in both.

Three columns of Table 2.1 show the correlations between three versions of the MACH scale and agreeing with each of the 14 statements. For example, for the first statement the correlations are 0.18, 0.10, and 0.22. These are positive numbers, indicating that people who scored higher on Machiavellians were more likely to agree that people are lazy, compared with people who scores low on the scale. While correlations range from -1.00 to $+1.00$, with questionnaire items that are phrased in different terms, the coefficients tend not to be very high. For 200 respondents, in data like this, correlations at or above 0.18 are considered statistically significant, because there is less than one chance in 100 that pure chance produced this result in the absence of any reliable connection between the variables.

The 0.18 is for the entire 10-item MACH scale; 0.10 is for the 6-item Tactics subscale, and 0.22 is for the 4-item Perspective subscale. Given that it has fewer items, the Perspective subscale measures less well than the two other scales, so the fact it has higher correlations than Tactics for six of the seven Theory X items indicates that Tactics are doing most of the work in connecting Machiavellianism with Theory X. In fact, the 200 modern managers score low on the overall MACH scale. The 10 MACH items were combined by adding the scores for the High-MACH items and subtracting the scores for the Low-MACH items. Each was rated on a five-point scale—strongly disagree, disagree, neutral, agree, and strongly agree—so the total scale could range from -20 to $+20$. The mean score for these 200 respondents was -6.8, meaning they tended to be low in Machiavellianism, and indeed only eight of them had positive scores.

Item X7, about giving detailed instructions, seems not to fit with the other six Theory X items, and experienced managers may have found that detailed instructions really are necessary, regardless of what their management philosophy might be. The pattern of correlations between the MACH scales and the Theory Y items is complex, but there is some tendency for believers in the Machiavellian perspective to disagree with some of the Theory Y statements, or at least agree less strongly. Clearly, the 24 items involved in Table 2.1 have complex relationships to each other, in the minds of this particular set of respondents, but there is also evidence of underlying themes that connect the ideas. The table also connects the thought processes and thus the personalities of two deceased human beings, Machiavelli and McGregor.

The MACH scale illustrates how theory-driven research, based ultimately on the thinking of one individual human being, can produce useful questionnaire measurement indexes by boiling down many statements to a few. To produce massive questionnaires designed to measure the great complexity of an individual personality, we need to go in the opposite direction, from a few items to many, in the process combining the contributions of many people.

2.2 Ethnographic Questionnaires

There are many ways to combine scientific methods, and one that I used in the 1974–1986 spaceflight studies might be called *ethnographic questionnaires*. Ethnography, of course, is the documentation of a culture, usually conducted by cultural anthropologists using traditional qualitative observation techniques. Close reading of ethnographies written by highly influential anthropologists of the past shows they also made very great use of *native informants*, members of the society being studied who are able to articulate their culture especially well, whether via formal interviews or informal conversations. In the first phase of the ethnographic questionnaire method, the people answering the questionnaire serve as native informants to some degree, while the people answering items in the second questionnaire serve more like traditional respondents.

An example that highlights modern Internet-based communication technology and connects to the central theme of this book was a pilot study to explore human conceptions of the afterlife. In the previous chapter we saw how questions about the afterlife from the General Social Survey could be used to chart the conceptions held by members of an unusual subculture, and here we shall see how the items could be derived directly from the culture rather than from the minds and theories of social scientists. At the same time, this pilot study explored how web-based questionnaires could play a role in personality capture.

On May 23, 1997, I launched a website called The Question Factory, to prototype methods of online questionnaire development. It lasted about 2 years, using an Internet service provider named Erol's which was absorbed into a different company about the time I was shifting over to a team effort to be described below that carried out a pair of major online surveys garnering data from tens of thousands of respondents [14]. In November 1997, a Phase I questionnaire was added to the site, focusing on the afterlife. The first three open-ended questions clearly sought to learn the respondent's own, personal views, shown here with answers from one individual:

What do you BELIEVE will happen to your personally, after you die?
"Nothing really; maybe I might be reincarnated and my memory would be erased about my past life."
What do you HOPE will happen to you personally, after you die?
"I hope that I will live again sometime."
What do you FEAR will happen to you personally, after you die?
"Nothing."

Three other open-ended items asked the person to take the role of respondent, reporting what other people think, although of course filtered through this particular individual's own beliefs and perceptions.

> Describe a belief that some people have about life after death, a belief with which you personally disagree.
> "People say they will go to heaven and hell."
> Describe a belief about life after death as you imagine it is held by people who belong to a very different culture and society from your own.
> "Above."
> Describe a belief about life after death that may have been held by people many centuries ago.
> "Egyptians might have thought that Osiris, god of the dead, would let them have life in some afterlife."

Clearly, this person is aware of a range of culturally defined possibilities, and does not happen to adhere to the dominant Christian religion. The structure of these responses is typical for a thoughtful respondent, quite apart from their content, including the fact that some items stimulate answers that are full sentences, while other items stimulate only a perfunctory response. Thus, collecting a rich corpus of data does require multiple questions and multiple respondents, not only to obtain a diversity of responses, but to have a sufficient number of expressions of each particular idea in order to understand it fully. In the case of the Phase I afterlife questionnaire, 131 people submitted responses.

Qualitative methods sometimes called *grounded theory* were then used to produce a Phase II questionnaire comprised of 90 statements about the afterlife. Frankly, sloppy social scientists often use this term to describe a theoretical stumbling-around inside a culture, hoping that insights will somehow appear. However, as originally developed by Glaser and Strauss, grounded theory was a highly rigorous qualitative approach, that gradually developed a system of conceptual categories [15]. One part of the method was developing each category incrementally, by adding spoken or written text generated by members of the culture under study, until that category had become *saturated* and no longer changed as more text was added.

The Phase II questionnaire garnered data from 198 respondents, who rated each of the 90 statements on a 7-point scale, following this instruction: "How likely do you think it is that this will happen to you after you die?" In order to understand how online ethnographic questionnaires work, we shall examine the most detailed factor analysis that was done on these data, following the same general approach as every other factor analysis reported in this book, but identifying fully 18 factors, six of which were dominated by only a single item. With naturally derived data, such as from this pilot study, where the items were not selected because they were believed to represent theoretically significant ideas, it is common for early-numbered factors to comprise many items, and later-numbered factors to identify very minor dimensions of variation. However, if the goal is personality capture, the minor factors may really be hints of major conceptualizations that do not happen to be fully represented among the respondents, and thus the starting points for future research and instrument development.

In this case, Factor 1 reflects the dominant Christian conception of the afterlife, supplemented by what may be other conceptualizations that might have split off into different factors for a different set of respondents. Fully 25 items loaded above 0.5 on this factor, going as high as 0.90, which can roughly be called *Heaven*:

Factor 1 Positive: *Heaven*
0.90 Praise and worship God for all eternity.
0.88 Spend eternity with God.
0.88 Be filled with awe and thankfulness at the goodness and mercy of God.
0.87 Stand before your God and account for the life you led on Earth.
0.86 Relax in a perfect place with no crime, no violence, no war, just peace.
0.83 Give and receive pure love.
0.82 Become pure and untouched by sin.
0.82 Grow in spiritual understanding.
0.81 Hear the voice of God say, "Well done, my good and faithful servant."
0.74 Finally know if there is life after death.
0.73 Rejoice because you are released from the aches, wants, and pains of a mortal body.
0.70 Hear angels and saints singing and playing harps.
0.70 Lovingly reunite with deceased loved ones.
0.67 Know the truth of things past and present that have occurred in this world.
0.67 Get to know what life is all about and why you lived the life you have lived.
0.64 Play, sing and dance with the angels.
0.64 Belong to a community based on harmony, equality and order.
0.62 Be freed from the flesh, carnality and sexuality.
0.61 See colors so beautiful that you will spend hours just enjoying them.
0.59 See streets of gold, beautiful gardens, glass churches and a crystal sea.
0.58 Enjoy total freedom.
0.56 Be free of pain, despair and all the cares of life.
0.56 Continue to live on in a different form, in another existence.
0.53 Have greatly enhanced senses with maximum potential for experiencing existence.
0.53 Live eternally in a real, physical, resurrected body. (also in Factor 13)

By a remarkable coincidence two items had exactly the same loading, 0.67, but also express very similar ideas that are not necessarily associated with the Christian conception of the afterlife: "Know the truth of things past and present that have occurred in this world." "Get to know what life is all about and why you lived the life you have lived." The most weakly loaded item, at the bottom of the list, reflects a controversy within Christianity: "Live eternally in a real, physical, resurrected body." This item also appears as the only item in Factor 13, having one of the rare negative loadings in this dataset, −0.57. Thus, Factor 13 represents rejection of this idea, while we see it included positively if weakly in Factor 1.

As we noted in the previous section, psychologists often reverse some of the items, for example taking something Machiavelli said was true and calling it false, to guard against response bias. An alternate corrective is to include a battery of items specifically designed to measure response bias, leaving items such as those from Machiavelli exactly the way he stated them originally. I think that second strategy is best for personality capture questionnaires, indeed including many scales that could detect response bias because those biases are part of the personality we are trying to capture. In any case, only after completing an ethnographic questionnaire study might one reverse the direction of some items, and then only for use in other studies having different goals. One consequence of this strategy is that we seldom see negative factor loadings, although here Factor 1 had negative loadings on four items that express one possible dissent from the Christian conception of the afterlife:

Factor 1 Negative: *Oblivion*
−0.83 Not experience anything, because there is no afterlife and death is final.
−0.74 Cease to exist, never thinking or feeling again.
−0.57 Feel nothing, and you will not even know that you are dead.
−0.52 Cease to exist except for the memories of you that remain in the hearts and minds of those who knew you and continue to live on Earth.

Factor 2 is negative in a different way, expressing what Christians fear, rather than what they hope which was covered in Factor 1. Hell becomes a second factor, rather than giving more items a negative loading on Factor 1, largely because Christians disagree greatly on the reality of Hell, even as most believe in Heaven:

Factor 2: *Hell*
0.94 Be burned in a raging fire that never ceases, where you endure agony forever.
0.94 Enter a terrible place filled with never-ending fear, pain, torment, hate, anger, cruelty, and sadness.
0.88 Become trapped forever in a torture chamber designed just for you, where you experience an exaggerated version of the suffering you have already encountered on Earth.
0.87 Be confined in a place of torture where you relive the pain and anguish that you lived or caused on Earth, over and over again.
0.76 See a devil with a pitchfork stoking the fires of hell, while other writhing creatures are screaming in pain.
0.76 Be engulfed by ugliness, decay and stench unimaginable.
0.73 Undergo inescapable doom, like being crushed helpless between two icebergs.
0.73 Be thrown into a place of torment for evil doers and unbelievers.
0.70 Agonize in unspeakable pain and anguish that grip you so intensely that you would explode rather than exist.
0.65 Writhe in the pit and lake of fire, seeing distant Heaven and knowing you can never have the happiness of the souls who are there.
0.63 Eternally have to feel the pain you caused others during your life (also in Factor 12).
0.57 Be forever trapped in the agony of the last moment of life (also in Factor 17).
0.54 Be forever lonely, with no one to love or who cares about you.
0.52 Endure total darkness in a very cold place (also in Factor 11).
0.51 Suffer eternal separation from God (also in Factor 15).

To be sure, Christianity is not the only religion on the Earth, and Asian traditions tend to consider the possibility of reincarnation. Whether or not there were many adherents of Asian religions among the respondents, they do recognize it as an alternative. The fact that reincarnation items clustered into Factor 3 suggests not only that they fit together in the minds of the respondent, but also that respondents have a range of views about them:

Factor 3: Reincarnation
0.89 Be reborn into a new child or animal.
0.86 Go through a series of lives, eventually reaching Nirvana.
0.84 Be reincarnated in a form you deserve, as a result of your behavior in this life.
0.81 Have another opportunity to choose a situation to be born into that will allow you to learn lessons you need to learn.

0.67 Exist as a spirit on the Earth, inhabiting an animal, tree, or other part of nature.
0.66 Be reborn near the family you love so dearly in this lifetime.
0.59 Return to Earth as a spirit guardian to guide people along the right path.
0.59 Move on to the next realm of existence to learn the lessons you did not learn on Earth.
0.52 Become part of a huge network of energy connecting each dead person to all the other entities, making a vast web that encompasses the whole universe.

Factor 4 seems to reflect an emotional response, perhaps worthy of the label *unease*, that is somewhat different from either hope or fear:

Factor 4: *Unease*
0.69 Feel intense uncertainty about what is going on and what will happen.
0.66 Feel unendurable boredom, lacking challenges and creativity.
0.63 Have a ghostlike existence with little sensory awareness or pleasure.
0.60 Regret missed opportunities, chances not taken, people not met, loves not loved, sights not seen, and questions unanswered.
0.56 Be only semi-conscious for several days before going to the next life.

The first four factors by no means exhaust the possibilities, neither the range of viewpoints promulgated by religions and philosophies, nor the range of personal emotions that contemplation of death may arouse. The remaining 14 factors all seem to make sense, although none collects more than three items, and thus could be the focus of subsequent research studies that went beyond the limited scope of this research study. For example, one could build them into Phase I questionnaires of open-ended items, in which each of the statements below elicited comments from respondents that could be edited to produce additional related statements for Phase II questionnaires. While I have given a label to each of these minor factors, only future research could really tell us what cultural and psychological phenomena they reflect:

Factor 5: *Nature*
0.75 See a beautiful sunset.
0.63 Dwell in a warm, beautiful land with trees, mountains, and an ocean that goes on forever.
0.58 Enter a world of green meadows, grassy plains, and plentiful buffalo you can hunt with your ancient ancestors.

Factor 6: *Flying*
0.78 See many white clouds with angels playing trumpets.
0.55 Get wings that allow you to fly everywhere and watch over all the people and animals on Earth.

Factor 7: *Cultic*
0.71 Be admitted to one part of a heaven that is divided into a hierarchy of realms of different qualities.
0.67 Teach others about "the plan," in a spirit world.
0.65 Become the God of your own universe.

Factor 8: Boundless
0.62 Achieve a state of consciousness without limitations.
0.54 Feel free from individual ego identification and completely unified with all other forms of energy.

Factor 9: *Corpse*
0.81 Decay in the grave and turn to dust.
0.76 Be buried in the cold, hard ground.

Factor 10: Indifference
0.75 No longer care about the things you saw or worried about in this world.

Factor 11: *Limbo*
0.56 Enter a gray, shadowy realm.
0.51 Endure total darkness in a very cold place (also in Factor 2).

Factor 12: *Guilt*
0.69 Regretfully decide you should have listened to the missionaries when they knocked
    on your door.
0.50 Eternally have to feel the pain and anguish you caused others during your life (also
    in Factor 2).

Factor 13: *Nonphysical*
-0.57 Live eternally in a real, physical, resurrected body (also in Factor 1, but negative
    here).

Factor 14: *Purgatory*
0.75 Stay in Purgatory for a while, then after paying your debt of sin, go to Heaven.

Factor 15: *Reluctance*
0.64 Suffer eternal separation from God (also in Factor 2).
0.52 Stay on Earth for a while after the funeral, visiting loved ones to comfort them.

Factor 16: *Vampires*
0.61 Be fed upon by vampire-like gods, slowly and painfully.

Factor 17: *Subjective*
0.63 Be trapped forever in the agony of the last moment of life (also in Factor 2).

Factor 18: *Despair*
0.69 Weep over the complete absence of good, of joy, of beauty, of hope.

As well as illustrating a methodology that will be useful for personality capture, this pilot study examined conceptions of the afterlife that already are embedded in cultures and subcultures on the Earth, even as personality emulation may possibly provide future alternatives we cannot fully articulate today. The next example takes the methodology to a higher level, with a much more massive questionnaire database, raising a great variety of questions about the human future.

2.3   The Year 2100

Although rooted in the past, human action is always directed toward the future. Thus by examining conceptions of the future, we can learn much about people's beliefs, values and other qualities that shape their behavior. In the 1960s, a *futurology* rage gripped American intellectuals, many of whom had been working for the Kennedy-Johnson administration or who wished to serve as advisors charting the course of its "New Frontier" and "Great Society." Among the results were two visionary books, *The Year 2000*, by Herman Kahn and Anthony J. Wiener, and *Toward the Year 2000*, edited by Daniel Bell [16, 17]. Based on the work of think tanks and university scholars, these books not only attempted to extrapolate trends but also to sketch scenarios describing futures that might result if different decisions were made by societal leaders.

A few of the prognostications proved to be on the mark, such as the predicted collapse of the Soviet Union, but others were far too optimistic, notably an aggressive space program at the dawn of the twenty-first century. Ultimately, all the visions of the year 2000 were little more than the informed guesses and personal hopes of intellectuals. As that supposedly fateful year approached, I joined a team headed by James Witte that conducted one of the largest and most innovative online questionnaire surveys carried out to that date, *Survey2000*, which collected responses from roughly 46,500 adults online. When the opportunity came to include an open-ended question about the future, we decided to do a project like those of the 1960s, but based on the predictions of thousands of ordinary people rather than a handful of famous pundits [18, 19].

On June 1, 1997, The Questionnaire Factory added a Phase I questionnaire, containing several open-ended questions about what might happen over the coming century. One worked especially well, and was included as the very last item in Survey2000: "Imagine the future and try to predict how the world will change over the next century. Think about everyday life as well as major changes in society, culture, and technology." Many respondents gave thoughtful answers to this question, producing more than 10 MB of text. I read carefully through all this text, copying out phrases and sentences that seemed to identify distinct ideas about how the future might be. Naturally, some ideas were expressed in about the same language by many different people, and I copied only the first or best expressions I encountered. This very time-consuming process eventually gave us a new file with just over 5,000 text extracts.

I then worked carefully through these 5,000 excerpts, combining and editing them into clear statements of single ideas. Some are simple declarative statements predicting that something will be true in the year 2100. Others are more complex, suggesting what will cause a particular outcome or combining factors to describe a general condition in the future. As I was completing the editing, I began to categorize the ideas in groups, initially having about 35 categories. Then came an iterative process of collapsing categories and regrouping items, until there were 20 groups with 100 items in each. These were then built into a computer program called *The Year 2100*, having 2,000 stimuli and with two responses to each for fully 4,000 measurements of a person's views of the future. Figure 2.1 shows the user interface when the respondent is rating a statement highly relevant to the subject of this book.

Clicking the [Help] button would temporarily switch to a special page where the user could try the interface, following these instructions:

FIRST: On a scale from 1=BAD to 8=GOOD how would you rate this statement about the future? Second: On a scale from 1=UNLIKELY to 8=LIKELY how would you rate this statement about the future? Click your mouse on a number between BAD and GOOD (1–8). Then click a button between UNLIKELY and LIKELY (1–8). Finally, click OK in the middle.

At the moment, the respondent is ready to click OK, having already rated this item 8 on both of the scales, as indicated by the fact the [8] buttons are brighter in both scales. However, the respondent is free to click a different number on a scale, changing the rating upon second thoughts. The [Back] and [Skip] buttons allow the respondent to see previous or subsequent items, without recording a response for this one, while [OK] records the responses and goes on to the next item.

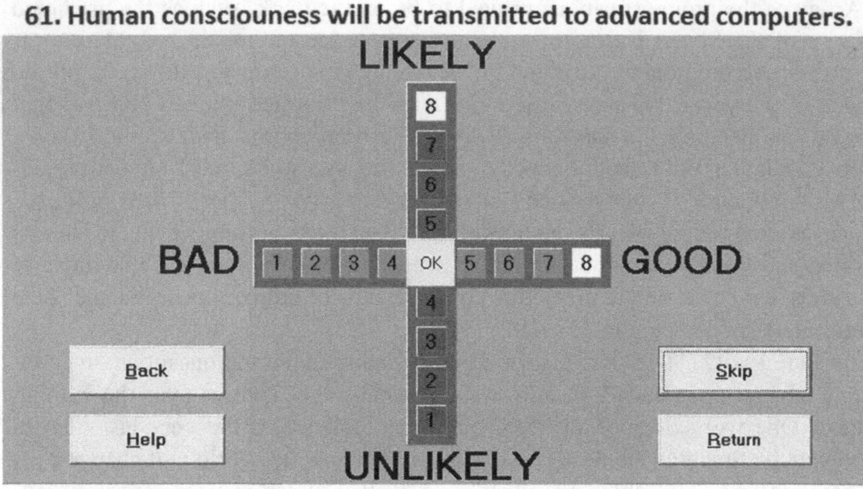

61. Human consciouness will be transmitted to advanced computers.

Fig. 2.1 The cross interface in the Year 2100 software

"Human consciousness will be transmitted to advanced computers" happens to be number 61 of 100 items in a category roughly called Knowledge. For ease in remembering, the 20 groups have simple names: Art, Business, Conflict, Domestic, Education, Family, Government, Health, International, Justice, Knowledge, Labor, Miscellaneous, Nature, Outer space, Population, Quality of life, Religion, Society, and Technology. This categorization is a little artificial. For example, the Domestic group not only has statements about people's homes but also includes ideas about urban and rural environments and about the food people will eat at home. However, each group other than Miscellaneous covers a definite conceptual territory and thus can guide the user in his or her exploration of the data. The Year 2100 software had three main goals. It sought to be:

1. An interactive book of the future based on the thoughts of thousands of people around the world, thus a time machine for the imagination.
2. A system for recording a person's opinions about issues that challenge decision makers today, thus a time capsule to preserve an important aspect of that individual.
3. An educational system for preparing essays concerning the major trends of our times, thus a method for consciousness expansion at both home and school.

At any point, the user can save the most recent data, stop with the intention of returning later, or see any one of a number of analyses of the data collected to that point. For example, one option displays the items in one of the 20 categories, followed by the respondent's rating of it in the form [GOOD, LIKELY]. Here are the seven Knowledge items that have in the middle the one about transmitting human consciousness into computers:

58. People will hold onto superstitions and myths all the more strongly, as the gap widens between science and public understanding of it. [3, 7]
59. Interest in science education will decline in the most developed nations, and they will import their scientists from other countries. [2, 7]
60. The solar system will be well understood. [6, 7]

61. Human consciousness will be transmitted to advanced computers. [8, 8]
62. For the first time in human history, human-computer interfaces will permit development of technologies of the soul. [8, 8]
63. Anthropologists will make amazing discoveries about human origins. [6, 7]
64. The golden age of science will have ended, but the age of conceptual logic and relative thinking will have just begun. [3, 6]

Some of the analysis tools pull out subsets of items the respondent rated in similar ways. An especially complex one gives the respondent the full matrix of 64 response pairs ([1, 1]; [1, 2]; [1, 3] etc.), but a simpler set of options includes the following four definitions:

Pollyanna: Predictions that are 6–8 Good and 6–8 Likely
Utopia: Predictions that are 6–8 Good and 1–3 Likely
Dystopia: Predictions that are 1–3 Good and 1–3 Likely
Threat: Predictions that are 1–3 Good and 6–8 Likely

For example the individual's utopia is that subset of predictions that the respondent wishes would prove true, but firmly doubts will indeed come about. Any of these categories, any of the 20 topical groups, and indeed the entire list of 2,000 items can be downloaded as a text file, either with or without the respondent's ratings of each item, to be edited in a word processor or other software.

The correlation between the Good and Likely ratings is a measure of the respondent's optimism—the belief that good things will happen, defining "good" in whatever way the user wishes. This optimism variable is calculated for each of the 20 topic areas, as well as for the entire group of 2,000. Table 2.2 ranks the 20 topic areas in terms of one respondent's optimism scores, and of course a different respondent would show a different pattern.

In expressing extreme optimism about the future of religion, this respondent was not expressing religious faith, nor was the extreme pessimism about outer space a rejection of the space program. The GOOD ratings by a respondent express that individual's values, and this possibly atypical respondent rated just two religion items 7 or 8 on the GOOD scale: "The spiritual deadness affecting prosperous societies will lead to a proliferation of strange cults and fanatic religious movements." "Science will become the official state religion, with scientists as high priests." And this respondent rated seven outer space items only 1 or 2 on the GOOD scale: "There will not yet be real breakthroughs in how to take humans to explore the planets of other stars." "People will not be able to establish permanent residences on extraterrestrial moons or planets." "All people will be living on distant planets, since the Earth will have been destroyed." "Humanity will not leave the Earth in meaningful numbers, because the technology required will be beyond its grasp." "Only very slight progress will be made in space." "Space exploration will be too expensive to continue." "Space exploration will stall, symbolizing the failed promises of technology." Thus, we cannot assume from the optimism-pessimism scores what the individual's values are, but must look at the meaning of the items given extreme ratings.

Because it is easy to download all the items and responses, more elaborate analysis can be done using a spreadsheet or special statistical software. Table 2.3 illustrates the possibilities. After this respondent had rated all 2,000 items, we down-

Table 2.2 Correlations between Good and Likely, defining optimisms of one respondent

Category	Contents of category	Optimism
Religion	Religion, spirituality, faith, secularization, denominations	0.61
International	International relations, nations, regions of the world	0.55
Domestic	Home life, houses, foods, urban and rural communities	0.54
Technology	Transportation, communications, computer technology	0.52
Miscellaneous	Miscellaneous aspects of technology, culture, society, life	0.51
Society	Relations between individual people and social classes	0.47
Business	Business, commerce, the economy, wealth, inequality	0.46
Art	Art, music, literature, culture, entertainment, sports, style	0.40
Conflict	Conflict between groups, including non-violent competition	0.37
Health	Health, medicine, sickness, genetics, drugs, specific diseases	0.30
Government	Government, politics, politicians, political systems, ideologies	0.28
Education	Students, schools, academics, languages, education in society	0.26
Justice	Crime, justice, courts, law, police, morality, punishment	0.26
Quality of life	Lifestyles, values, social problems, general quality of life	0.23
Nature	Environment, climate, natural resources, flora, fauna	0.13
Family	Marriage, families, children, reproduction, sexuality	0.10
Knowledge	Knowledge, science, beliefs, philosophies, world views	0.08
Labor	Jobs, labor relations, occupations, working conditions, careers	0.08
Population	Demography, life span, fertility, mortality, migration, cloning	−0.14
Outer space	Space exploration, space technology, and human future in the universe	−0.36

loaded them into a spreadsheet and asked the respondent to go through them and assign each to one of these new categories: Internet, Electronic, Space, Biotechnology, Nuclear, and Other. The 0.15 optimism score for the Nuclear category, not very far from the zero point on the scale and less reliable than others because it is based on a small number of items, says that the respondent is neither optimistic nor pessimistic in that area. The negative score of −0.30 on Space items means the respondent is specifically pessimistic about future space technology development, believing that good things are unlikely to happen.

Ethnographic questionnaires designed to expand the options for personality capture can be integrated with existing psychological and social science measurement instruments, to achieve the best of both methods. That is best illustrated by building upon a set of classical questionnaire scales called the Semantic Differential, which resembles the work we have just described, but has very important differences.

2.4 The Semantic Differential

This is a commonly-used kind of questionnaire scale, developed back in the 1950s, that asks the respondent to judge something in terms of several pairs of opposite adjectives [20–22]. Through a series of studies, using factor analysis and progressively refining the list of antonyms, Charles Osgood and his associates came to the

Table 2.3 Recategorization of the Year 2100 Items by one respondent

Category	Examples of statements in the category	Number of Items	Mean good	Mean likely	Optimism (r)
Internet	The art of letter writing will revive through use of e-mail. E-commerce will provide consumers around the world with the best products and services at the cheapest prices. The Internet will allow gifted individuals to be heard without being controlled by the marketplace and nay-sayers	99	5.1	5.6	0.44
Electronic	Digitized art will be the most influential approach in fields as diverse as painting, movie making, and music. Everyone will be required to have some type of microchip implanted under their skin in order to buy and sell. The typical house will be controlled by a main computer that does the basic tasks around the home	120	4.7	5.3	0.48
Space	Arrays of solar panels on the Moon will provide much of the Earth's electric power. There will be a defense system to protect Earth from asteroids. The meek will inherit the Earth, and the brave will travel to other worlds	128	6.2	4.3	−0.30
Biotechnology	Genetic engineering will be extremely useful in agriculture. Alzheimer's and other forms of senility will have been wiped out. A vaccine to prevent AIDS will have unleashed a second sexual revolution	120	5.1	5.2	0.41
Nuclear	A major nuclear world war will occur between the West and Islamic states. Energy will be chiefly supplied by nuclear fusion facilities that operate on hydrogen derived from water. There will be a political crisis over the disposal of spent fuel from nuclear power plants	17	3.9	4.4	0.15
Other Technology	Terrorists having weapons of mass destruction will force nations to become police states in order to provide security for their people. Engineers will be able to build microscopic machines, assembled molecule by molecule, to do useful work. More and more women will enter the fields of engineering, science, research, computing, and technology	148	4.9	5.0	0.24
Non-technology	Natural foods and herbs will be used widely for good health and fitness. The typical person will experience multiple divorces and remarriages. Radical politics will draw strength from the alienation of vast numbers of people who are disconnected from their neighbors	1368	4.2	4.8	0.29

conclusion there existed primarily three dimensions of meaning. *Evaluation* was the first dimension, measured through scales like good-bad, beautiful-ugly, true-false, and kind-cruel. The second dimension, *potency*, emerged in such distinctions as strong-weak, hard-soft, heavy-light, and masculine-feminine. Some respondents have difficulty distinguishing the third dimension, *activity*, from potency, but it was measured by dichotomies like active-passive, fast-slow, and excitable-calm.

Osgood's research team was able to find other dimensions, using such methods as partial correlations to remove the effect of the first three dimensions before looking for others, but much Semantic Differential research is limited to evaluation, potency, and activity. In the early days, Osgood described these as three general dimensions of meaning for human beings, but later he came to speak of *affective meaning*, implying they were emotional reactions to stimuli. While any noun or verb can be rated through the Semantic Differential, many studies investigated how respondents judged people playing various roles in their lives. For example, research by Jon Hoelter employed a brief version of the evaluation dimension to study how high-school students judged themselves, their friends, their parents, and their teachers [23].

David Heise has showed how Semantic Differential data about a person can be used to emulate aspects of that person's framework of judgment [24, 25]. Of course, it is easy enough to have the individual rate a number of key concepts, such as *mother* and *child*, on a set of Semantic Differential scales. Heise's key step was to postulate *affect control theory*, a system for predicting how ratings of separate concepts could combine in a particular, novel situation [26]. For example, suppose Heise already has a person's ratings of *mother*, *child*, *tired* and *scold*. His theory then allows him to predict how the person would rate the entire sentence, "The tired mother scolded her child." To do so requires development of a kind of grammar, specifying the algorithms for combining the meanings of words into the meanings of sentences. Furthermore, Heise's approach would allow scientists to evaluate and improve the theory, on the basis of any discrepancies between such predictions and actual ratings of whole sentences.

Central to Heise's research program was the use of personal computers to allow people to invest many hours rating a large number of concepts in terms of the Semantic Differential, doing so in short bursts of activity whenever they happened to have time during the day. Inspired by Heise's extension of the Semantic Differential, but seeking to add complexity in a different direction, I developed a questionnaire software program called *Self* that presented 1,600 stimuli, each seeking two responses, for a total of 3,200 measurements. Self was freely available online, and the Appendix to this book explains where it and the nine related programs can be found. Self-sought to achieve three main goals for the user:

1. An interactive tool for private exploration of a person's own psychology, thus a microscope for the mind.
2. A system for recording a person's self-image and values concerning the qualities a good person should have, thus a time capsule to preserve an important aspect of that individual.
3. An educational system for preparing essays in courses such as the psychology of personality, introductory psychology, and social psychology.

The software is designed to make it easy for users to save files containing particular kinds of qualities, then call them up into a word processor for printing, editing, or to use as the nucleus of an essay the user might write. A file of the qualities the user considers best for a person to have can be the basis for a term paper in philosophy, psychology or sociology. In the context of the course perspective, the essay could explain what the qualities have in common. One qualitative analysis option, "Character Analysis," automatically writes a little essay about the user's qualities.

Because the data are based on personal judgments, they say much about the user. Are "bad" qualities those that the user thinks indicate weakness or wickedness? Or are judgments determined by unique aspects of one's personal life history, by individual needs, or by moral instruction the person received? Especially interesting are the qualities judged to be very good, but which the respondent thinks he or she lacks. How can any of those ideal qualities be gained? Or should the user recognize that some are unrealistic? Or is the person too modest, and actually possesses them?

One option, "Biography," creates the seed of an autobiography. It produces a text file of all the qualities that describe the person well, along with brief instructions on how to use them in writing part of an autobiography. Good biographies generally have two themes: chronology and character. The *chronology* is the timeline of events, settings, and people in the individual's life. *Character* is the nature of the personality as reflected in the individual's actions, reactions, and interpretations.

In the first phase of the research, a battery of 18 fresh paired-opposite items was administered to 512 respondents who were members of small work groups. The 18 items were developed with the help of 36 students in classes on the Sociology of Organizations and on Small Group Processes. I asked students to think about the qualities they would like to see in people they were working with. Each student wrote down as many as 20 of these terms, then next to each one he or she wrote its opposite (antonym). Then the classes discussed the words and selected 18 pairs that seemed to cover the most important dimensions of personality that were important for co-workers.

Statistical analysis of many respondents' data confirmed that this process of item-generation was working, so the second phase of the project returned to the full list of qualities the students had mentioned, identifying many more pairs of opposites. The third phase of the work involved employing four standard thesauri to generate as many pairs of opposites as possible that described personal qualities, without reusing any of the words or employing any obscure terms.

The fourth phase of the work involved creating and refining a categorization of these terms that places them in 20 groups of 80 words (40 pairs) each. For ease of remembering, the groups have simple names: Ascendant, Benevolent, Convention, Dominance, Erotic, Feelings, Goal-direction, Harmony, Intellect, Judicial, Kinetic, Likeable, Miscellaneous, Notional, Organization, Physical, Quality, Random, Sociability, and Temporal. This final categorization is a little artificial, and both the Miscellaneous and Random categories lack any fundamental coherence. However, each of the other 18 groups covers a definite conceptual territory and thus can guide the user in his or her exploration of the data.

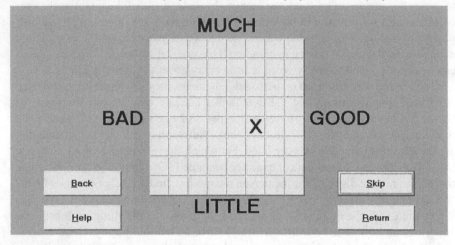

Fig. 2.2 The block interface in the self software

Although the computer linked each antonym pair, the two words were presented to the user separately, 40 steps apart in the list of 80 words in each group. For example, "approachable" was the 3rd word in the Sociability set, and "unapproachable" was the 43rd. The questionnaire administration part of the software gave the users two options, the first of which—*cross*—was shown in Fig. 2.1. Now, Fig. 2.2 shows the other option—*block*—that would be used by people already familiar with *cross* and the logic of the process, allowing one mouse click to answer two questions, and avoiding the need to click an extra time to register the response.

As shown in Fig. 2.2, the user was asked to click inside a checkerboard whose dimensions measured two variables. The horizontal scale asked how Bad or Good it generally was for a person to be approachable. The vertical scale asked how Little or Much the person had this quality. The figure shows the situation after the respondent has clicked the box representing both 6 box on the Bad-Good scale, and 4 box on the Little-Much scale. This would automatically move on to item 4, which happens to be "diplomatic."

The Self software was written for the most common Windows operating system, for use on desktop and laptop machines. The user can easily enter, respond to a few items, then exit, even running the program simultaneously with other software, as I did when I copied the two figures above. The program offers many ways to analyze the qualities and the respondent's judgments of them, both quantitative and qualitative.

In The Year 2100, the correlation between the two scales measured optimism, and here it measures self-esteem. It is the correlation between how Good the respondent rated the qualities and how Much the respondent believed to possess them. Thus, self-esteem is defined straight-forwardly as the extent to which a person feels he or she has good qualities. And it is measured relative to the individual's own personal standards of goodness, rather than imposing other people's standards.

Another subtle but informative measure concerns how distinct a group of qualities is in the respondent's mind. Each of the groups of 80 qualities is composed of 40 pairs of antonyms. This measure is the average of the differences in the ratings of the two qualities in each antonym pair. It can be as little as 0.0 or as much as 7.0, but usually is between these extremes. A very low number indicates confusion about the concepts, that the respondents not care about them, or that they are not very meaningful to the particular person. A high number means that the particular group of antonyms is very clear in the individual's mind, who makes very strong distinctions between these opposite concepts. For each of the 20 areas comprising 40 antonym pairs, the software automatically generates a character analysis like the following for one respondent:

2.5   Sociability

What is your self-image in the general area of "sociability" qualities? How do you communicate with others? Do you encourage interaction, or not?

Your self-image has 30 of the qualities in this group: embarrassed, diplomatic, civil, good-natured, attentive, frank, remote, shy, gentlemanly, isolated, diffident, withdrawn, lonesome, courteous, affable, formal, cordial, private, secretive, unsociable, gallant, polite, connected, expressive, tactful, genial, solitary, introverted, antisocial and uncomplaining.

The opposites of these qualities are: audacious, undiplomatic, uncivil, sullen, inattentive, secretive, intimate, forward, ungentlemanly, connected, expressive, involved, festive, discourteous, surly, informal, grim, public, frank, sociable, rude, impolite, isolated, diffident, blunt, cranky, gregarious, extroverted, social and complaining.

There are 3 apparent contradictions here, because your self-image seems to be torn between these pairs of opposites: "frank" or "secretive," "isolated" or "connected" and "diffident" or "expressive."

On average you judge your 30 sociability qualities to be 4.7 on the scale from bad=1 to good=8. Roughly speaking, you feel these qualities are an almost equal mixture of good and bad.

Your self-esteem is measured by the correlation between rating qualities good and saying that you have them. With respect to "sociability" qualities, your self-esteem is 0.20. That is, you have slightly high self-esteem.

You rated all 40 pairs of opposites. The average difference in your rating of the antonyms in each pair was 2.0 on the 8-point Little to Much scale. This is a very small difference. Apparently your characteristics in this area are weak or ambiguous.

On the 8-point Bad to Good scale, the average difference in your rating of the antonyms in each pair was 3.4. Your values are rather clear, but not striking, when it comes to "sociability" qualities.

Another one of the many analysis tools provides a display such as shown in Fig. 2.3, comparing the statistics for one of the 20 groups of items against all the others. The clickable buttons at the bottom can switch the bar graphs between the Good and Much measures, provide raw numbers or percents, and switch to a listing of all items and their ratings in this set of qualities.

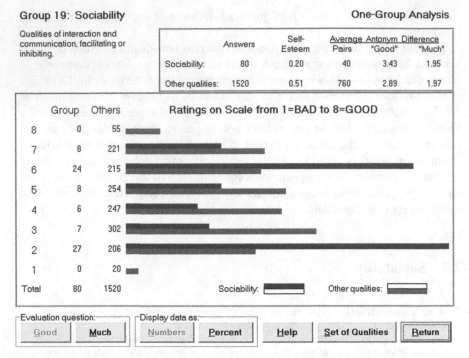

Fig. 2.3 One statistical analysis display in the self software

2.6   Conclusion

In the following chapter, we will return to the original Semantic Differential, and branch off from it in a different direction, but here we have explored expanding the number of scales from 12 to 800, in a way producing 3,200 measurements, without worrying about how many of them group into clusters, or how many personality dimensions are represented. We have shown how questionnaire items can be derived from the thinking of specific individuals, such as Machiavelli and McGregor, and then introduced methods for deriving very large numbers of questionnaire items through a rigorous equivalent of ethnographic research of a substantial human culture. We have begun to see how computer administration of questionnaires, online or via special software programmed for desktop and laptop computers, can facilitate administration and analysis of very large number of items, and we can now continue that exploration into the modern realm of mobile and ubiquitous devices.

References

1. Bainbridge, W. S. (1989). *Survey research: A computer-assisted introduction*. Belmont: Wadsworth.
2. Bainbridge, W. S. (1976). *The spaceflight revolution*. New York: Wiley Interscience.
3. Bainbridge, W. S. (1991). *Goals in Space: American values and the future of technology*. Albany: State University of New York Press.
4. Machiavelli, N. (1940). *The prince and the discourses*. New York: Modern library.
5. http://en.wikipedia.org/wiki/Machiavelli. Accessed 19 Jan 2013
6. Christie, R., & Geis, F. L. (1970). *Studies in machiavellianism*. New York: Academic Press.
7. Cronbach, L. J. (1951). Coefficient alpha and the internal structure of tests. *Psychometrica, 16*, 297–334.
8. Couch, A., & Kenniston, K. (1960). Yeasayers and naysayers: Agreeing response set as a personality variable. *Journal of Abnormal and Social Psychology, 60*, 151–174.
9. Berg, I. A. (Ed.). (1967). Response set in personality assessment. Chicago: Aldine.
10. Bainbridge, W. S. (1989). *Survey research: A computer-assisted introduction* (pp. 282–285). Belmont: Wadsworth.
11. http://en.wikipedia.org/wiki/Sucker_(slang). Accessed Jan 19 2013.
12. McGregor, D. (1960). *The human side of enterprise*. New York: McGraw-Hill.
13. McGregor, D. (1966). *Leadership and motivation*. Cambridge: MIT Press.
14. Bainbridge, W. S. (2000). Religious ethnography on the world wide web. In J. K. Hadden & D. Cowan (Eds.), *Religion and the internet* (pp. 55–80). Greenwich: JAI Press.
15. Glaser, B. G., & Strauss, A. L. (1967). *The discovery of grounded theory: Strategies for qualitative research*. Chicago: Aldine.
16. Kahn, H., & Wiener, A. J. (1967). *The Year 2000*. New York: Macmillan.
17. Bell, D. (Ed.). (1968). Toward the year 2000. Boston: Houghton Mifflin.
18. Witte, J., Amoroso, L., & Howard, P. N. (2000). Method and representation in internet-based survey tools: Mobility, community, and cultural identity in Survey 2000. *Social Science Computer Review, 18*(2), 179–195.
19. Witte, J., & Pargas, R. (2004). Online questionnaires. In W. S. Bainbridge (Ed.), *Berkshire encyclopedia of human computer interaction* (pp. 520–525). Great Barrington: Berkshire Publishing Group
20. Osgood, C. E., Suci, G. J., & Tannenbaum, P. H. (1957). *The measurement of meaning*. Urbana: University of Illinois Press.
21. Osgood, C. E., May, W. H., & Miron, M. S. (1975). *Cross-cultural universals of affective meaning*. Urbana: University of Illinois Press.
22. Bainbridge, W. S. (1994). Semantic differential. In R. E. Asher & J. M. Y. Simpson (Eds.), *The encyclopedia of language and linguistics* (pp. 3800–3801). Oxford: Pergamon.
23. Hoelter, J. W. (1984). Relative effects of significant others on self-evaluation. *Social Psychology Quarterly, 47*(3), 255–262.
24. Schneider, A., & Heise,.D. R (1995). Simulating symbolic interaction. *Journal of Mathematical Sociology, 20*, 271–287.
25. Heise, D. R. (2004). Enculturing agents with expressive role behavior. In S. Payr (Ed.), *Agent Culture (pp. 127–142). Florence: Lawrence Erlbaum Associates.*
26. *Heise, D. R. (1999). Controlling affective experience interpersonally. Social Psychology Quarterly, 62, 4–16.*

Chapter 3
Mobile and Ubiquitous Capture

Traditionally, *personality* is conceptualized in psychological terms as a persistent predisposition to feel and behave in ways characteristic for the individual [1]. Over the span of nearly a century, psychologists developed sets of questionnaire items designed to measure the dimensions of personality and comparable qualities of the human self. Their work is an excellent starting point for twenty-first century personality capture, but only a starting point. Some of the strengths of their approach were also limitations, and some of their assumptions were arbitrary. Most significantly, the development of modern information technologies makes it possible to move beyond the practical and theoretical boundaries that constrained traditional personality psychology. This chapter will demonstrate how mobile and ubiquitous computing, combined with some the best methods from the social and psychological sciences, can surmount those barriers. In particular, the focus will repeatedly shift from desktop computers, to mobile devices, to Internet, thus not merely introducing the value of mobile devices, but showing how many forms of information technology can cooperate.

At this point in the progress of human-centered computing, there appear to be two main areas of rapid development. One is the emergence of online communities and subcultures, using social media that exploit the mature technology that is Internet, innovating in design and social organization rather than in computer science. Included are not only recreational social environments like Facebook and *World of Warcraft*, but very serious alternatives to traditional social institutions. In what I call *Digital Government 2.0*, Internet is not used merely as a channel for communicating information from government agencies to the public as in Digital Government 1.0, but as a platform on which citizens can create their own decision-making and action-oriented systems to replace traditional government agencies. *Citizen Science* is an evolving domain in which professional scientists and serious enthusiasts collaborate to discover new truths about reality, for example astronomical classifications in Galaxy Zoo and data collection concerning living organisms as in eBird [2]. The following chapter considers another technology related to refinement of artistic subcultures, *recommender systems* that currently are used to target advertising to the interests of particular customers, but could become an alternative to the academic humanities in the future.

W. S. Bainbridge, *Personality Capture and Emulation,* Human-Computer Interaction Series,   51
DOI 10.1007/978-1-4471-5604-8_3, © Springer-Verlag London 2014

The other area of rapid development is mobile and ubiquitous computing and communication, also based on the existing Internet infrastructure and on other supportive infrastructures such as cell phone networks. While much human-centered computing research has already been completed in this field, it is frankly rather confusing and many questions remain wide open. One reason is that many specific technologies, and indeed corporations, are competing in a volatile global marketplace, so we cannot predict which will dominate even just a very few years in the future. Another is that mobile machines generally have far less memory, computing power, and graphics capabilities than desktop machines, which means that the software they run is often rather limited. For example, the popular games run on cell phones and pocket computers tend to resemble those run on videogame systems two decades ago, rather than having the vast scope of the massively multiplayer online games that require high-end personal computers. This chapter will explore the ways we can adapt this rapidly changing mobile technology for personality capture, in the context of ubiquitous computing that links the mobile devices to all kinds of other information technology.

3.1   Psychology's "Big Five"

A key goal of questionnaire-based personality research in the middle of the twentieth century was to chart major dimensions of variation that applied to the entire population, which had the effect of taking attention away from factors that defined the uniqueness of individual human beings. Supporting this priority was a methodological limitation of the research, namely that practical considerations required the questionnaire to be rather short, never taking more than about an hour to complete. The number of people who could be studied with the old paper-and-pencil methods was low, again making it impossible to examine factors that might apply only to small subsets of the population. Today, using personal computers and mobile devices, it is possible to administer very long questionnaires, in segments of time spaced out over weeks and months, to use Internet to reach thousands of respondents, and to build complex contingencies into the administration program that selects modules appropriate for the given individual, on the basis of the person's answers to earlier questions.

Another limitation of the traditional questionnaire approach was that it relied upon verbal self-reports, rather than observations of the individual's behavior. Later chapters will outline several ways it is possible to record a person's actual behavior in a range of more-or-less realistic settings, but the new computer technology also makes it easier to administer questionnaires in which a person describes their friends and family members, at least in part reflecting the behavior of many people other than the immediate respondent. Furthermore, a key theme of this book is that each person has his or her own personality theory, which should not be ignored in an analysis of the person, and that must be reflected in any emulation. This chapter begins, however, with what for many years seemed the best candidate for a general theory of personality variations, which emerged and consolidated in the five decades 1945–1995.

Research using questionnaires to explore personality began prior to the Second World War, but immediately after it this approach blossomed, especially through the work of Raymond Cattell who claimed to have discovered fully 16 primary dimensions of personality [3, 4]. Although a version of Cattell's questionnaire test was still being used 60 years after its creation, his specific findings were never replicated by other psychologists, and one reason may be the primitive nature of computing technology at the time he worked. He employed that computationally-intensive form of statistical data reduction called *factor analysis*, which ideally is used iteratively, in a process by which the items in a questionnaire are constantly refined through continual reanalysis, and which placed very heavy demands on computing power, at least during the early years of digital computers [5, 6]. Of course modern computers have no difficulty with factor analysis, and the version built in the Statistical Package for the Social Sciences (SPSS) functioned almost instantly on personal computers 20 years ago, but this was not the case 40 years earlier.

Factor analysis is not only demanding, but also makes very definite assumptions about the structure of reality. It begins with responses from a few hundred people who filled out a personality questionnaire containing from a dozen to several dozen items. It then calculates the correlations among all pairs of items, using the Pearson's r correlation coefficient which assumes the items have particular qualities such as being real-number variables with a normal distribution of cases. Then it goes through a series of steps, including a crucial iterative process called *rotation*, to arrive at a smaller number of new variables called *factors*, each of which represents a dimension of variation across all of the original items. We have already seen examples that demonstrated how valuable this method can be.

In the physical sciences it was very common to employ the metaphor of dimensions, for example considering the mass of an object as a dimension comparable to its length, but it is not clear this assumption can be made about human personalities. After the development of electronic computers, many other methods were invented, including notably *multi-dimensional scaling* that also conceptualized variation in terms of dimensions. However, to a significant extent, dimensionality is a metaphor, and it is also possible to do various computerized forms of *cluster analysis* or to group items in hierarchical tree structures.

While many psychologists criticized Cattell's specific findings, many adopted his general methods. The gradual result was consolidation on five key dimensions of personality, the so-called "Big Five" personality dimensions that are central to personality psychology [7]. Several different versions of the Big Five exist, and one is called the OCEAN version because the initials of the five dimension names spell this word: Openness to experience (fantasy, aesthetics, feelings), Conscientiousness (competence, order, dutifulness), Extraversion (warmth, gregariousness, assertiveness), Agreeableness (trust, straightforwardness, altruism), Neuroticism (anxiety, angry hostility, depression).

These five dimensions are social and emotional, as well as individual. Anger, interpersonal warmth, altruism, and a sense of duty all involve feelings about how to relate to other people. Openness to experience specifically means a willingness to experience new feelings in new settings, including with new people. Conscientiousness and Agreeableness describe the willingness to do what other people want, the first relating to task performance and the second more a matter of interpersonal style, whereas Neuroticism implies a degree of estrangement from others.

Many psychological tests are protected by copyright, but Lewis R. Goldberg has been a pioneer of creating and validating versions of psychological scales, then placing them in the public domain for anybody to use, indeed available online [8, 9]. A leading Big Five researcher, Goldberg offers 100 Big Five items, 20 measuring each of the five dimensions. Each item is a phrase describing a characteristic a person might have. The respondent rates each item in terms of how accurately it describes him or her, using a 5-point scale from 1 to 5. Here are Goldberg's Big Five, along with characteristics from the dimension's list of 20 items [10]. The second example for each dimension is scored negatively:

Extraversion:
+Make friends easily
−Am a very private person

Agreeableness:
+Sympathize with others' feelings
−Am indifferent to the feelings of others

Conscientiousness:
+Love order and regularity
−Find it difficult to get down to work

Emotional Stability (opposite of Neuroticism):
+Am relaxed most of the time
−Get stressed out easily

Imagination (comparable to Openness to experience):
+Love to think up new ways of doing things
−Have difficulty understanding abstract ideas

Some of these scales have very long histories in psychology, especially the first one, Extraversion, sometimes also called Surgency. It features prominently in the 1921 classification of personalities offered by Carl Gustav Jung, Sigmund Freud's early disciple and later rival [11]. Jung, in turn derived some of his ideas about personality types from Friedrich Nietzsche's 1872 book, *The Birth of Tragedy*, and Nietzsche looked to the ancient Greeks for inspiration [12].

Goldberg has a short version of the Extraversion scale, using the ten items listed below. A person's responses to the ten are combined into a single score. One way to do this is by adding the ratings for the five positive items, and subtracting the ratings for the five negative ones. More usually in personality psychology like this, the coding scale for the negative items is reversed, after the person has given the ratings, so that 5 is recoded as 1, 4 as 2, 3 remains 3, 2 is recoded as 4, and 1 as 5. Then the average of all the items is calculated. This gives the whole scale the same range as each item, 1 through 5, with 5 meaning most Extraverted. This method also has the advantage that different dimensions can be compared, even if the numbers of positive and negative items are not equal in some scales. Notice that Extraversion is a symmetrical scale, and we could easily turn it into an Introversion measure by reversing how we combined the scores of individual items.

Scored positively for Extraversion:
+Am the life of the party
+Feel comfortable around people
+Start conversations
+Talk to a lot of different people at parties
+Don't mind being the center of attention

Scored negatively for Extraversion:
−Don't talk a lot
−Keep in the background
−Have little to say
−Don't like to draw attention to myself
−Am quiet around strangers

In the case of almost any self-report battery of items, the language used may be more meaningful to some people than to others, the conditional validity issue mentioned earlier. For example, not everybody may recognize the metaphor, "the life of the party," or realize that "keep in the background" refers to social distance. Thus, any questionnaire written in a human language may be biased toward the assumptions of a particular language and cultural community, although the hope was that the underlying dimensions of variation were real enough that they would shine through any problems of item wording. However, this problem suggests again that to some degree personality capture systems need to adjust to the language, culture, and perceptual framework of the individual.

Another way of looking at this is to say that psychological scales like the Big Five are rigorous distillations of concepts that already exist in natural language. This observation has several implications, including: (1) The dimensions of personality that are measured concern qualities of the person that affect social interactions, and thus that other people tend to notice and remark upon, rather than those aspects of the person that are important in themselves but less salient for social life. (2) While many features of human life are universal, there are enough differences across social groups in their culture and material conditions that personality dimensions will differ somewhat across different social groups. (3) There is no one best model of personality dimensions, and several variants may be equally suitable to describe a given individual.

Goldberg's version of the Big Five is not exactly identical to the OCEAN version, and Goldberg also offers an alternate version with seven dimensions, including a "Negative Valence" factor. If we ask people to go through a list of personality descriptions, asking how well each describes them, they are likely to engage in two contradictory mental activities simultaneously. First, they will follow instructions, and try to say how well each phrase describes them. Second, they will consider how good each described quality is generally considered, and try to give a positive impression of themselves as they answer. This second motive is social desirability bias, the tendency of a respondent to give socially acceptable answers to questions, which was discussed in the previous chapter.

Goldberg's Negative Valence measure measures social undesirability, and thus can serve to separate that bias from the other factors. However, concern with social desirability may be itself a personality variable, of value in personality capture,

rather than just being a distorter for measurements of other dimensions. Once we realize that, we can imagine a very different approach—asking the respondent to rate
how good or bad it is for a person to have the quality described by the phrase. It may
turn out that this approach measures the values the individual holds dear, as well as
that individual's perception of social desirability for the community to which that
person belongs. The following section uses two small pilot studies administered to
a total of three people through rather traditional methods, before jumping online and
garnering a thousand times that number of research subjects.

3.2 Big Five Pilot Studies

Using the same approach as for the Self study described in the previous chapter, a
Self II program was created for desktop or laptop personal computers, incorporating
1,000 of Goldberg's items reflecting many scales, including his 100-item version of
the Big Five and the two others just mentioned. As before, the respondent rates each
stimulus phrase twice, once asking how good each quality is, and a second time
asking how much the respondent possesses the quality. Table 3.1 reports the mean
responses on a scale from 1 to 8 for each scale of three different Big Five models of
personality, given by one respondent.

One of the debates concerning the Big Five is whether the factor that seems to
measure intellectual orientation should be called "Intellect" or "Openness to Experience." A motivating issue behind the debate is the fact that many personality psychologists wanted to identify dimensions of variation that were independent from
intellectual skills, such as might be measured by an IQ test. With that goal in mind
they included items that measured a person's interest in new experiences, rather
than concentrating on the person's interest in solving mental puzzles. Openness
to new ideas, however, fits into both conceptions, so the Intellect and Openness to
Experience dimensions of different measurement instruments give similar results.
In the case of the test subject for this pilot study, however, Intellect is scored significantly higher on both how much this individual claims to possess the trait, and how
good it is in that individual's value system.

Of course personality is not just a person's self-image and values; it is also reflected in what other people feel about us. Table 3.2 summarizes responses from
two sisters who were asked to rate each other as well as themselves, on Goldberg's
100 Big Five items, using traditional paper questionnaires that had been printed out
from a desktop computer. Note how the two siblings rate on Extraversion. Subject
A rates herself at 2.7 on the scale from 1 to 5, whereas her sister rates her higher at
3.5. In contrast, both agree that Subject B should be rated around 2.0 or 2.1. Both
research subjects rate the other higher on Agreeableness than the other rates herself,
and indeed they rate each other higher than they rate themselves. This is logical,
because agreeableness directly concerns behavior toward another person, and privately each sister may occasionally suppress negative feelings rather than expressing them and making the other sister fully aware of them.

Table 3.1 Mean responses by one subject to three personality models

Personality factor	How MUCH the quality describes the respondent	How GOOD the respondent judges the quality to be
The OCEAN version of the Big Five		
Openness to experience	5.60	5.70
Conscientiousness	4.60	6.10
Extraversion	3.75	5.15
Agreeableness	4.15	4.45
Non-neuroticism	3.85	5.50
Lewis Goldberg's version of the Big Five		
Intellect	6.60	6.60
Conscientiousness	4.85	5.55
Extraversion	3.65	5.25
Agreeableness	3.80	4.30
Emotional Stability	4.25	5.30
An alternate model		
Intellect	6.60	6.40
Conscientiousness	5.20	4.70
Extraversion	3.80	5.20
Agreeableness	4.00	4.60
Emotional stability	4.00	5.70
Attractiveness	4.60	5.80
Negative valence	4.80	4.50

Table 3.2 Five personality dimensions of two siblings

	Subject A		Subject B	
	Rated by:		Rated by:	
	Self	Sibling	Self	Sibling
Extraversion	2.7	3.5	2.1	2.0
Agreeableness	2.9	3.5	3.1	3.7
Conscientiousness	3.1	3.9	2.9	2.7
Emotional stability	3.7	3.5	3.0	2.9
Imagination	3.5	4.7	4.4	4.0

Subject B rates Subject A higher on Conscientiousness than Subject A rates herself, and research indicates that this dimension is especially important for relations between people during adolescence, the period of life when the sisters' conceptions of each other may have consolidated [13]. Each rates the other higher on Imagination than the rater rates herself, which may reflect the fact that individuals may be more aware of the sources of their own ideas, realizing that some were not self-invented but borrowed from a book or a friend.

The fact that one person's description of another may not perfectly match the individual's own self-description does not invalidate the approach. Rather, the two kinds of data reflect different aspects of the person, and thus provide a more complete description. It should be kept in mind that the Goldberg items concern perceptions of the individual when they are combined. Very different measures would be used to capture attitudes, beliefs, preferences, observable behavior, and meanings. For example, with good reason the general public tends to believe that certain people are naturally violent, yet propensity for violent behavior tends to be ignored by the academic community in designing questionnaires, although it may be hidden inside the Neuroticism dimension, and indeed filling out a questionnaire does not often stimulate violence [14].

Throughout this book, we shall see that the science of personality capture is more advanced than the technology of personality emulation, but we have begun to see efforts to give artificial intelligence characters the Big Five personality dispositions of real people. Sumedha Kshirsagar and Nadia Magnenat-Thalmann used Bayesian methods to model mood changes in non-player characters in computer games, based on three of the five dimensions of the Big Five theory: "A Neurotic person will change moods often, and tend to go into a negative mood easily. On the other hand, an Extravert person will tend to shift to a positive mood quickly in a conversation. An Agreeable person will tend to go to positive mood more often, but frequent mood changes may not be shown." [15]

Su, Pham, and Wardhani also based their research on the Big Five theory, building a fuzzy rule-based system to combine the influence of different personality characteristics to control the interactions and movements of a virtual character [16]. Starting with the assumption that a character can be high or low on each of the five dimensions, the system produced 32 different rules, such as: If (Openness is Low) and (Conscientiousness is Low) and (Extraversion is Low) and (Agreeableness is Low) and (Neuroticism is Low) then (CharacterType is Hinder) and (BehaviorType is Cold).

3.3   Online Android Application

After both Self programs had been completed, an opportunity presented itself to explore a novel method for collecting personality capture data, in the new mobile computing environment. This opportunity came when Martine Rothblatt, the head of the United Therapeutics biotechnology company, asked one of his associates, Michael Clancy, to transform Self II into an Android application, and a version of the program using just Goldberg's 100 Big Five items was distributed for free over Internet. As programmed expertly by Clancy, the application worked very well, allowing the respondents to send the data to the central archive instantly. In addition to the 200 bytes of data in which a respondent rated the Big Five items twice, the dataset included two measures of the respondent's location: (1) a text field where the respondent wrote this information, and (2) the latitude and longitude automatically provided by the respondent's device, if the respondent has allowed it to do so. Most respondents lived in the United States, and the data reported here were for the 50 US states, cases in the two geolocators agreed. *Geolocation* could be of importance in the future, as individuals send vast numbers of questionnaire ratings through such a system, over a period of years, including for example the emotional rating of events as they happen in the real world. Also, we can use geolocators to look at regional cultures and other local conditions that shape people's experiences of life, such as rural versus urban environments.

Clancy was able to provide the data in a form requiring very little preprocessing before placing it in a standard statistical analysis program. The chief preparation necessary was calculating the correlations for all respondents between the two sets of responses to the 100 Big Five items, because statistical analysis packages do not calculate correlations within rows of the data. For the 3,267 respondents whose data are reported here, there was a mean correlation of 0.43 and a standard deviation of 0.34. Correlation coefficients ranged from -1.00 to $+1.00$, so 0.43 implies positive self-esteem for the typical respondent: The person's rating of how much he or she has each quality correlates positively with judging the quality to be good. However, this correlation may also reflect response biases such as social desirability.

A standard deviation of 0.34 implies that about a sixth of respondents have correlations below 0.09 ($0.43 - 0.34 = 0.09$), which suggests lack of self-esteem, so there is ample scope for future analysis of how the two sets of measures correlate. Here we shall focus on the first set, people's descriptions of themselves, to replicate the classic factor analyses as both a quality check and an opportunity to explore the complexity of personality with an unusually large number of respondents. There are many kinds of factor analysis, but one key distinction is between confirmatory and exploratory approaches.

A *confirmatory factor analysis* starts with a theory and seeks to test it. In this case, that meant telling the computer to reduce the data on people's ratings of themselves to exactly five dimensions, and indeed Goldberg's version of the Big Five did emerge. However, as the differences among the three models of personality in Table 3.1 suggest would happen, the results were not exactly his. Notably, the first factor was the opposite of his Emotional Stability factor. Table 3.3 lists the items with the strongest loadings on this factor. A factor loading can be conceptualized roughly as the correlation between the item and the factor, although the numbers tend to be larger than ordinary correlations. Originally, the Non-Neuroticism factor of the OCEAN version was called the Neuroticism factor, but was renamed by psychologists and its codings reversed, so that a high rating on each factor was socially desirable. But here, our 3,267 respondents have returned us to the original meaning of this factor.

An *exploratory factor analysis* seeks to discover meaningful structures without many preconceptions about what they will be, as we first saw in Chapter 1. I asked the computer to do a factor analysis of people's ratings of themselves, without specifying how many factors there should be. Technically, this meant using principal components analysis, selecting for rotation all factors with eigenvalues greater than 1, and using the varimax rotation method. Table 3.4 shows the rather complex results, which can be called the Small Fifteen.

The rotation part of the analysis converged very quickly, perhaps a testimony to how well a large number of respondents compensates for measurement errors in the data. The result was fully 17 factors, of which the last two were essentially noise. Thus, the table lists 15 factors, and I have attempted to label each. All items with factor loadings above 0.5 are included. A negative loading means that the opposite

Table 3.3 Confirmatory
factor 1: Neuroticism (3,267
respondents)

Factor 1 Item	Loading
Get irritated easily	0.72
Get angry easily	0.72
Have frequent mood swings	0.72
Get upset easily	0.71
Get stressed out easily	0.69
Panic easily	0.65
Change my mood a lot	0.65
Get overwhelmed by emotions	0.65
Get caught up in my problems	0.64
Am easily disturbed	0.63
Take offense easily	0.60
Often feel blue	0.60
Worry about things	0.50

of the descriptor belongs to the factor. For example, the positively loaded items in factor 1 represent extraversion, whereas the negative ones represent introversion.

Clearly, the Big Five have expanded into 15 smaller measures, some of which would require further development for future use, finding other items to combine with the ones listed to do a better job of measuring the quality. As in the third version of the Big Five in Table 3.1, this approach to some extent handled the negative valence, by producing some factors that were distinctively negative in connotation. In future, one could add to the questionnaire one of the response bias measures that can be used to control for such things as social desirability—but with awareness that social desirability bias is not so much a defect of questionnaire items as a dimension of individual personality that needs to be measured in its own right.

Factor 13, which I call Inhibition, consists of just one item, "Bottle up my feelings," and it is a good example of how we can go beyond these summary measures. I suspect that people differ in whether they interpret bottling up to be a bad thing, although the subculture of psychotherapists has a vested interest in calling it bad. We can learn more by listing all the other items that correlated at lest 0.25 with this item: Am a very private person (0.31), Am quiet around strangers (0.30), Keep in the background (0.27), Often feel uncomfortable around others (0.26), Don't talk a lot (0.26), Find it difficult to approach others (0.25), Have little to say (0.25), and Often feel blue (0.25). Some of these seem obviously negative, even reflecting depression, but the first three and some of the others are not necessarily negative.

Of course, the item about bottling up feelings might be considered an indicator of Introversion, with perhaps a touch of Neuroticism. But it could be the proper strategy for dealing with some kinds of social environment, not unlike the Perspective dimension of Machiavellianism. Especially in some cultures, but also in many people's experience of life, being a quiet person can be the best practical choice. Perhaps there is a general dimension of personality that could be called Tactic, but it might not be easy to measure without an understanding of the specific social environment which determines which tactics are effective. To the extent that the Big

Table 3.4 Fifteen dimensions of personality (3,267 respondents)

Factor	Representative items (loadings)
1. Extraversion	POSITIVE: Start conversations (0.70); Am the life of the party (0.70); Talk to a lot of different people at parties (0.70); Feel comfortable around people (0.66); Don't mind being the center of attention (0.63); Feel at ease with people (0.62); Make friends easily (0.62); Am skilled in handling social situations (0.61)
	NEGATIVE: Have little to say (−0.55); Often feel uncomfortable around others (−0.56); Find it difficult to approach others (−0.61); Don't talk a lot (−0.64); Keep in the background (−0.66); Am quiet around strangers (−0.66)
2. Neuroticism	Have frequent mood swings (0.74); Get stressed out easily (0.74); Get irritated easily (0.73); Get upset easily (0.72); Get angry easily (0.70); Get caught up in my problems (0.67); Get overwhelmed by emotions (0.67); Change my mood a lot (0.66); Panic easily (0.66); Often feel blue (0.61); Take offense easily (0.59); Am easily disturbed (0.59); Worry about things (0.54)
3. Benevolence	Sympathize with others' feelings (0.71); Think of others first (0.69); Take time out for others (0.66); Love to help others (0.66); Inquire about others' well-being (0.64); Feel others' emotions (0.62); Have a soft heart (0.59); Know how to comfort others (0.57); Have a good word for everyone (0.50)
4. Intellect I	Am quick to understand things (0.71); Catch on to things quickly (0.62); Can handle a lot of information (0.62); Am good at many things (0.60); Pay attention to details (0.56)
5. Organization	Do things according to a plan (0.75); Follow a schedule (0.70); Make plans and stick to them (0.68); Love order and regularity (0.63); Am always prepared (0.52); Like order (0.52).
6. Messiness	POSITIVE: Leave a mess in my room (0.71); Leave my belongings around (0.70); Often forget to put things back in their proper place (0.69)
	NEGATIVE: Like to tidy up (−0.62).
7. Indifference	Am indifferent to the feelings of others (0.59); Feel little concern for others (0.57); Am not interested in other people's problems (0.55).
8. Unimaginativeness	POSITIVE: Have difficulty imagining things (0.71); Do not have a good imagination (0.63)
	NEGATIVE: Have a vivid imagination (−0.61)
9. Literacy	POSITIVE: Have a rich vocabulary (0.73); Use difficult words (0.73); Love to read challenging material (0.65)
	NEGATIVE: Avoid difficult reading material (−0.53)
10. Laziness	Find it difficult to get down to work (0.58); Neglect my duties (0.58); Waste my time (0.58).
11. Implacability	Seldom get mad (0.74); Rarely get irritated (0.66)
12. Agreeableness	Am on good terms with nearly everyone (0.55); Make people feel at ease (0.50)
13. Inhibition	Bottle up my feelings (0.61)
14. Intellect II	Am exacting in my work (0.55); Love to think up new ways of doing things (0.55)
15. Superficiality	Will not probe deeply into a subject (0.56); Try to avoid complex people (0.52)

Five represents a constraining orthodoxy, it is because it reflects the values shared by most people in our society—or most academic psychologists—but once we allow the Big Five to expand into the Small Fifteen, and we collect data from thousands of individuals, then there is ample room for the values of different subcultures to be represented.

3.4   Mobile Pilot Studies

The previous section showed how Internet-connected mobile devices can allow very large numbers of individuals to participate in personality research, with the byproduct that their self-ratings become permanent parts of a data archive. This section offers two examples in which a pocket computer collected large amounts of data from single individuals, but delivering the data not over Internet but by plugging the mobile device into a desktop that had the software to interface with it. The first of the two pilot studies was an extension of the Self program, described in the previous chapter.

The Self software was delivered via email to four volunteers, who answered all 3,200 questions. The software presented the stimuli in 20 groups of antonym pairs, but the groups were not really assembled on the basis of a very clear theory. Given responses from a large number of respondents, one could construct a universal theory arranging the antonym pairs into dimensions or clusters, using methods like factor analysis. But a very different approach is also possible: A person-specific personality theory can be developed, and then applied to data from that person, and data from other people as well.

A spreadsheet was loaded with the 800 antonym pairs—giving both terms in a pair together, rather than separated as in the Self program. One research subject, called Subject 1 in Fig. 3.5, was given the pocket computer and asked to categorize them in about a dozen groups, using any principles the subject wished. Over a period of several days, the subject carried the pocket computer and from time to time worked on the categorization task, which in itself was yet another way of capturing aspects of the subject's personality. This particular subject happened to arrive at 13 categories, not exactly 12, with different numbers of pairs in each. Table 3.5 summarizes responses from four subjects, Subject 1 and three others, analyzing the data in terms of Subject 1's categorization.

The labels of the 13 categories are the three words that garnered the highest total "Good" score from all four subjects. A respondent judged how bad or good it was for a person to have the quality described by each word, and how little or much he or she actually possessed the quality. Because we have so many data points for each individual, it is possible to correlate people with each other, to see how similar or different their ratings are. For example, Subject 1 and Subject 2 correlate 0.67 with each other on their bad-good ratings, and 0.52 on the little-much ratings of the 1,600 qualities. The averages for the 6 coefficients linking the 4 subjects are 0.67 again (ranging from 0.61 to 0.74) for bad-good, and 0.47 (ranging from 0.37 to 0.56) for

Table 3.5 Adjectives describing a person's character, categorized by subject 1

Most "Good" items in subject C's category	N of Pairs	Self-Esteem (correlation GOOD and MUCH)			
		Subject 1	Subject 2	Subject 3	Subject 4
1. Alert, alive, motivated	36	0.57	0.77	0.95	0.83
2. Clear, dedicated, focused	55	0.63	0.78	0.94	0.89
3. Unique, credible, exceptional	51	0.71	0.78	0.89	0.82
4. Healthy, complete, durable	41	0.12	0.58	0.92	0.58
5. Enlightened, innovative, aware	45	0.87	0.92	0.95	0.95
6. Future, real, instinctive	44	0.59	0.70	0.93	0.71
7. Courageous, hopeful, inquisitive	75	0.13	0.44	0.87	0.77
8. Constructive, inspiring, true	142	0.61	0.82	0.91	0.85
9. Spiritual, affectionate, loveable	57	−0.21	0.37	0.87	0.75
10. Resourceful, best, energetic	89	0.39	0.80	0.81	0.83
11. Able, capable, honest	98	0.87	0.91	0.90	0.93
12. Celestial, cosmic, eternal	28	0.38	0.80	0.87	0.87
13. Good-natured, initiating, approachable	39	0.33	0.73	0.95	0.90

little-much. The difference between 0.67 and 0.47 is actually quite interesting. Apparently the four subjects share cultural assumptions about how good or bad the qualities are, but they have different self images, each stressing a somewhat different collection of personal qualities.

For each subject, Table 3.5 gives the correlations between the Good and Much scales in each of the categories, which as we have seen is a plausible measure of topic-specific self-esteem. For example, category 7 includes qualities like courageous and hopeful (and their antonyms, fearful and despairing). Subject 1 placed 75 pairs of items in this category. Among the ratings given these 150 items by Subject 1, the correlation between the Good and Much scales is only 0.13, which means essentially no correlation between rating a quality good and feeling that one possesses it. This is much lower than the self-esteem coefficients for the three other subjects: 0.44, 0.77, 0.87.

However, it may not be appropriate to say that Subject 1 has abnormally low self-esteem, because we do not have population norms for the coefficients. In addition, it is important to remember that self-esteem can be abnormally high, as well as abnormally low. This can occur, for example, during a clinically manic episode, as was in fact the case for one of the high-esteem subjects. More importantly, we can compare the self-esteem coefficients within the data for a given respondent. Subject 1's self-esteem is lowest for qualities like "spiritual, affectionate, loveable" (−0.21), and highest for qualities like "able, capable, honest" (0.87).

Notice that this pilot study used a mobile pocket computer, multiple desktop computers, and Internet email connecting the desktops. The pocket computer lacked both the data and the computing power to do the full analysis, yet it played an essential role. The second pilot study used the same pocket computer, but for more intensive data collection, on the basis of a complex prior data collection effort using multiple Internet-connected computers.

The second pilot study used the 2,000 items from a program similar to the ones described before, called Emotions. The starting point was a list of 10 emotional antonym pairs: love-fear, joy-sadness, gratitude-anger, pleasure-pain, pride-shame, desire-hate, satisfaction-frustration, surprise-boredom, lust-disgust, and excitement-indifference. This is a rather conventional list, but was fine-tuned with advice from developmental cognitive scientist, Bennett Bertenthal. Each of these items was handled separately, although the pairs could easily be recombined during data analysis. The idea was to give the respondent 100 descriptions of situations that might stimulate a given emotion, asking how Bad or Good the situation would make the respondent feel, and how Little or Much it would stimulate the particular emotion. Thus, Emotions adjusted the Little-Much scale to focus on a different emotion for each of the 20 groups of stimuli.

One thousand stimuli came from a pair of questionnaires administered through The Question Factory website which had been created to develop survey items. Each questionnaire listed ten emotions, and asked respondents: "For each of these ten emotions, we will ask you to think of something that makes you have that particular feeling. By 'things' we mean anything at all—actions, places, kinds of person, moods, physical sensations, sights, sounds, thoughts, words, memories—whatever might elicit this emotion. We will also ask you to think of what makes someone else—a person very different from you—have the same feelings." The surveys gave respondents spaces to write "one of the things that might produce an emotion, whether in you or in somebody else. A phrase or short sentence is enough, if it expresses what is in your mind. We will protect the confidentiality of your answers, so please answer honestly and openly." Hundreds of people responded to these surveys, and I edited 1,000 stimuli from what they wrote.

The other 1,000 stimuli came from 20 searches of the World Wide Web using various search engines to find texts describing situations that elicited each of the emotions. By this means, a large number of works of literature and online essays were located that used the words in context. Each of the stimuli in this set were written on the basis of the entire context around the quotation, although in many cases the phrase is a direct quotation. Thus, the 2,000 stimuli were all derived from Internet, but by two very different means.

The research subject for this pilot study first responded to the 4,000 questions in the Emotions program, using a desktop computer, in several medium-duration sessions. Table 3.6 organizes the responses in terms of the antonym pairs, including correlations between the two scales within each of the 20 groups of 100 stimuli. Not surprisingly, most show a big difference between the first term in a pair and the second. For example we generally assume love is good, and the 100 stimuli in the love category have a positive correlation of 0.59 between being rated good and the degree to which they elicit the emotion in this respondent. In contrast, the fear terms have a negative -0.72 correlation, which is one way of saying that fear is bad. The two antonym pairs that do not show this clear pattern, surprise-boredom and excitement-indifference both concern the intensity of the stimulus, and thus apparently measure a very different dimension of emotional reactions than the bad-good Evaluation dimension.

Table 3.6 Emotion ratings by one subject using a desktop computer

Category defining words in Ten near antonym pairs		Mean rating of 100 stimuli in each of 20 categories on 1–8 bad-good scale		Correlation between saying 100 stimuli are good and they elicit the given emotion	
		First category	Second category	First category	Second category
Love	Fear	5.07	4.32	0.59	−0.72
Joy	Sadness	5.09	3.59	0.79	−0.56
Gratitude	Anger	5.34	3.80	0.60	−0.34
Pleasure	Pain	4.78	3.83	0.66	−0.53
Pride	Shame	5.53	3.88	0.75	−0.50
Desire	Hate	4.56	4.13	0.44	−0.66
Satisfaction	Frustration	5.00	3.74	0.73	−0.53
Surprise	Boredom	4.51	4.62	−0.03	−0.26
Lust	Disgust	4.61	3.90	0.55	−0.60
Excitement	Indifference	4.30	4.27	0.05	−0.01

For the mobile computer version, the respondent was asked to rate each of the 2,000 events in terms of all 20 emotions, for a total of 40,000 ratings rather than just 4,000. The respondent found it quite comfortable to answer this vast number of questions, because the pocket computer allowed answering a few at a time, while waiting for a bus or during some other wasted time during the day, wherever the respondent happened to be. Rather than being a burden, this task turned out to be an antidote to boredom, given that every life has lots of down time during which the person wishes something more interesting were available.

The resulting 40,000 measures can be analyzed in many ways, but one obvious step was to factor analyze the data to see how the respondent conceptualizes the 20 emotions. The data turned out to have primarily three dimensions in it, one collecting positive emotions, the second collecting negative emotions, and the third collecting four emotions that describe the energetic character of the stimulus: excitement, surprise, indifference, and boredom. The respondent then rated all 2,000 items again, in terms of the three main dimensions traditionally associated with the Semantic Differential, for another 6,000 measurements.

The bad-good question administered a second time asked about the Evaluation dimension of the Semantic Differential, and the pocket PC program asked the respondent to rate each stimulus in terms of additional weak-strong and passive-active scales, to capture the Potency and Activity dimensions. In fact, this particular respondent did not distinguish between Potency and Activity, combining them mentally in what I am here calling an *energetic dimension*. Figure 3.1 graphs the 20 emotions in terms of the average Evaluation at the two points in time versus the average of the Potency and Activity scales (energetic), based on correlations with how much the 2,000 stimuli had each connotation for this individual.

The map for another person would be both similar and different. Many members of many cultures would distinguish Potency from Activity, but this person does not. Interestingly, this respondent considers most positive emotions to be more energetic than most negative emotions. Fear is the only exception. This is consistent with the

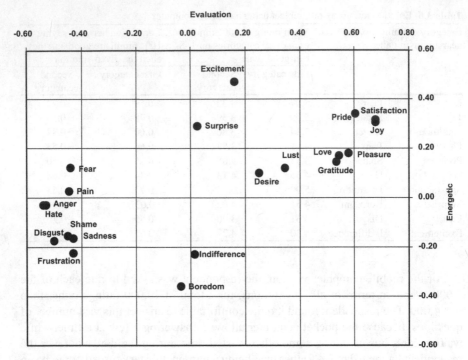

Fig.3.1 Map of emotions by one subject using a pocket computer

prevalent American ideology that people can actively achieve good things for themselves, but if they remain passive they may become victims to bad things. Note that
some emotions generally considered similar occupy almost exactly the same spots
on the map, anger and hate, satisfaction and joy.

3.5   A Mobile Game Machine

Citizens of modern societies carry around with them a great variety of comput-
er-like machines that might be useful for personality capture, from tablets to cell
phones, both of which today may access Internet and incorporate cameras. This
section will examine a popular but unusual device, the Nintendo 3DS portable game
console that was released in February 2012, because it illustrates both the poten-
tialities for the future technologies, and the limitations that current technologies
have for personality capture. This section will highlight a few games that assess a
person's perceptions, cognitive abilities, and reaction time, and thus are proxies for
future software designed specifically for personality capture.

The 3DS is an advanced version of the "double screen" DS that was released
more than 7 years earlier, replacing the main display screen with one that shows

three-dimensional images, using a technology that does not require the user to wear special glasses. All models of both machines have a geometry similar to a minia-ture laptop computer, with the main display screen on a lid that hinges open, and a stylus-operated or touch-screen input device in the place of a keyboard, framed with a few mechanical input devices like those of a videogame controller. The 3DS in-corporates three cameras, two pointing forward to permit taking three-dimensional photographs and to capture images of the real world to combine with graphics in games that employ augmented reality. A motion sensor and some computer vision capability also support augmented reality applications. The 3DS used for this explo-ration was about $3 \times 5 \times 3/4$ inches in size, so a tremendous number of features are crammed into a small volume.

If their users wish, two or more 3DS machines can link up via local radio they generate and manage themselves, and I had no difficulty doing this or linking to my home wireless system to access Internet. Some software can be downloaded from Internet stores, but the main format for distributing games was tiny ROM cartridges. Photos and other material can be exchanged via radio between machines belonging to different users, or uploaded to Facebook, but the main way of transferring data to a personal computer is by removing a memory card and physically plugging it into the PC. The 3DS is an amazing prototype of multi-feature mobile systems, less capable than tablet computers because of the smaller display and limited ability to run non-game software, but nonetheless a harbinger of future developments. Brief consideration of three game ROMs can suggest how such systems could accomplish personality capture.

Crosswords Plus builds on the tradition of crossword puzzles, such as those pub-lished in daily newspapers and solved by commuters on trains and busses for many decades, but with multi-player capabilities. In addition to 1,000 crossword puzzles, the game includes "wordsearch" puzzles that require searching a grid of letters for hidden words, anagrams that require rearranging a set of letters to form several words, and a "word of the day" educational component. In the main crosswords interface, the upper screen displays the puzzle, more-or-less filled in depending upon how far the player has progressed, while the lower screen is the input device. To add a letter, the user employs the game's stylus to click on a square in the lower screen, which then increases in size so the user can write a letter. The interface can be set to display a letter in red if it is wrong, but in general the player needs to watch carefully to see that the machine properly recognized the letter the user was trying to write.

For example, in one of the medium size puzzles, the open square in the upper left corner had two open squares to the right, and two open squares below, with room for two three-letter words to share their initial letter. To the right of the image of the whole puzzle on the upper screen, was a clock counting how long the player had been working on the puzzle, plus two definitions: across = "lyrical tribute" and down = "motor lubricant." Clicking the corner square allowed the player to draw a circle, placing an "O" in that square. Clicking the square to the right of it, allowed placing a "D," and the system correctly distinguished the drawing from "O." But the first attempt to write "E" in the next square across produced a "Z" so a second attempt was needed, to produce "ODE." Drawing in the two squares below the upper left produced the correct word down, "OIL." Other controls on the stylus screen move from square to square, allow seeing all the hints, and offer somewhat costly clues.

As the word of the day feature of *Crosswords Plus* suggests, a prime ability required to solve crossword puzzles is an extensive vocabulary, but there is no standard list of terms that all human beings should know. Most obviously, humans speak many languages, and a Spanish-speaker would write "ODA" rather than "ODE." By their very nature, these puzzles often force their designers to employ abbreviations or obscure words, to complete regions of the puzzle. In this case, the three-letter word going down from the D in ODE is "DNA." The three squares across in the upper right corner of this puzzle must be filled with CPU, defined by the hint "main brain of a computer, for short." A five-letter word going down from the C is defined "Star Wars The _____ Wars (TV series)." The answer is the word "CLONE." Note that this word was defined in terms of a popular culture TV program that children would be likely to know, but perhaps not older people, rather than "organism whose genetic information is identical to that of a parent organism from which it was created." [17] This puzzle also defined "EYED" as part of the name of the musical group Black Eyed Peas, and often crossword puzzles include the names of people or other terms that belong to very specific subcultures. For personality capture, this is not necessarily a disadvantage, because we want to record a person"s subcultural membership as well as command of standard vocabularies.

Nikoli's Pencil Puzzle does for numbers what *Crosswords Plus* does for words, incorporating four kinds of number puzzles bearing Japanese names: *sudoku*, *shikaku*, *akari*, and *hashi*. Nikoli is the Japanese company that popularized or invented these similar games, and unlike crosswords these puzzles are not bound to a particular language. Sudoku is well known in English-speaking countries, and can often be found in newspapers alongside crosswords. Sudoku puzzles require the player to arrange the digits 0 through 9 in all the squares of a 9×9 checkerboard, such that no digit is duplicated in any row or column across the board, or in any of the nine 3×3 subregions of the matrix. Note that this is not identical to magic squares, because the player does not need to add up specified sums, which in any case would always be 45. Indeed, instead of the ten digits ten letters could be used, or ten icons, or ten colors. Each game starts with some of the squares already containing numbers, and the difficulty of the particular puzzle is determined by their pattern.

Sudoku puzzles are commonly created by computers today, so it seems fitting to solve them on one as well. Mathematicians have analyzed them, and there are different strategies for solving them, but it is not clear what they capture about a person's mind other than the ability to do so [18]. It may be that spatial perception, a good working memory, and fast scanning abilities are involved, but I tend to think these could be measured separately with greater accuracy, using psychological experiment methodology specifically designed for this purpose.

American Mensa Academy is a remarkable, if frankly controversial, game based on the subculture of an organization called Mensa that originated in Britain in 1946, enhancing social life for people of unusually high intelligence. Mensa's Wikipedia page calls it "a non-profit organization open to people who score at the 98th percentile or higher on a standardized, supervised IQ or other approved intelligence test" currently having 110,000 members world wide [19]. Half the membership belongs to American Mensa, which proclaims: "As a member, you have the opportunity to meet other smart people at local, regional and national levels. You can attend entertaining, intellectually stimulating events and exchange ideas with others through a variety of publications and our online Community. You can also work to help others in your community by volunteering for community-oriented activities and working with the Mensa Foundation." [20]

However, the overwhelming majority of people are ineligible to join, because their IQs are too low. Chap. 5 of this book will offer a brief critique of IQ tests, but of course our aim is to cherish human differences, as we must if we are to capture individual personalities, rather than to single out a tiny elite for attention. Many science fiction stories have imagined psychometric societies, in which social class is assigned according to the result of intelligence tests, and British sociologist Michael Young criticized this possibility in *The Rise of the Meritocracy* [21]. Tests not very different from IQ tests are used to screen applicants to elite universities, although considerable effort as well as native talent is required to earn their diplomas. So our real society is only partly cognocratic, and Mensa shows no signs of intending to seize power.

The in-game manual hints that playing may improve cognitive abilities, but begins by stimulating the player's competitive instincts: "Using puzzles that are similar to actual IQ test questions, *American Mensa ACADEMY* is designed to push your brain to its limits, challenging your grasp of language, numeracy, logic and more. With multiple play modes and a range of testing mini-games, *American Mensa ACADEMY* offers the perfect opportunity to prove once and for all that you're smarter than your friends!"

The language puzzles not only require the user to possess a huge vocabulary a advanced levels, but to be able to scan written text very quickly from the very beginning. One missing letters question starts with "ear?h?uake" and requires swiftly selecting the pair of letters that will make a word from: hk, kq, qt, ry. In one "mixed up" challenge, the player is supposed to quickly select which of the following spells the word *against*: aastgsi, aitnasn, tgapnai, or atnsgia. "Shuffleword" does not specify the target, but, for example, requires arranging the following three letter clusters to form a word: IF, ORM, UN. One "odd one out" question asks which of the following does not fit the others: tiger, panther, lion, bison. "Word deductions" offers four words and four different sets of four numbers, asking the player to identify a match. A match for "dozen, pair, trio, and bicycle" is "12, 2, 3, 2."

An "opposites" question requires the player to identify the antonym pair in: peace, small, big, bad. Yes, *big* and *small* are antonyms, but what if a pacifist believes that size is unimportant and a more significant opposition is *peace:bad*? Or what if a giant believes that *big* and *bad* are antonyms? These questions may not do a good job of criticizing the validity of this particular item, but in general IQ tests do assume that a right answer exists, but highly intelligent people may be able to construct logical justifications for alternative answers. More significant for our present purposes, items could be created that intentionally combine two sets of approximate antonyms, to see which is the clearer distinction for the particular person.

Especially noteworthy are the logic questions in *American Mensa ACADEMY*. Rather than using words, or numbers as in the numeracy items, these employ colors. This is reminiscent of the Vygotsky test mentioned in Chap. 1, which includes logic problems in which the symbols are colors. Personally, I found this kind of test vastly more difficult than the language or numeracy tests, because I simply could not remember the colors from one instant to the next, and had to struggle to name them, which slowed the process down considerably and often meant time ran out before I could finish. Of course the point of using colors or shapes in an IQ test is precisely to avoid contaminating the results with, for example, which language the person knows best, and whether they might be dyslexic while otherwise intelligent.

The Nintendo 3DS is not limited to commercially sold games, because it incorporates a web browser, and thus for example it was easy to log into the website www.quickiqtest.net and do a shape-oriented test supposedly measuring IQ online. As it happened, the test fit well into the small frame of the 3DS display, but the device's browser makes it easy to zoom in or out and to look around on a larger image. Clearly, one could post many kinds of personality capture systems online, designed to harmonize with the limited display capabilities of mobile devices. The main problem of the existing commercial 3DS games is that they save the player's total score, but not the responses to individual items. With the exception of a few of the "visual" questions in *American Mensa ACADEMY*, where quickly identifying objects amidst a complex scene was required, the three-dimensional capability of the hardware was valueless for the games described here.

3.6 Ubiquity of Meaning

A brief pilot study can illustrate some of the vast potential of multi-method, multi-location personality capture. The general concept was to ask a person to select people and things of interest to that individual, then rate them in terms of a traditional version of the Semantic Differential. The people and things were represented by photographs, and the media were intentionally mixed to illustrate the range of possibilities. The study could have asked the subject to take pictures of people the subject knew well, but it was felt that a pilot exploration of the mechanics of methods should not attempt to deal with the significant privacy and informed consent issues that doing so might raise. Therefore, the subject used a portable laptop computer to access websites offering pictures of 20 famous people selected by the subject. Then the Nintendo 3DS was used to take photographs of 20 objects selected by the subject that were around the house, including the house itself. Via wireless, the pictures of people were transmitted to a desktop machine, which copied the 3DS pictures directly from its memory chip.

A questionnaire combining the pictures with Semantic Differential scales was constructed on that desktop computer, then emailed to another that had a nice color printer, and the subject answered the questions on two traditional paper question-naires. The responses were manually entered and analyzed on a third desktop computer which had the right statistical software. Of course, the questionnaire could have been administered in purely electronic form, or the paper questionnaires could have been designed so that optical scanning could capture the data, and a great variety of methods could have been used for the pictures. The version of the Semantic Differential used was taken from research by David Heise published in 1970, and the use of paper questionnaires was intended to symbolize the importance of basing personality capture on the science of the past as well as the technology of the present [22]. However, modern computer-operated printing produced excellent color images of the 20 people and 20 objects, something that would have been prohibitively expensive years ago.

The same kind of factor analysis used throughout this book was applied to the data, but in two totally different ways. First, a confirmatory analysis was done of the 12 scales that formed Heise's version of the Semantic Differential, calling for exactly three factors. The scales most highly rated on the first factor were the Evaluation dimension: good-bad (loading 0.94), nice-awful (0.94), sweet-sour (0.91), and helpful-unhelpful (0.86). However, four other scales were loaded in the range 0.67 to 0.42, and the second factor was a mixture of Potency and Activity. Only one scale was heavily loaded on the third factor, young-old (0.89), and the research subject was observed debating how old several of the 20 people were, and some of the things also had objective ages. Thus, this respondent, like the other one described above, did not clearly distinguish the second and third dimensions of the Semantic Differential, and the young-old scale illustrates how some antonym pairs may have distinctive meaning.

Second, an exploratory factor analysis was done to determine the cognitive and emotional structure of the 40 stimuli in the respondent's mind. Procedurally, for both analyses the data were assembled into a spreadsheet, which was saved in a form appropriate for the SPSS statistical analysis software, to do the analysis of scales. Then the data matrix in the spreadsheet was rotated 90 degrees, and saved again, to do the analysis of stimuli. This time, SPSS was asked to find and rotate all factors having eigenvalues greater than 1, and the result was the 9 dimensions of variation, shown in Table 3.7.

Factor 1 is clearly the Evaluation dimension. For this respondent, the Virgin Mary and Jesus Christ represent perfect goodness, and none of the more ordinary 18 other people have this prime virtue. Several things are loaded positively, and it is known that this respondent treasures these personal possessions. Loaded negatively are trash bags and two pictures of dead mice that were caught in different kinds of traps inside the respondent's home, clearly reflecting the negative end of the Evaluation scales. The third factor also includes Jesus Christ, along with a recent pope, and reflects goodness in people, recognizing that Jesus was both a symbol and a man. The second factor collects people the respondent admires but has somewhat less emotional attachment to, indicating that all three early factors represent positive Evaluation, but differing in terms of dimensions that are not part of the classical Semantic Differential, such as the degree of abstractness versus personhood.

Table 3.7 Factor analysis of 20 people and 20 things

Factor	People	Things
1	The Virgin Mary (loading 0.71), Jesus Christ (0.59)	POSITIVE: expensive buffet cabinet (0.93), bowl of fresh fruit (0.89), snowman doll (0.85), potted miniature tree (0.83), monkey doll (0.79), elegant table decorations (0.76), vase of yellow roses (0.61), flowers in the garden (0.56), NEGATIVE: trash bags (−0.50), dead mouse in glue trap (−0.69), dead mouse in snap trap (−0.93)
2	Wolfgang Amadeus Mozart (0.93), Eva Peron (0.93), Joan of Arc (0.90), Queen Isabella (0.89), Abraham Lincoln (0.87)	Telephone (0.90)
3	Violeta Chamorro (0.90), Pope John Paul II (0.89), Albert Einstein (0.87), Frida Kahlo (0.78), Sarah Jessica Parker (0.77), Jesus Christ (0.74), John F. Kennedy (0.59)	NEGATIVE: dead mouse in glue trap (−0.69)
4	Salome (0.90), Marie Antoinette (0.82), Napoleon Bonaparte (0.77), Adolf Hitler (0.76)	POSITIVE: trash bags (0.52), NEGATIVE: vase of yellow roses (−0.51)
5	None	POSITIVE: alarm clock (0.90), hair dryer (0.82), NEGATIVE: trash bags (−0.50)
6	POSITIVE: John F. Kennedy (0.58), NEGATIVE: Joseph Mengele (−0.54), Marilyn Monroe (−0.56)	Outdoor broom (0.96)
7	NEGATIVE: Joseph Mengele (−0.63)	Animal burrow in back yard (0.81), Christmas figurines (0.59), the respondent's home (0.53)
8	Ludwig van Beethoven (0.85)	Angel statuette (0.57)
9	Marilyn Monroe (0.57)	Telephone (0.74)

Factor 4 is the negative end of the Evaluation dimension. While rating Marie Antoinette, the respondent quoted the famous words, "Let them eat cake," often attributed to Marie Antoinette and expressing her contempt for the needs of common people. The picture of Salome selected by this respondent is the painting by Titian showing her holding the severed head of John the Baptist, taken from Salome's Wikipedia page [23]. Napoleon and Hitler were both cruel aggressors, in this respondent's mind, and indeed we can imagine each of these two dictators admiring the other and becoming friends, now that they both are in Hell.

Factors 5 through 9 may or may not have clear meanings. The affair between President John F. Kennedy and movie star Marilyn Monroe provides a real but ambiguous conceptual connection between them. The fact that this respondent selected as obscure a person as Nazi concentration camp doctor Joseph Mengele as one of the 20 human stimuli suggests he may have a specific personal meaning. The fact that the respondent was encouraged to select negative as well as positive stimuli may have been responsible for the inclusion of Mengele, and strengthened the salience of the Evaluation dimension. To be sure, this is only a pilot study, and a really complete study might begin by asking respondents to list all the people they know by name, both to avoid this possible bias, but more importantly to permit measurement of many more than 3 or even 9 dimensions of personal meaning.

The main point of this pilot study was to explore the mechanics of mobile and ubiquitous measurement of meaning, and the focus on the Semantic Differential was merely a convenient way to anchor the data collection conceptually. It is easy to imagine software written for tablet computers having nice cameras that would allow respondents to photograph and rate people, things, places, and events out across their communities, in realtime, according to whatever questionnaire scales were appropriate for the given case and purpose.

3.7 Conclusion

The pilot studies reported in this Chapter have an admittedly piecemeal quality, and even the large study of the Big Five using an Android app focused on relatively narrow issues. Can we imagine how the full range of mobile and ubiquitous computing and communications could be used to capture the personalities of individuals in a more comprehensive manner? The most obvious prerequisite is a social organization to support and coordinate the work, whether in academia or industry. One radical but stimulating idea would be to create an organization called OPT, Online Personal Therapy, designed for people of average or even superior mental health who wanted to strengthen their self-awareness. The Big Five app had given immediate feedback to respondents, and OPT would do that as well, while respondents used mobile devices not only to respond to a large number of personality and attitude questions, but also to rate people, places and events in real time. A component of the software would assist the user in thinking about the results, and recording intellectual or emotional reactions. For an experienced user, this system would have the side effect of putting Freud's disciples out of business, because OPT would discourage self-deception and vicious circles of depression, allowing people to be their own best therapists.

References

1. Lindzey, G., & Aronson, E. (Eds.). (1968). *The handbook of social psychology*. Reading: Addison-Wesley.
2. http://www.galaxyzoo.org/, http://ebird.org/content/ebird/. Accessed 27 July 2013.
3. Cattell, R. B. (1948). Primary personality factors in the realm of objective tests. *Journal of Personality*, 16(4), 459–486.
4. Cattell, R. B. (1949). *Handbook of the 16 personality factors questionnaire*. Champaign: Institute for Personality and Ability Testing.
5. Cattell, R. B. (1965). Factor analysis: An introduction to essentials I, The purpose and underlying models. *Biometrics*, *21*(1), 190–215.
6. Cattell, R. B. (1965). Factor analysis: an introduction to essentials II. The role of factor analysis in research. *Biometrics*, *21*(2), 405–435.

7. Wiggins, J. S. (Ed.). (1996). *The five-factor model of personality: Theoretical perspectives*. New York: Guilford Press.
8. Goldberg, L. R. (1993). The structure of phenotypic personality traits. *American Psychologist, 48*, 26–34.
9. Goldberg, L. R. (1999). A broad-bandwidth, public domain, personality inventory measuring the lower-level facets of several five-factor models. In I. Mervielde, I. Deary, F. De Fruyt, & F. Ostendorf (Eds.), *Personality psychology in Europe* (vol. 7, pp. 7–28). Tilburg: Tilburg University Press.
10. http://ipip.ori.org/newBigFive5broadKey.htm. Accessed 29 Oct 2013.
11. Jung, C. G. (1923). *Psychological types*. New York: Brace & company (Translation of a 1921 book originally published in German).
12. Bishop, P. (1995). *The Dionysian self: C. G. Jung's reception of Friedrich Nietzsche*. New York: W. de Gruyter.
13. Jensen-Campbell, L. A., & Malcolm, K. T. (2007). The importance of conscientiousness in adolescent interpersonal relationships. *Personality and Social Psychology Bulletin, 33*, 368–383.
14. Jensen-Campbell, L. A., Knack, J. M., Waldrip, A. M., & Campbell, S. D. (2007). Do big five personality traits associated with self-control influence the regulation of anger and aggression? *Journal of Research in Personality, 41*, 403–424.
15. Kshirsagar, S., & Magnenat-Thalmann, N. (2002). A multilayer personality model. In *Proceedings of the Symposium on Smart Graphics* (pp. 107–115). New York: ACM.
16. Su, W.-P., Pham, B., & Wardhani, A. (2007). Personality and emotion-based high-level control of affective story characters. *IEEE Transactions on Vizualization and Computer Graphics, 13*, 281–293.
17. http://en.wikipedia.org/wiki/Clone. Accessed 16 Mar 2013.
18. Delahaye, J.-P.(2006 June). The science behind sudoku. *Scientific American, 294*, 80–87.
19. *http://en.wikipedia.org/wiki/Mensa_International*. Accessed 16 Mar 2013.
20. http://www.us.mensa.org/learn/about/. Accessed 16 Mar 2013.
21. Young, M. (1958). *The rise of the meritocracy, 1870–2033*. London: Thames and Hudson.
22. Heise, D. R. (1970). The semantic differential and attitude research. In G. F. Summers (Ed.), *Attitude measurement* (pp. 235–253). Chicago: Rand McNally.
23. http://en.wikipedia.org/wiki/Salome. Accessed 3 Aug 2013.

Chapter 4
Recommender Systems

A major new kind of tool and data resource for social science research came into existence a few years ago, usually called *recommender systems* [1, 2] but also sometimes referred to as *collaborative filtering* [3]. These systems are now a well-developed part of online commerce, targeting advertising to specific customers on the basis of the individual's probable preferences, but they have not yet seen much use across the social sciences. The data for a recommender system come from actual buying patterns or from ratings of items contributed by customers, augmented by categorizations often assigned by professionals in the field. Such data are in many ways comparable to questionnaire data and can be extremely valuable to social scientists, even as they already represent a form of personality capture and emulation. The goals of this chapter are to introduce the main features of recommender systems, show how they preserve and emulate the preferences of individuals, connect preferences to other features of a person's character, and embed the individual in the wider culture.

One of the most familiar examples, which will feature in the first sections of this chapter, is the Netflix movie rating system [4, 5]. Much of the research literature emphasizes a system's ability to predict the future behavior of a person, and thus could be used directly to emulate that person, even after death. A very few studies have been based on general measures of the individual's personality, but typically only to start a recommendation history that shifts to pure preference ratings later on [6–8]. Thus, the research and the systems themselves tend not to make much use of social and cognitive theory, and do not therefore feed back into the human sciences to achieve wider advances. Also, the focus of each system on predicting one particular kind of behavior, such as renting and liking movies, narrows the scope of the behavior they can predict. Real emulation requires understanding, which requires the integration of theory with data. Ultimately, this will require convergence of science and scholarship in cultural anthropology, sociology, the arts, and the humanities. One way to conceptualize the necessary intellectual revolution is to say that we need to establish a new *cultural science*.

We could take inspiration from the anthropology journal *World Cultures*, which is the current manifestation of a research program dating back to George Murdock's work developing the *Ethnographic Atlas* in the late 1940s and the *Human Relations*

W. S. Bainbridge, *Personality Capture and Emulation*, Human-Computer Interaction Series, 75
DOI 10.1007/978-1-4471-5604-8_4, © Springer-Verlag London 2014

Area Files at Yale [9, 10]. In a sense this is a questionnaire approach, in which social scientists read carefully through the ethnographic reports on a society, answering concrete questions about it: Does the culture have pottery? Does the culture have kings? Thus, the effective unit of analysis – analogous to the respondent in ordinary questionnaire research—is the culture, not the individual. But in its first issue, the editor of *World Cultures* stressed that the goal was to achieve a more sophisticated, multi-level understanding of culture: "… we are looking for systems that operate at multiple levels in human behavior and meaning systems, which involves both the testing of concrete hypotheses about covariation, the positing of general processes, and the observation of patterns which may manifest themselves in different ways at different levels and in different contexts." [11]

Cultural science could come into being in the same manner achieved by cognitive science decades ago, following the same two principles: (1) This new science must approach its subject matter in a far more rigorous manner than has been traditional. (2) It must be created through the convergence of subfields existing across several traditional disciplines, combining their best theories and methods as the basis for developing entirely new ones. The quantitative *World Cultures* approach would be perhaps the main contribution from cultural anthropology. Political science and political sociology could contribute their best efforts in the area of cultural ideologies. Social psychology and communications could examine how culture is developed and transmitted through intimate social interactions. This chapter is not the place to create an entirely new science, but the vision of this possibility is necessary to understand the potential of recommender systems.

As they would best be applied to personality capture and emulation, recommender systems would not only collect preference data from an individual, not only use similar data from similar individuals to predict additional preferences for the target individual, but also place the individual's values and desires in a meaningful cultural context. Humans classify and evaluate the phenomena in the surrounding world not only on the basis of their own direct experience, but also through socially-constructed language developed over a very long period of time by a vast number of other people. In the case of artworks such as a motion picture, the creators of the movie had their own conceptions of it, which were a mixture of their analysis of the market for a particular film and their own expressive desires. The individual viewer rating that film for Netflix has some perhaps intuitive understanding of a cultural background that is shared with the producers, as well as other cultural influences that the individual brings to bear on the personal judgment. We can best explore these issues through a pair of analysis using small portions of the immense Netflix dataset.

4.1   The Universal Human Condition

The Netflix dataset that was shared openly with researchers consists of 17,770 text files, each one for a different movie. Each line of a text file reflects the rating of that movie by one respondent who is identified by an ID number. The data reflect responses from fully 400,000 people who rated movies they had seen, on a scale from 1 to 5 in terms of how much the respondent liked the movie. Before any analysis can be done, multiple files need to be combined, in such a manner that all the ratings by each individual are connected. The challenge here will be to see how far we can legitimately go from these rather pedestrian preference data, toward identifying different cultural perspectives from which to view the position of humanity in the universe [12].

I will illustrate this methodology first by starting with the 2005 film *Constantine* starring Keanu Reeves, who had earlier starred in dystopian, surrealistic "cyberpunk" movies, notably *Johnny Mnemonic* (1995) and *The Matrix* (1999). My research interest in this film was two-fold. First, it is an expression of a very substantial subculture in the contemporary world, associated with computer technology, videogames, and unorthodox, supernaturally-oriented fantasies. Second, the major theological premise of the film is dualist, comparable to the theology of The Process Church of the Final Judgement about which I wrote my second book [13]. The Process promoted the unity of Christ and Satan, beyond good and evil. The protagonist of the movie, John Constantine, struggles to find the right course in a world where Satan is the moral equivalent of God. For comparison, I will also look at the contemporaneous 2004 film, *The Passion of the Christ*, directed by Mel Gibson, which has some aesthetic similarities while being theologically more orthodox.

To explore the utility of working with the Netflix recommender system preference data, I randomly selected 40,000 respondents who had rated *Constantine*. I then added ratings these respondents had given for six highly varied movies about religion, including *The Passion of the Christ*. I also included one (*Super Mario Bros.*) based on a video game, because *Constantine* was issued as a videogame as well as in the form of a movie. Indeed, while the game was based on the movie, the movie was based on a graphic novel, so the story exists in three parallel genres. In addition to watching the movie, I played the game through to conclusion, gaining a personal "feel" for its cultural environment. While the emphasis here will be on analysis of quantitative data, direct familiarity with an artwork may be necessary to place it in the proper conceptual framework. Here is the description of the game I wrote for my book *eGods*, a study of religious culture in electronic games:

> In the solo-player game called *Constantine*, the very first thing a player must do is go to Hell. Based on a movie and graphic novel, the story concerns John Constantine, a faithless soldier in the war between Heaven and Hell, at a time when infernal demons have broken a truce and begun invading Earth. Many of his weapons have biblical origins: a pistol that fires stones from the road to Damascus, a machine gun shooting nails used to crucify martyrs, holy water grenades, a bomb called the Shroud of Moses, and, finally, the spearhead that slew Jesus. Constantine's mission requires him to shuttle back and forth between terrestrial Los Angeles and Hell's devastated version of the city, where infernal explosions hurl melting cars and buses through the sulfuric air. At the end, Constantine must fight against both the angel Gabriel and Mammon, the son of Satan. Then he discovers that God had engineered the demonic invasion to strengthen religious belief, which only reinforces his view that God is really no better than Satan [14].

Table 4.1 shows that the 40,000 raters gave *Constantine* a mean score of 3.41 on a scale from 1 (did not like) to 5 (liked very much), and 16,264 of these *Constantine*-raters gave the *Passion of Christ* a mean of 3.79. As Table 4.1 shows, liking *Constantine* correlates most highly with liking *Super Mario Bros.*, which with a mean of

Table 4.1 Connections among selected movies rated by Netflix customers

Movie (Year released)	Cases	Mean	Correlation (r) with:		Passion cases
			Constantine	Passion of Christ	
Constantine (2005)	40,000	3.41	1.00	0.18	16,264
The Passion of the Christ (2004)	16,264	3.79	0.18	1.00	16,264
The Exorcist (1973)	12,746	3.93	0.13	0.10	7,077
The Ten Commandments (1956)	4,057	4.03	0.13	0.31	2,632
Super Mario Bros. (1993)	1,285	2.40	0.36	0.15	724
Jesus Christ Superstar (1973)	815	3.58	0.13	0.15	484
Elmer Gantry (1960)	666	3.43	−0.01	0.09	392
The Chronicles of Narnia: The Lion, the Witch and the Wardrobe (1988)	594	3.19	0.19	0.16	340

2.40 is the lowest-rated of the set, and we can suggest three possible explanations. First, both movies are connected to video games and have some of the quality of a quest game in which many minor enemies must be dealt with on the way to the "boss." Second, both may appeal to the same audience, primarily adolescent and young-adult males. Third, both movies concern evil monsters coming up from beneath the Earth, and the heroes must descend into their realm to do battle with them.

Table 4.1 also reveals a strong correlation (0.31) between liking both *The Passion of the Christ* and *The Ten Commandments*, two more conventional religious epics produced nearly half a century apart, among the 2,632 respondents who had seen both films and had seen *Constantine*. Many other correlations in the range 0.10 through 0.19 may represent a weak tendency for movies with a religious theme to cluster together, regardless of their style or theology. However, it is worth pointing out that preference scale data tend to exhibit small positive correlations, akin to a yea-saying/nay-saying bias [15]. Put simply: some people like movies more than other people do. Thus, the weak to zero correlations with *Elmer Gantry* may actually represent negative correlations, obscured by this bias, perhaps because this film about an errant preacher does not take a positive stance toward religion. Whatever the interpretations, the strength and range of associations seem quite typical for preference data, thus suggesting that a much more extensive study to chart the cultural clustering of religion-related movies would be quite feasible.

Three obvious points deserve emphasis. First, the Netflix dataset is a prime illustration of the fact that some kinds of online quantitative data concern very much larger numbers of cases than we traditionally see in questionnaire research. The 16,264 respondents who rated both *Constantine* and *The Passion of Christ* are about 11 times the number of people who respond to any particular year's General Social Survey. Large numbers of cases allow us to "drill down" deeper in our analysis, potentially disentangling more different factors that shape people's preferences.

Second, people may indeed have many different reasons for liking or disliking a film or other work of art. When I studied preferences for science fiction films, rated by people attending the 1978 World Science Fiction Convention, the key factor dis-

Table 4.2 Analysis of 20 frequently seen spaceflight movies

Spaceflight movie	Year	Mean	Raters	Factor 1	Factor 2	Factor 3	Factor 4	Factor 5
Mission to Mars	2000	3.01	14,596	0.80				
Red Planet	2000	3.09	11,397	0.78				
Deep Impact	1998	3.33	14,058	0.65				
Lost in Space	1998	2.96	13,431	0.63				
Space Cowboys	2000	3.35	14,610	0.57				
Pitch Black	2000	3.60	14,780	0.43	0.40			
Stargate	1994	3.89	13,062	0.41				
Contact	1997	3.72	15,791	0.40				
Alien	1979	4.20	15,709		0.60			
Total Recall	1990	3.73	18,677		0.59			
Dune	1984	3.56	9,890		0.42			
Apollo 13	1995	4.11	17,494			0.74		
The Right Stuff	1983	3.99	11,185			0.71		
The Hitchhiker's Guide to the Galaxy	2005	3.11	6,878				0.71	
Spaceballs	1987	3.51	16,020				0.68	
Galaxy Quest	1999	3.60	14,721				0.45	
Solaris	2002	2.52	8,740					0.75
2001: A Space Odyssey	1968	3.75	15,326					0.68
The Last Starfighter	1984	3.62	13,587					
Starship Troopers	1997	3.42	13,719					

tinguishing films was the decade in which they were produced [16]. Their topic did not seem to matter. Of course, that study was done before services like Netflix made it easy to watch a desired film from any decade, which suggests that factors potentially affecting preferences may be switched on or off by conditions surrounding the watching and rating of films. Other factors include which star actors appeared in the films, such that we would predict people who liked *The Ten Commandments* would also like *Ben Hur*, because Charleton Heston starred in both [17]. People who liked *Constantine* include some who simply are Keanu Reeves fans.

Third, if we use the large numbers of respondents as a tool to disentangle multiple factors, we may find that some factors are really interesting conceptions of the human place in the universe, embodied in works of art and appreciated by at least some of the people expressing themselves through a recommender system. A second analysis using the Netflix data illustrate how this might be accomplished.

For a more general project looking at public opinion data on the exploration of outer space, I identified 20 very popular movies in the Netflix database that depicted human space travel, were not sequels of other movies, and did not belong to the *Star Wars* and *Star Trek* franchises. I combined their data, and then selected all 20,987 respondents who had rated at least 10 of them. Table 4.2 lists the 20 films, along with their release dates, their mean preference ratings, and the number of raters, followed by a factor analysis. This was the same kind of exploratory analysis used earlier in this book, in this case reporting all factor loadings of 0.40 or greater.

There are several ways to interpret the factors that emerge in this kind of factor analysis. Back in Chap. 1, I relied upon my direct familiarity with the Children of God to assign meanings to the factors that went only a short distance beyond the literal meanings of the descriptions of the afterlife connected with each of three dimensions. Here I can draw upon my perspective seeing each of the films, but also on information posted at the Internet Movie Database (IMDb) [18]. The first two films in Factor 1 date from the same year, 2000, all but one of the other six films in the factor are within three years of that date, and their mean year of release is 1998. So one thing they have in common is that they were popular sci-fi films of the same period. The first two films happen both to be about the planet Mars. The IMDb classifies both as Sci-Fi, but also puts *Mission to Mars* in the Adventure and Drama categories, while assigning *Red Planet* to Action and Thriller [19, 20].

The Netflix data were obtained in 2006, and the ratings were made during the 2003–2006 period, often right after the respondent had rented the film. The date when a film was made may still be a significant determinant of whether a specific individual rated it, and if so what preference rating is given, but perhaps less of a factor than back in 1978 when I did my initial movie preference study. Still, Factor 1 appears to be general spaceflight movies from around 1998, that have a diversity of styles, artistic merit, and mean preferences. The situation is very different for the four other factors, suggesting that Factor 1 is a general dimension related to a film's release date, essentially a *confounding factor* that left the other factors free to express distinctive meanings.

Factor 2 consists of emotionally intense movies focused on superheroes, blending action with depth psychology. Note that *Total Recall* did not wind up in Factor 1, despite the fact that the interplanetary travel takes the hero to Mars. *Pitch Black* is almost equally loaded on Factor 1 and Factor 2, was also released in 2000, and was assigned by IMDb to the same categories as *Red Planet*. *Pitch Black* led to a 2004 sequel, *The Chronicles of Riddick*, and the two films garnered almost the exact same mean preference rating in the full dataset, 3.57 and 3.56, and here the mean rating of *Pitch Black* is about the same, 3.60 for the sci-fi fans who rated at least 10 of the 20 spaceflight movies covered here. I have studied a computer game based on this pair of movies, and find very substantial cultural content hidden beneath the intense action, suggesting morbid conceptions of the human place in the universe not very different from those in *Constantine* [21].

Factor 3 connects two factual historical movies dramatizing real spaceflight somewhat accurately. *The Right Stuff* depicts the first American astronauts in the Mercury Program who briefly entered outer space in the 1961–1963 period, while *Apollo 13* concerns the 1970 flight in the Apollo Program in which an accident prevented a lunar landing and nearly killed the crew. Factor 4, consisting of *The Hitchhiker's Guide to the Galaxy*, *Spaceballs*, and *Galaxy Quest*, measures liking comedy or light entertainment space movies. Of these, *Galaxy Quest* has an interesting philosophical premise, being a parody of *Star Trek* that imagines a real alien species assumes a sci-fi television program is real and comes to Earth seeking help from its actors.

Factor 5 combines two mystical movies about the meaning of existence, *Solaris* and *2001: A Space Odyssey*. The 2002 American version of *Solaris* is a remake of a 1972 Russian film based on a 1961 novel by Polish writer Stanislaw Lem which Wikipedia says "is about the ultimate inadequacy of communication between human and non-human species [22, 23]." In my own possibly idiosyncratic reading of the novel, it appears to be a metaphor of the psychopathological relationship between a citizen of Poland and the Soviet Union that then dominated the country. IMDb summaries the plots of the 1972 and 2002 movies thus: "A psychologist is sent to a space station orbiting an alien planet in order to discover what has caused the crew to go insane [24]." "A troubled psychologist is sent to investigate the crew of an isolated research station orbiting a bizarre planet [25]." The planet, it turns out, is a living being that telepathically interferes with human mental processes, just as the Soviet Union sought to control the ideology of the inhabitants of its "satellites."

In the 1978 questionnaire study of movie preferences among science fiction fans, it proved impossible to use factor analysis to categorize *2001: A Space Odyssey*. The reason was that essentially all the respondents loved it, so there was no variation to form the basis of calculating correlations. On a preference scale from 0 to 6, the mean was 5.17. An alternative way of analyzing Netflix data is to focus not on the preference ratings themselves, but on whether each respondent rated a film, a proxy for whether they had seen it. This also did not work for the science fiction fan data, because 99% rated *2001*.

Solaris has been described as the Soviet Union's answer to *2001*, although this claim is debated by critics, who may use finer categories to classify films than ordinary audiences or science fiction fans use [26]. In *2001*, a superior extraterrestrial intelligence interacts with humanity in a mysterious manner that seems comparable to a relationship with a distant god, but the film and Arthur C. Clarke novel connected with it may just be suggesting that exploration of space is required to discover the meaning of human life [27]. This implies both that great works of art may be ambiguous as to meaning, which causes problems for using them to capture a human personality, and that they deal with deep issues, which makes them essential for complete personality capture.

4.2 Cultures and Subcultures

The human mind prefers simple models of reality, but it produces complex cultural constellations that may not be capable of simple mapping. The plot thickens considerable if we seek to understand the relationship between an individual personality and the culture in which the individual developed. The default cognitive strategy, of social scientists and ordinary citizens alike, is to frame phenomena in terms of well-defined, closed categories. For example, Friedrich Nietzsche, who will feature prominently in Chap. 7, believed classical Greek society had two choices, to be

Apollonian or Dionysian, individualist and rational or collectivist and sensual. Sociologist Alvin Gouldner, in contrast, viewed classical Greece as a contest society in which individuals battled for supremacy in competitions of which the Olympic Games were but one minor manifestation, thus employing a great variety of tactics but within one over-arching strategy [28–30]. Already we have seen that both the Big Five and the Semantic Differential have some value, and they are dimensions rather than category boxes. But especially when we are working with large numbers of research subjects, and large numbers of measurements of a single subject, we can discover many more dimensions of variation than the five or three that those approaches originally offered.

Recommender system data offer an embarrassment of riches, but are fragmentary in the extreme. An obvious problem with the Netflix data is missing cases, the fact that most respondents saw and rated only a tiny fraction of the 17,770 movies. This is not a fatal flaw if the goal is to recommend one more movie a given customer might like to rent. Many different computational procedures could suffice, but a common approach is to identify a group of respondents who gave ratings similar to those of the target individual, often called a *neighborhood* [31]. For example, given one customer, his ratings of a dozen films could be used to scan through the data base for other customers who gave similar ratings. The measure could be as simple as the average difference between this customer's ratings and those of other customers who rated at least a half dozen of the films. The customers similar to that one could be called his neighbors, and the group could stabilize as a neighborhood over time to reduce the computational cost. Then it would be a simple matter to note which films were highly rated in the neighborhood, but the customer had not seen them, perhaps especially films that were rated more highly in the neighborhood than by all the customers in the database. In fact, a diversity of algorithms are used by recommender systems, but none seem well designed to map the culture in a way that can be expressed through meaningful concepts.

Examining the Netflix data for the 20 spaceflight films in a different way can help identify potential directions for future work. First, to escape for the moment the problem of missing data, we will focus exclusively on respondents who rated all 20 films. We can think of several potential flaws of this approach. Perhaps the number who rated all 20 is simply too small. Well, it is exactly 215, which is a sufficient number for our purposes here. Perhaps the only people who would watch all 20 spaceflight movies are such rabid fans they would give a top 5 rating to everyone, thus rendering correlation analysis impossible. In fact their average rating was 3.6, on the 1 to 5 scale, somewhat positive but not bumping up against the ceiling. Perhaps each rater gave the same score to all 20 films, not taking the task seriously. But the standard deviation, averaged across the 215 raters, was fully 0.9. As we get into the analysis, we shall see that the results are conceptually meaningful.

For present didactic purposes, we will focus on the three respondents that gave the greatest diversity of ratings, as measured by the standard deviation across each one's 20 scores, and approach the movies through a simpler classification, based on a factor analysis like the others presented in this book, but designed to extract just two factors, the minimum possible with this technique. We will give sci-fi names to

Table 4.3 Movie analysis for the 215 respondents who rated them all

Spaceflight Movie	Mean	Factor 1	Factor 2	Buck's Rating	Flash's Rating	Buzz's Rating
Lost in Space	3.14	*0.74*	−0.06	1	4	1
Red Planet	3.20	*0.71*	0.10	2	4	2
Mission to Mars	3.07	*0.70*	−0.08	3	5	2
Deep Impact	3.37	*0.63*	0.12	1	5	5
Pitch Black	3.61	*0.63*	0.07	5	5	3
Starship Troopers	3.61	*0.59*	0.22	1	5	4
Space Cowboys	3.40	*0.57*	0.13	2	4	3
Stargate	4.02	*0.57*	0.31	4	5	4
The Last Starfighter	3.68	*0.51*	0.39	3	5	1
Total Recall	3.91	*0.54*	0.24	5	5	5
Dune	3.76	*0.50*	0.26	3	5	1
Spaceballs	3.43	*0.40*	0.26	5	1	5
Alien	4.26	0.34	0.30	5	5	1
Contact	3.87	0.34	0.30	2	2	1
Solaris	2.41	0.30	0.24	3	1	2
The Hitchhiker's Guide to the Galaxy	3.17	0.27	0.33	3	3	3
Galaxy Quest	3.67	0.22	*0.41*	4	1	5
2001: A Space Odyssey	3.86	0.07	*0.62*	5	5	5
The Right Stuff	3.92	0.06	*0.78*	4	3	4
Apollo 13	4.14	−0.07	*0.57*	5	4	3

the three respondents, although of course we do not know their actual names: Buck (Buck Rogers), Flash (Flash Gordon) and Buzz (Buzz Corey from the 1950 television series, *Space Patrol*). Their summary statistics were as follows: Buck (mean score = 3.3, standard deviation = 1.5), Flash (3.9, 1.5), and Buzz (3.0, 1.6). Table 4.3 gives their scores, along with the means and factor loadings for all 215 of these respondents. Of course, small errors are introduced by rounding off to one or two decimal places, and the numbers of ratings and respondents are small, so we should not place confidence in minor differences.

Table 4.3 rearranges the movies in descending order of their loadings on Factor 1, giving all the loadings rather than just those 0.40 or greater, and marking in *italics* those that meet that criterion. The majority of the movies load at or above 0.40 on Factor 1, suggesting it measures general preference for sci-fi movies, although it may also measure a positive bias in giving ratings in general, which could be determined if we compared a random sample of movies about other topics. Only one fifth of the twenty movies load heavily on Factor 2, and it clearly reflects appreciation for the real space exploration program. Both *The Right Stuff* and *Apollo 13* are docudramas about actual spaceflight history, *2001* depicts space technology realistically, and *Galaxy Quest* toyed with the contrast between sci-fi and real spaceflight.

There are several ways we could compare Buck, Flash and Buzz, both with each other and with the 212 other respondents who rated all 20 movies. Among the more sophisticated is in terms of their factor scores on the two factors. This book has frequently used factor analysis, because it is one of the standard methods, has been used far more extensively in social and psychological sciences than the more recent machine learning or clustering methods, and achieves a degree of coherence across chapters. It does assume that the measurements being analyzed can be understood in terms of continuous dimensions, and in the variants of factor analysis used here, that those dimensions are indeed at right angles to each other. Thus, when we introduce factor scores it is only to use this method as an intelligible extension of the methods we have emphasized, in full awareness that contemporary computer science offers many alternatives.

Flash, for example, has a factor score of 1.81 on Factor 1, and -1.44 on Factor 2. This means, relative to all 215 respondents, he is more favorable than the average about Factor 1, and less favorable about Factor 2. The averages of factor scores across all the respondents are, by definition 0.00 and 0.00. Buck's factor scores go the other way, -1.53 on Factor 1 and 1.19 on Factor 2. Buzz is between the other two, at -1.22 and -0.25. It is a simple matter to calculate the differences in factor scores between each of these three and the other respondents, thereby providing a way of identifying their neighbors in terms of preferences.

If we consider two respondents to be neighbors if the total difference in their factor scores is less than 1, then these three are not neighbors of each other, but Flash has 10 neighbors, Buck has 11, and Buzz has fully 29. We could look to see what other movies these neighbors had seen, and what ratings they gave, in order to advise Flash, Buck and Buzz what to rent next. Alternatively, we could focus just on Factor 2, ignoring the more general Factor 1, and consider to be neighbors those with factor scores on Factor 2 that are close to that of the target individual. Or we could extend the factor analysis to consider what cultural themes motivate other genres of movies, thus achieving cultural science while also recording and emulating the personalities of the respondents. In going beyond this set of 20 films, we would be extending the analysis beyond the original preference variables, and this can easily be done even when the additional data do not concern preference ratings.

4.3 Integrating Preference with Another Variable

Most existing data about individual preferences concern commodities that are bought and sold, because recommender systems are tools of the advertising industry. However, people have preferences with respect to all kinds of things and actions, and preferences have implications for a wide range of attitudes and behaviors. To illustrate these points, I shall use data I originally obtained from students at Harvard University, in the first of two questionnaires I administered in the weeks following the first Space Shuttle disaster, with a primary aim of discovering their thoughts about the legitimate goals of space exploration. The first questionnaire included open-ended questions about the goals of space, and the second questionnaire included 125 fixed choice items asking a second sample of students to rate ideas collected by the first questionnaire. However, the bulk of the first questionnaire consisted of fixed-choice preference questions.

After completing a book based on the Harvard students' responses concerning the space program [32], I used a subset of the data for a social-science methodology textbook for which I wrote a set of statistical analysis demonstration programs. A total of 1,077 students completed the first questionnaire, March through May, 1986, but I used a subset of 512 cases for the statistical package, the exact number being chosen for programming efficiency with the computers of the period, but making sure there were equal numbers of male and female respondents, that most respondents had answered each preference question, that all respondents had answered an item taken from the General Social Survey:

> We hear a lot of talk these days about liberals and conservatives. Below is a seven-point scale on which the political views that people might hold are arranged from extremely liberal (point "1") to extremely conservative (point "7"). Where would you place yourself on this scale? Please circle the ONE number that best indicates your general political views.
> 1. Extremely liberal
> 2. Liberal
> 3. Slightly liberal
> 4. Moderate, middle of the road
> 5. Slightly conservative
> 6. Conservative
> 7. Extremely conservative

Strictly speaking, this is not a preference question, but it could just as equally have been phrased as one, or even as a pair of preference items, one asking how much the respondent likes "conservative politics," the second asking about "liberal politics," and the pair allowing the researcher to do a sophisticated analysis that could identify not only liberals and conservatives, but also those respondents who loved or hated both. Here, in Table 4.4, we shall use the respondent's gender and political orientation, as measured by the GSS item, as non-preference items to help us understand preferences.

Table 4.4 focuses on preference questions for 30 academic subjects, preferences that presumably are very salient for the Harvard student respondents because they were at that moment taking classes in those fields, and periodically needing to make decisions about what classes to take during the next semester, and indeed which subjects to major in. They were in a section of the questionnaire explicitly titled Preferences for College Subjects, and the respondent was asked to rate each one on a 7-point scale:

> Following is a list of various subjects that are taught at universities. Please tell us how much you like each one of them, whether you actually have taken a course in it or not. Please circle the number 1 if you do not like the subject at all. Please circle the number 7 if you like it very much—if it is one of your very favorite subjects. Otherwise, please circle the one number in between that best indicates how much you like it [33].

Table 4.4 Academic preferences, gender, and political orientation

Subject	Mean Rating for:		Correlation with:	
	Women	Men	Male	Conservative
Engineering	2.68	3.67	0.28	0.15
Economics	3.37	4.18	0.23	0.27
Physics	3.28	4.04	0.20	0.00
Business	3.33	3.96	0.16	0.38
Political science	4.43	4.96	0.15	0.08
Geology	3.05	3.51	0.15	0.06
Chemistry	3.40	3.80	0.12	0.06
Astronomy	4.29	4.62	0.11	−0.04
Mathematics	3.77	4.14	0.10	0.05
Oceanography	3.68	3.96	0.09	−0.03
Architecture	4.02	4.24	0.07	−0.02
Law	4.45	4.48	0.01	0.10
History	5.32	5.35	0.01	0.09
Medicine	4.07	4.06	0.00	0.05
Zoology	3.77	3.77	0.00	−0.04
Botany	3.22	3.13	−0.03	−0.14
Classics (ancient civilization)	4.32	4.17	−0.05	0.04
Music	4.90	4.67	−0.07	−0.08
Biology	4.72	4.40	−0.10	−0.11
Drama	4.43	4.06	−0.10	−0.18
Education	4.43	4.05	−0.11	−0.10
Communications	4.44	4.08	−0.11	−0.01
Sociology	4.40	3.98	−0.13	−0.12
Nursing	2.82	2.36	−0.16	−0.06
Psychology	5.01	4.48	−0.17	−0.19
Art	5.23	4.60	−0.19	−0.21
Anthropology	4.88	4.27	−0.19	−0.24
Social work	4.44	3.76	−0.20	−0.25
Literature	5.86	5.13	−0.25	−0.16
A foreign language	5.44	4.56	−0.27	−0.12

The 30 academic subjects in Table 4.4 are listed in the order of descending correlation with the respondent being male. Thus, men tend to give higher ratings to Engineering, Economics and Physics, and women tend to give higher ratings to Social Work, Literature, and a foreign language. Right away, this reminds us that momentary preferences are shaped by a person's enduring characteristics. Looking down the last column in the table we see that conservatives tend to like Business and Economics more than liberals do, while liberals favor Art, Anthropology and Social Work. Thus, some preferences, but in this example rather few of them, are associated with a general ideological dimension. To be sure, Harvard students are more liberal than the general population, but they still show variation. Only 1.4% called themselves extremely conservative, compared with 9.2% who were very liberal. Combining the fine-grained response categories, 26.6% were conservative, 10.5 were moderate, and 62.9% were liberal.

Arranging the list in terms of gender correlations tends also to arrange them in terms of political correlations, but not exactly. In this Harvard student dataset, men are more likely to be conservative than women, and the correlation between male and conservative is 0.24. The correlation between the 30 pairs of correlations is fully 0.79, although correlations of correlations can be very strong. In this they are comparable to factor loadings, because by aggregating lots of data into a single coefficient we reduce the effect of random variations—and indeed of individual differences.

In social statistics, we often speak of *statistical significance*. Students tend to understand this as a reflection of how big or noteworthy a coefficient is, and that is frankly the way professionals tend to think of it when talking casually. But it really measures the chance that a correlation of X in data from a random sample could result from a population where the real correlation is zero, merely magnified by errors in sampling. In this table and the next, correlations at least 0.15 above or below zero achieve 0.001 level of statistical significance, as usually calculated. Unfortunately, even the most assiduous real pollsters never achieve random samples, and this has caused some social statisticians to suggest we should abandon statistical significance, although it does provide a way of talking about the confidence we have in our results. Of course, if our focus is a specified individual human being, rather than the general population, such concepts become rather problematic.

4.4   Individuals and Categories

As we saw in the cases of Crone and Geezer in the first chapter, well-preserved datasets can be used to understand some aspect of a particular person even after their deaths, and without necessarily knowing their names. Above we called three anonymous respondents Buck, Flash and Buzz. Page 252 of the textbook that incorporated the Harvard student preference data displayed all the responses from the student who happened to be listed first. She was female, so let us here called her Prima. Politically, she described herself as extremely liberal. She was a college junior, and now three decades later we can imagine that she not only graduated but went on to have a fine career and a full family life, with decades still to live. We do not know what that career is, but she rated 6 of the academic subjects the maximum 7 on the preference scale: anthropology, biology, foreign language, literature, medicine, and zoology. Did she go to medical school? Did she become a combined anthropologist-zoologist studying the interactions of people and animals in exotic lands? She knows what her actual fate was, and if people are able to preserve links to all the data archives containing information about themselves, they could provide such updates.

Table 4.5 covers a wide range of preference questions, beginning with two very broad items that concluded the academic preferences section of the questionnaire, the science and humanities in general. We see that women tend to rate the humani-

Table 4.5 Comparing one respondent with all respondents across several preferences

Preference for:	Prima's rating	Mean rating		Correlation with	
		Women	Men	Male	Conservative
The sciences, in general	5	4.56	4.89	0.09	0.01
The humanities, in general	6	6.08	5.65	−0.20	−0.16
Spy and detective stories	2	4.67	4.97	0.09	0.16
Stories of love and romance	5	4.84	3.44	−0.39	0.00
Science fiction stories	5	4.15	4.79	0.17	0.02
Television soap operas like "Dallas" and "Dynasty"	7	3.02	2.36	−0.18	0.10
War stories	2	2.90	4.45	0.42	0.39
Driving very fast in a car	6	4.02	5.08	0.27	0.20
Complete personal security	3	4.76	4.52	−0.07	0.01
Taking physical risks	7	4.16	4.82	0.21	0.06
Taking risks in your relationships with people	5	4.39	4.27	0.04	−0.06

ties somewhat higher than men do, but men give the humanities a higher rating than they do anything else in that table. Thus, we always need to be careful not to over-interpret a difference, for example wrongly concluding that women like the humanities while men hate them. The next five rows concern genres of entertainment fiction, while the final four concern general policies for action in human life, documenting how widely we may apply preference question methodology to diverse sectors of human life.

Prima seems to be a risk-taker, and a soap-opera fan. The table appears to confirm stereotypes, notably that women like stories of love and romance, while men and conservatives like war stories and taking the physical risk of driving very fast in a car, yet Prima likes physical risks despite being a woman and a liberal. Note that politics does not correlate with preferences for stories of love and romance, despite the fact that gender does and gender correlates with politics. I also calculated the correlations with politics for men and women separately, finding that among men politics does not correlate with liking this kind of story, but among women liking these stories correlates somewhat (0.17) with being conservative. This illustrates the fact that human characteristics and experiences can combine in complex ways to produce any particular behavior, including expressing a preference.

Many years ago when I was teaching at the University of Washington, I had access to students' grades in a dataset that also gave their genders. Sadly I discovered that overall, the grade point average of sociology majors was lower than majors in most other departments. I analyzed the data using a method to control for the gender of the student, and the grade point difference for sociology got even worse. Women had higher grade point averages than men, and women liked sociology more than men did. But people who liked sociology tended to have low grades. This illustrates the concept *suppressor variable*, a situation in which one variable in a dataset effectively conceals relationships between other variables [34].

In 1981, I recruited 730 female students and 578 male students at the University of Washington to complete a questionnaire that included the same battery of prefer-

Table 4.6 Loadings in two factor analyses of academic science subject preferences

Academic subject	730 female college students			578 male college students		
	Factor 1	Factor 2	Factor 3	Factor 2	Factor 5	Factor 3
Medicine	0.82			0.68		
Nursing	0.76			0.44		
Biology	0.63			0.72		
Zoology	0.62			0.71		
Chemistry	0.51		0.57	0.51		0.58
Oceanography		0.67		0.41	0.54	
Botany		0.61		0.50		
Astronomy		0.58			0.49	
Geology		0.54			0.50	
Anthropology		0.42			0.49	
Physics			0.72			0.80
Engineering			0.71			0.69
Mathematics			0.59			0.68

ence items about academic subjects later administered to Harvard students. While males and females may have somewhat different preferences, they may conceptualize the map of academic subjects in an identical manner, if they belong to the same culture. Or, there may be subtle differences in classification as well. Table 4.6 gives all the factor loadings above 0.40 for separate analyses by gender, focusing on many of the sciences. The table is arranged in terms of the first three factors that emerged in the female data, then arranging the male coefficients in the same way, ignoring for this analysis the social sciences and humanities, about which there also were some disagreements. Random factors will prevent the loadings from being identical across genders, but the table appears to show that women conceptualized the life sciences differently, placing at the center of Factor 1 two human-helping professions, medicine and nursing. Men put biology and zoology at the center and added oceanography and botany to the same factor, defining it more as an abstract life sciences dimension. They agreed in their conceptualization of the very rigorous non-life sciences.

In the Netflix section, we noted that movies of different periods will be judged differently, not only because of topical or stylistic differences, but simply because people of different ages would have experienced them differently. Returning to the Harvard data, consider the soap opera item in Table 4.5. This name comes from the fact that daytime radio dramas decades ago were aimed at housewives, and many were sponsored by soap companies. Naming two very popular night-time TV examples, *Dallas* and *Dynasty*, was intended to give the item a somewhat broader meaning. Originally, Dallas ran 1978–1991, and Dynasty, 1981–1989. During the years both aired, they competed in the Nielsen ratings, which were followed very closely by advertisers and thus determined the longevity of a series. According to the Wikipedia page for the Nielsen ratings, *Dallas* was the top rated show in America in 1983–1984 with 25.7% of the viewing audience, while *Dynasty* won in 1984–1985 with 25.0% [35]. The company today proclaims it uses an advanced automatic method for documenting the viewing habits of the households in its sample:

Using data from set top boxes, Nielsen delivers a constant, real-time stream of information, revealing tuning behavior during programs and commercials. We can tell clients which commercials are being watched and which have the strongest engagement and impact. We even analyze which position in the program or commercial block is most effective for a specific brand [36].

We can imagine a similar system that privately documented all of a person's television watching, over the entire life course. Of course, many of the people who rated the two shows during their original broadcast years are now deceased, but their data may live on. Similarly, many actors from the shows have passed away, while their performances are often rebroadcast or available to purchase. Consider the example of Larry Hagman, who played the lovable villain in *Dallas*, J. R. Ewing. At the end of the 1979–1980, J. R. Ewing was shot, leaving the audience on a cliffhanger, not knowing who fired the gun or whether Ewing would survive. Reportedly, Hagman used the huge public excitement generated to increase his salary markedly, and both he and Ewing did indeed return to life. *Dallas* was revived in 2012, with Hagman briefly reprising his role, before actually dying that November.

Prima was a woman and a liberal, but was she a science-fiction fan? Her rating of 5 for "science fiction stories" was only slightly above the male average, which was a little above the female average, and she was not among the students who rated it 7. However, science fiction is not a unitary concept; there are many kinds. Indeed, the more salient a topic is for people, the finer the distinctions they tend to make about it. Thus, when I administered a preference-based questionnaire about SF literature to participants at the 1978 world science fiction convention, I found very fine distinctions indeed. The main body of the questionnaire consisted of preference questions about 140 authors—two of which were bogus to catch respondents who were not being careful.

Factor analysis of the authors allowed me to confirm that there were three main dimensions—or major categories—of science fiction literature, each of which could be defined by correlations between its formal name and other items, and I included several of those other items in the Harvard student questionnaire. The three main ideological dimensions of science fiction, as understood by devoted fans in 1978, were generally called Hard-Science, New-Wave, and Fantasy, terms that are unfamiliar to most non-fans. In Table 4.7, the final column of the table shows SF fan correlations between these obscure terms and items that could properly be included in a questionnaire administered to non-fans. The table compares Prima with the entire student group of which she is a part, and with the science fiction fans who rated the same items at their convention. The preference scale for students ranged 1–7, while the one for fans ranged 0–6, so I have added 1 to all the SF fan mean ratings to render them comparable.

The study of science fiction fans is a clear example of *cultural science*, examining the perspective a subculture has about its main focus of interest. The results could be described as a *folk ontology*, a set of categories native to the subculture. Here, a folk ontology has been applied to a more general population, with special attention to one member of it whom we have named Prima. This illustrates the potential for capturing the personality of one person in terms of multiple cultures,

Table 4.7 Students' preferences for items derived from a study of science fiction fans

Preference for:	Prima	512 Students	595 SF Fans	Correlation with:
Fiction based on the physical sciences	5	3.74	5.26	Hard-Science (0.66)
Stories about new technology	1	4.24	5.60	Hard-Science (0.51)
Factual science articles	4	3.92	4.92	Hard-Science (0.49)
Stories in which there is a rational explanation for everything	2	4.17	4.57	Hard-Science (0.46)
Avant-garde fiction which experiments with new styles	1	4.37	4.14	New-Wave (0.65)
Fiction based on the social sciences	5	4.78	4.74	New-Wave (0.40)
Fiction that is critical of our society	5	5.24	4.65	New-Wave (0.38)
Fiction which deeply probes personal relationships and feelings	7	5.52	5.30	New-Wave (0.37)
Feminist literature	7	3.53	3.65	New-Wave (0.31)
Utopian political novels and essays	5	4.18	3.56	New-Wave (0.25)
Fantasy stories involving swords and sorcery	3	3.93	4.84	Fantasy (0.66)
Stories about magic	4	4.21	5.00	Fantasy (0.61)
Tales of the supernatural	1	4.35	4.08	Fantasy (0.44)
Myths and legends	6	5.24	5.22	Fantasy (0.58

with which that individual may have varying degrees of relationship. Science fiction is by its own self-definition rather exotic, as cultures go, and fans often contrast themselves with ordinary people, whom they pejoratively call *mundanes*. This suggests we should now consider a much more mundane example to anchor our work in ordinary life.

4.5 A Culinary Pilot Study

This section is based on the development of a questionnaire software module about food preferences, named Taste and using much of the same code as Self and The Year 2100, and a pilot study applying it to one test subject. As explained in Chap. 2, the National Geographic Society sponsored Survey 2000, a major web-based questionnaire project. The version administered to children under age 16 included a simple open-ended item that asked, "What's your favorite food?" A total of 10,298 children responded. After accounting for duplications, a total of 1,537 different foods were mentioned. Any with which I was unfamiliar were checked by looking the term up in Metacrawler, which employed several of the most popular web search engines. I completed the list up to 2,000 items by drawing upon web-based grocery catalogs, restaurant menus, and cook books. I especially made sure to add a number of items that adults might have mentioned but children would not, such as alcoholic beverages and cooking spices.

Some of the terms are occasionally used as synonyms for each other, such as "grinder" and "submarine" or "ramen" and "lo mein." However, people also make distinctions between these terms, and they reflect regional and ethnic differences as well. Many terms are very simple and refer to broad categories, such as "beans" and "bread." Others make very fine distinctions, for example: "chocolate chip cookies," "chocolate chip cookie dough," "cookie dough ice cream," and "chocolate chip cookie dough ice cream." If we included all the distinctions and combinations that people make, we would have tens of thousands of items, but it was important to include at least some very fine distinctions to measure how simple versus complex a person's food categorization system is.

A standard problem in questionnaire research is that some respondents will not be in a position to answer some questions. In the case of this roster of foods, the test subject was personally familiar with just 1,434 of the 2,000 items. The Taste software was written such that there was an additional response category, "don't know," and the analysis modules were adjusted to discount missing data. Studies with this feature should clearly state what it means to be familiar with a stimulus. For example, this respondent could attach a meaning to phrases like "pumpkin leaves" or "cooked fiddleheads," but did not recall ever eating these delicacies.

On a scale of 1 = Dislike to 8 = Like, the respondent's average rating of 1,434 foods was 4.81, only modestly above the 4.5 mid-point on the scale. A second scale asked the respondent to judge the food on a scale of 1 = Unhealthy to 8 = Healthy. The average Healthy score was 3.49, far below the 4.5 mid-point. Whether correctly or not, this respondent feels that much food is unhealthy, and this scale may measure a general difference between people, in terms of how health-conscious or critical they are about the things they eat. The correlation between the Like and Healthy ratings across the rated foods was 0.29, not extremely high but positive, suggesting that this individual's preferences are partly based on health considerations.

Another way of analyzing this preference-health relationship is to consider the foods the respondent rates highest on both scales. A total of 89 were rated at least 6 on both scales, and exactly 20 were rated 7 or 8 on both scales: apricots, baby carrots, Brussels sprouts, carrots, cherries, cranberries, cranberry juice, grapefruit juice, kidney beans, lettuce, lima beans, Mandarin oranges, oranges, orange juice, pears, peas, steamed vegetables, succotash, tangerines, and tomatoes. Just one item was rated very healthy but strongly disliked, namely guacamole. Fully 308 foods were counted as *vices*, scoring 6 or higher on the Like scale, but 3 or lower on the Healthy scale. One could go through all the specific ratings to make sense of them. For example, these three presumably were rated unhealthy because an otherwise healthy vegetable has been fried: corn fritters, onion rings, and vegetable tempura.

For convenience in using the Taste software, the 2,000 foods and beverages had been roughly categorized in 20 groups. As was the case for the modules described earlier, this categorization is rather artificial. However, each group covers a definite conceptual territory and thus can guide the user in his or her exploration of the data. For ease in remembering, the categories have simple names, listed in Table 4.8.

Table 4.8 Ratings of 2,000 foods by one research subject

Category	Description	Items rated	Mean like	Mean healthy	Like–Healthy correlation
Assorted	Soups, stews, casseroles, and salads	80	5.09	4.09	0.34
Breads	Bread, rolls, sandwiches and similar foods	90	4.47	3.50	0.63
Chicken	Chicken dishes and other poultry foods	84	3.89	3.05	0.33
Desserts	Pies, cakes, ice cream, and other after dinner foods	77	5.30	3.27	0.03
European	French, German, Italian and other European cuisines	48	4.29	2.96	0.22
Fruits	Nuts, fruits, and dishes made from them	82	5.38	4.98	0.27
General	Broad categories including some national cuisines	84	4.76	4.42	0.43
Hispanic	Latin American, Latino, and Mexican dishes	42	4.83	3.60	0.13
Ingredients	Spices, flavorings, toppings and various cooking materials	81	5.10	3.86	0.04
Jelly beans	Candy of all kinds, hard and soft	94	5.54	2.32	−0.06
Kangaroo	Wild game, deer, rabbits, and other hunted animals	10	3.70	3.90	0.59
Liquids	Juices, milk, alcoholic beverages, and soft drinks	83	4.88	4.02	0.41
Meats	Types and cuts of common meat and meat dishes	76	4.47	2.80	0.35
Non-classified	Miscellaneous foods including potato dishes	65	5.09	2.98	−0.14
Oriental	Asian dishes and national cuisines	50	5.60	3.16	0.01
Pasta	Rice, noodle, and pasta dishes	77	4.73	3.30	0.24
Quiche	Eggs, cheese, omelets, and similar foods	90	4.52	2.60	0.31
Random	Snacks, fast food, eaten at random times of day	79	4.01	2.47	0.50
Seafood	Fish, shellfish, and foods from the ocean	65	4.17	3.29	0.36
Tomatoes	Vegetables of all kinds, cooked and uncooked	77	5.48	5.34	0.56

As with the similar software modules described in other chapters, a correlation between the two measures can be calculated for each category, indicating how much the person's preferences for the food in the category are connected to health judgments. The category judged most unhealthy by the respondent is jelly beans (i.e. candy of all kinds, hard and soft), but the respondent admits liking candy, and shows no correlation between liking and judging a particular kind of candy to be more or less healthy. While we can infer the reasons for preferences to some extent by this questionnaire method, it might be instructive to supplement this method by qualitative interviews, for example asking the respondent to explain unhealthy-healthy ratings for a sample of the foods. While food preferences are an individual matter, eating often occurs in a social context, especially for children who eat the food prepared by their parents at the family dinner table, and many lifetime food preferences may be established in childhood. This suggests we need to consider the social aspects of preferences.

4.6   Subcultures and Networks

Individual people differ in their preferences, yet preferences have a social dimension. Some activities are inherently shared, such as playing games like chess or tennis. Others, like watching movies, are often but not always done in social settings. The University of Washington data allow us to explore this social dimension of preferences, because it was a linked-respondent survey [37]. Each student in a very large introductory Sociology class who chose to participate got a packet of four identical questionnaires. One was for the student, two were for close friends of the student, and one was for an acquaintance. A total of 1,439 questionnaires were completed, 554 by students in the class, 612 by close friends, and 273 by acquaintances. The friends and acquaintances were asked a question about how close a friendship they had with the student, on a scale from 0 to 6, and sealed their questionnaires in an envelope so they could answer candidly despite the fact the student delivered the questionnaire back to us. Here we will focus on 424 pairs of respondents in which the friend gave a closeness rating of 5 or 6.

The main topic of the study was religion, and the most active religious force on campus was the Born Again movement, so respondents were asked whether they considered themselves Born Again. Here we will also consider the 219 close friend pairs in which neither of the two linked respondents considered themselves to be Born Again. Thus, we can look at how individual preferences related to two different kinds of social connection: (1) a dyadic bond between two people, and (2) membership in a subculturally distinct group. Table 4.9 does this for nine preferences, reporting the concordance between the preferences of two individuals, expressed as the gamma correlation between their responses to the give preference question.

Respondents who like beer tend to have friends who like it, too. The gamma of 0.32 for all 424 close friend pairs is a solid if not spectacular correlation. The gam-

Table 4.9 Correlations in preferences of close-friend pairs of students

Preference for:	424 close friend pairs	219 not born again close friend pairs
Beer	0.32	0.33
Diet soda	0.27	0.28
Rock music	0.25	0.22
Tobacco cigarettes	0.50	0.44
Marijuana	0.45	0.41
The Physical Sciences	0.01	0.00
The Social Sciences	0.04	-0.02
Religious books and articles	0.25	0.03
Hymns and spirituals	0.22	0.07

ma for the 219 pairs in which neither friend is Born Again is almost identical, 0.33. This suggests that friendship and beer-drinking are salient for each other, while beer-drinking and the Born Again movement are not connected. We might have expected a significant difference between the two coefficients, because historically the Born Again movement is connected to the forms of Protestantism that advocated prohibition of alcohol. But in the lives of these respondents, beer and religion appear to be separate aspects of life. Of course, they don't drink beer at church meetings, but that tendency does not transfer over to other settings where beer drinking might be appropriate. We see similar patterns for diet soda and rock music.

Tobacco cigarettes and marijuana show high concordances, while preference for academic subjects do not. The two religion-related items at the bottom of Table 4.9 show solid correlations among all students, but not among the pairs in which neither friend is Born Again. This reflects the fact that liking religious writings and religious music is practically a requirement for membership in the Born Again subculture, and Born-Agains tend to have other Born-Agains for friends. While this may seem perfectly obvious, it is a nice illustration of a general principle: Some preferences are primarily determined at the level of the individual, while other preferences are properties of groups.

A wide variety of existing questionnaire datasets include explicit preference items, and many kinds of other attitudinal items could be rephrased as preferences. Thus, it is possible to calibrate various types of preference items to the demographic characteristics of respondents, or their group memberships. For example, the U.S. Congregational Life Survey, administered to thousands of church members in 2001, measured preferences for the kinds of music listed in Table 4.10. The question specifically asked "While you may value many different styles of music, which of the following do you prefer in congregational worship? (Mark up to two options.)." Another question asked, "What is your race or origin? (Mark all that apply.)" The data are freely available for anyone to download and analyze from the online digital library of the Association of Religion Data Archives, and anybody may print out the questionnaire and answer it for their own records [38].

These data are structured rather differently than those we considered earlier, thus illustrating the range of measurement approaches that may be used. Each respondent could check as many as two kinds of preferred religious music, which

Table 4.10 Preferences for religious music across "Races"

Preference for:	Asian or Pacific Islander	Black or African American	Hispanic, Latino, or Spanish origin	Indian (American) or Alaska Native	White or Caucasian
Traditional hymns	46.0%	35.6%	39.9%	46.8%	64.8%
Praise music or choruses	33.6%	42.9%	39.3%	32.9%	30.4%
Contemporary hymns	20.7%	16.4%	14.6%	20.1%	27.4%
Other contemporary music or songs (not hymns)	11.6%	11.3%	8.7%	13.7%	13.6%
Sung responsorial psalms	12.6%	3.0%	15.6%	7.4%	9.7%
Classical music or chorales	9.2%	3.1%	7.1%	7.5%	10.1%
Contemplative chants (Taize, Iona)	1.5%	0.8%	1.4%	2.7%	2.0%
Music or songs from a variety of cultures	12.3%	12.3%	14.3%	15.1%	7.8%
African-American gospel music	3.9%	42.4%	4.4%	10.5%	3.1%
No music or songs	1.1%	0.5%	0.9%	1.4%	1.3%
Don't know	5.8%	2.7%	5.7%	4.9%	2.5%
Total	158.3%	171.0%	151.9%	163.0%	172.7%
Respondents	4,957	5,481	14,884	1,416	88,935

explains why the totals near the bottom exceed 100%. Also, a respondent could check multiple "race or origin" boxes, which means the total number of respondents is somewhat less than 88,935, although this certainly has one of the biggest numbers of cases in any conventional questionnaire survey. In the context of cultural science, as well as modern political correctness, we might prefer to describe the "race" categories as very rough measures of "culture of origin," recognizing that the categories offered do not include many options that might be salient for particular individuals.

4.7 Emulating Preferences

Already today, recommender systems allow people to influence the behavior of others, long after providing preference ratings, and even after death. Thinking back to the liberal-conservative GSS item used in some of the questionnaires, and the fact it can be conceptualized as a preference item, reminds us that people's political preferences can have long-lasting impacts on other people. Voting in an election expresses a preference that has obvious consequences. The farmers of the Constitution of the United States are recognized to have had great influence lasting for more than two centuries.

Consider the following radical possibility, whether or not we wish to implement it, as a logical extension. A politically radical but technically easy option would allow you to vote posthumously in elections of your nation, community, or organization. Today, you would answer several thousand questions about political issues, policies, and your general philosophy of life. Long after your demise, a random sample of the population would answer these same questions plus new questions that were part of a referendum on some key decisions of the day. Statistical analysis of the future respondents' answers would make it possible to predict how you would answer the new referendum questions, and your vote could be included with theirs.

Any innovation that overturns prevailing social norms will meet opposition, but often innovations can get started in especially conducive contexts, and spread out from there. For example, opponents might argue that only living people should vote, because the dead have no interest in how society is run. Taken to the extreme, this argument implies that old people, who will die before the full effect of new laws has been felt, should have only fractional votes, whereas young people with many years to live under the regime should have full votes. Posthumous voting, however, could get started in voluntary organizations, before gradually invading the society's political process.

For example, imagine that an elderly rich person named Bill Getty wanted to leave a billion dollars in a foundation for struggling artists. A scientifically designed art appreciation test would measure his tastes and aesthetic sensitivities, perhaps by having him rate a hundred carefully selected works of art in terms of a preference scale. After his death, every year hundreds of artists would submit works of art that would be displayed to the public. Visitors to the exhibition would rate each of the 100 old works that Bill Getty had rated, and they also would rate each of the new works on display. A statistical technique such as multiple regression analysis would produce an equation, based both on Bill's scores and those of the given year's exhibition visitors, that would estimate which artists Bill would have wanted to support, and they would win grants from his foundation. Because the money belonged to Bill in the first place, no one could complain about the fact that his tastes continued to determine the grants made by his foundation after his death. Once it was established in the special case of individual legacies, posthumous voting could gradually be adopted by university clubs, churches and other private organizations, before being tried out with political districts.

Alternatively, the development of a rigorous and comprehensive cultural science could become the basis of the liberal arts education of the future. Employing data from a diversity of recommender systems, preference questionnaires, and works by humanistic scholars, a dynamic classification of human cultural productions could become the basis of a reformed university curriculum. The goal would not merely be to put science fiction literature and movies in one course, and religious movies and music in another course, but to understand the fundamental issues addressed by all forms of artistic expression, designing capstone courses that bridge across genres on the basis of profound insights about human existence. Graduates could live their lives in terms of what they learned in their liberal arts education, modified by their personal experience, and express their judgments in ways that feed back into the evolving cultural science.

4.8 Conclusion

Recommender systems already accomplish personality capture and emulation, but always submerging the individual into a group, often a subgroup of the total population of respondents who happen to have preferences very similar to those of the user. Thus, this is a very democratic approach, stressing incorporation and personalization, at the expense of apotheosis. The chief current limitation is that recommender systems are tied to commercial enterprises, so they ignore very many spheres of life about which people have preferences, such as academic subjects. One can naturally imagine creating recommender systems in other areas of human life, for example one focused on sciences and humanities for use by advisors and students in academic institutions. But the really significant development would be the establishment of a new, quantitative cultural science, building upon the methodologies described in this chapter, incorporating appropriate, sophisticated theories, and contributing to a better understanding of the social world in which we live.

References

1. Resnick, P., & Varian, R. H. (1997). Recommender systems. *Communications of the ACM, 40*, 56–58.
2. Basu, C., Hirsh, H., & Cohen, W. (1998). Recommendation as classification: Using social and content-based information in recommendation. *Proceedings of the fifteenth national conference on artificial intelligence*. Madison: Wisconsin.
3. Goldberg, D., Nichols, D., Oki, B. M., & Terry, D. (1992). Using collaborative filtering to weave an information tapestry. *Communications of the ACM, 35*, 61–70.
4. Bell, R. M., Koren, Y., & Volinsky, C. (2007). Modeling relationships at multiple scales to improve accuracy of large recommender systems. In, *Proceedings of the 13th ACM SIGKDD International Conference on Knowledge Discovery and Data Mining* (pp. 95–104). New York: ACM.
5. Ekstrand, M., & Riedl, J. (2012). When recommenders fail: Predicting recommender failure for algorithm selection and combination. In, Proceedings of the sixth ACM conference on recommender systems (pp. 233–236). New York: ACM.
6. Hu, R., & Pu, P. (2009). Acceptance issues of personality-based recommender systems. In, *Proceedings of the third ACM conference on recommender systems* (pp. 221–224). New York: ACM.
7. Kawamae, N., Sakano, H., & Yamada, T. (2009). Personalized recommendation based on the personal innovator degree. In, *Proceedings of the third ACM conference on recommender systems* (pp. 329–332). New York: ACM.
8. Hu, R., & Pu, P. (2011). Enhancing collaborative filtering systems with personality information. In, *Proceedings of the fifth ACM conference on recommender systems* (pp 197–204). New York: ACM.
9. Murdock, G. P. (1949). *Social Structure*. New York: MacMillan.
10. Ethnographic Atlas. (1967). *A Summary*. Pittsburgh: University of Pittsburgh Press.
11. White, D. R. (1986). The world cultures database. *World Cultures, 1*(1), 14.
12. Bainbridge, W. S. (2007). Expanding the use of the internet in religious research. *Review of Religious Research, 49*(1), 7–20.
13. Bainbridge, W. S. (1978). *Satan's Power*. Berkeley: University of California Press.
14. Bainbridge, W. S. (2013). *eGods* (p. 199). New York: Oxford University Press.

15. Couch, A., & Kenniston, K. (1960). Yeasayers and Naysayers: Agreeing response set as a personality variable. *Journal of Abnormal and Social Psychology*, *60*, 151–174.
16. Bainbridge, W. S. (1992). Social research methods and statistics: A computer-assisted introduction (p. 478). Belmont: Wadsworth.
17. en.wikipedia.org/wiki/Charleton_Heston. Accessed 3 Feb 2013.
18. www.imdb.com/. Accessed 16 Apr 2013.
19. www.imdb.com/title/tt0183523/plotsummary?ref_=tt_stry_pl. Accessed 9 Feb 2013.
20. www.imdb.com/title/tt0199753/plotsummary?ref_=tt_stry_pl. Accessed 9 Feb 2013.
21. Bainbridge, W. S. (2011). *The virtual future*. London: Springer.
22. Lem, S. (1970). *Solaris*. New York: Walker.
23. en.wikipedia.org/wiki/Solaris_(novel), accessed April 14, 2013.
24. www.imdb.com/title/tt0069293/, accessed April 14, 2013.
25. www.imdb.com/title/tt0307479/, accessed April 14, 2013.
26. Palmer, L. (15 June 2009). Culture Warrior: Kubrick's '2001' vs. Tarkovsky's 'Solaris'. www.filmschoolrejects.com/features/culture-warrior-kubricks-2001-vs-tarkovskys-solaris.php. Accessed 5 Apr 2013.
27. Clarke, A. C. (1968). *2001: A space odyssey*. London: Hutchinson.
28. Nietzsche, F., der Tragödie, D. G. (1872). Munich: Goldmann
29. Gouldner, A. W. (1965). Enter Plato New York: Basic Books
30. The Hellenic World. (1969). New York: Harper and Row.
31. Bell, R. M., Koren, Y., & Volinsky, C. (2007). Modeling relationships at multiple scales to improve accuracy of large recommender systems, In, *Proceedings of the 13th ACM SIGKDD international conference on knowledge discovery and data mining*. New York: ACM, pp. 95–104.
32. Bainbridge, W. S. (1991). *Goals in space: American values and the future of technology*. Albany, New York: State University of New York Press.
33. Bainbridge, W. S. (1992). Research methods and statistics: A computer-assisted introduction. Belmont, California: Wadsworth, p. 520.
34. Rosenberg, M. (1968). *The logic of survey analysis*. New York: Basic Books, p. 85.
35. en.wikipedia.org/wiki/Nielsen_ratings, accessed March 19, 2013
36. nielsen.com/us/en/nielsen-solutions/nielsen-measurement/nielsen-tv-measurement.html, accessed March 19, 2013
37. Bainbridge, W. S., & Stark, R. (1981). Friendship, religion, and the occult, *Review of Religious Research*, *22*, 313–327.
38. www.thearda.com/Archive/Files/Descriptions/USCLSRA.asp

Chapter 5
Cognitive Abilities

Much research, and much heated discussion, has focused on intelligence tests, especially the so-called IQ. The extensive use of aptitude tests in education has perhaps exaggerated the importance of such concepts [1–3]. Indeed, IQ stands for *intelligence quotient*, and a quotient is the result of doing mathematical division. The original idea was to categorize school children in terms of their mental development, and IQ was the result of dividing their mental age by their chronological age, and multiplying the result by 100 as if calculating a percentage. Mental age would be figured in terms of how the particular child scored in comparison with the average of other children of various age groups [4].

All this is very reasonable, except for three problems. First, once people become adults, the average test scores do not differ much by age, so the quotient loses its original justification. Second, it is unclear how much the tests are culture-bound, measuring the extent that a maturing child has learned the specific skills expected by the dominant groups in the surrounding society, and perhaps just by the academics who run the schools and devise the tests. Third, despite decades of research and debate, the IQ concept tends to be one dimensional, ignoring specialized intellectual skills and different ways of being smart. That last point is especially damaging for personality capture, because our goal here is to find ways of measuring diversity, and one number per person, distributed across the population according to the normal curve, with a mean of 100 and standard deviation of 15, tells us very little.

Once we have test results, the problem arises how we can use them to emulate the individual. It is relatively easy to write a computer program that would do arithmetic as well as a given individual, for example failing half the time on long division problems, but this does not take us very far. As Chap. 7 will explore, computer-based natural language processing and related technologies can emulate a person's language behavior, although at present only in limited ways. Here our goals are to identify a few general issues about capturing and emulating cognitive skills, and propose methods that might be used to achieve some progress. There should be no doubt that this is a tremendously challenging area, demanding but also deserving research and development by many people.

W. S. Bainbridge, *Personality Capture and Emulation,* Human-Computer Interaction Series, 101
DOI 10.1007/978-1-4471-5604-8_5, © Springer-Verlag London 2014

At various points, this chapter will link the ideas and pilot studies we discuss to the cognitive science literature, not with any expectation that we can nail down the ultimate truth, but rather to suggest intellectual resources we might draw upon for future research that might, eventually, do so. At one point, we will consider neural network simulations of human learning, and we shall replicate one particular classic experiment on short-term memory. Much of the existing research was aimed at determining the general principles by which normal human brains operate, but our focus will be on individual variations within and beyond the normal range. Consideration of expert systems will be an efficient way to begin to think about capturing cognitive skills that few people possess, but that exist in so many variants that they define the intellects of almost everybody.

5.1   Consciousness

Sometimes called *short-term memory* or *working memory*, some module or function in the brain serves to organize behavior in the present, while making plans for the future and drawing upon memories of the past. The more one reads of the relevant scientific literature, the more different models of this module one finds, and the greater the number of variations of each model, leading to the conclusion that we really do not understand with any certainty what it is and how it works. It may represent what people traditionally perceived as the spirit, soul, or consciousness of the person. Thus, it is a crucial topic for consideration here, possibly representing the essence of the personality we wish to capture and emulate.

Back in 1956, George A. Miller pointed out that the normal human brain can process perhaps between five and nine separate pieces of information at once, and this was generally taken to be the size of working memory [5]. Both in artificial intelligence and in cognitive science, the concept of *chunking* was introduced, referring to our ability to package several pieces of information together, thereby treating them as one and effectively increasing the size of our working memory [6]. For example, I just asked myself to recall quotations from William Shakespeare, and these were the first three that came to mind, in this order: "Let me not to the marriage of true minds admit impediments." "To be or not to be, that is the question." "The evil that men do lives after them, the good is oft interred with their bones." The fact that I was writing this paragraph for this book may have biased my recall toward quotations relevant to our topic here. Each quotation comes to mind as a unit, and the words arrive in a particular order.

A different person would have retrieved different quotations, indeed if any at all, and speakers of other languages would not memorize quotations in English. I have never read a German translation of Hamlet, but just now Google and Gutenberg allowed me to find the second of the three quotations in that language: "Seyn oder nicht seyn–Das ist die Frage." My first attempt to search the text failed, because I thought *seyn* should be spelled *sein*, since that is the modern way of spelling *to be*, but of course Shakespeare was not modern. I succeeded when I searched for

Fig. 5.1 The interface for the short-term memory pilot study

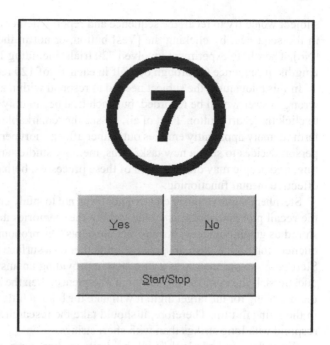

oder nicht, which means *or not*. It seems very unlikely that the human mind actually scans some neuron-based text of Shakespeare for common phrases like *or not*, which warns us that the fact both computers and humans can accomplish a task does not mean they do it in the same way.

An especially interesting early computerized study of human short-term memory by Saul Sternberg was published in the pages of the journal *Science* in 1966. For an ancillary book titled *Experiments in Psychology* and published in 1986 in connection with James Kalat's textbook, *Introduction to Psychology*, I wrote a computer program that allowed students to try Sternberg's experiment on themselves and their friends [7, 8]. Then, more recently I updated that program for serious pilot research related to personality capture. Sternberg reported data from 8 and 6 subjects in two different experiments, combining their data to perform preliminary tests of general hypotheses. My pilot study of just two subjects is intended to suggest ways of measuring how people differ, and my references to hypotheses are meant to suggest an intellectual context, not to test the ideas.

While the software I wrote was somewhat complex, and included many options, what the experimental subject had to deal with was very simple. As shown in Fig. 5.1, near the middle of a computer screen were three rectangular buttons, initially with nothing showing above them. To start each trial of the experiment, the subject would click the [Start] button, which would cause single digits from the range 0 through 9 to appear, one at a time, with a set delay between them. At random, there were from 1 to 6 digits, with no repetitions. Then after a pause a single digit would appear, inside a circle, like the 7 shown in the figure. The research subject would try to recall the sequence and report whether the target digit had been in the sequence, by clicking the [Yes] button, or not in the sequence, by clicking [No]. The whole experiment involved 720 trials, including 120 trials for each of the lengths of sequence (1 through 6), half in each set of 120 requiring a Yes answer.

In this pilot study, the subject needed to respond within a couple of seconds, or a wrong answer would be recorded, but each trial began only when the subject chose to click the [Start] button. First of all, we see the remarkable fact that people's short-term memory apparently empties out, either after a short period of time, or when the person decides to start a new task. Thus, memory studies are also studies of forgetting, and people may differ in both of these processes, both of which are needed for effective mental functioning.

Sternberg's marvelously creative goal was not to study error in memory, but how the recall process works, as a clue to how the memories are stored. Are the digits stored as graphic images? As abstract concepts? As pronounceable words? In a sequence from first to last, or spread out together on a surface seen by the mind's eye? Sternberg's experiment was a first step in providing an answer to just one of these questions. If the numbers are stored in a sequence, then the mind must scan through them looking for the target digit. It will take the brain a little time to check each digit in the string in turn. Therefore, it should take the research subject a little longer to respond with long strings than with short strings.

But if the mind can look at all the digits in short-term memory simultaneously, then the subject will take no longer to respond with long strings than with short ones. Thus the first research question is whether long strings of digits require a longer response time than short strings. If so, then the mind probably scans the digits in short-term memory. If not, then it probably can survey them all simultaneously. Sternberg's research supported the hypotheses that the mind scans, and his computer was primarily timing the delay between the display of the target digit and the subject's choice of a response.

Sternberg also examined a second hypothesis about how the scan operates. If the mind scans short-term memory, and has the capacity to stop the scan as soon as the target digit has been found, then it should take less time to come up with YES answers on long strings than with NO answers. But if it lacks the capacity to stop scanning until it has gone through the whole string, the response time might be the same for a given number of digits, regardless of whether the answer is YES or NO. Sternberg's experiment suggested that the scanning is exhaustive, because the YES answers did not come more quickly than the NO answers.

I had written the new version of the short-term memory program primarily to explore the possibility of measuring individual differences with the goal of including memory processes in personality capture, but the project took on a new dimension when a person with unusual memory abilities volunteered to be studied. We shall call this person Sharp, and one ordinary person who did the trials for comparison, Dull.

Sharp may possess an *eidetic memory*, although this concept has become somewhat controversial within psychology. The Wikipedia article about it asserts that proof is lacking, and cites one 1970 report in the journal *Nature* as the only scientific study apparently demonstrating a true photographic memory, while raising a number of serious questions about the validity of that study [9–12]. As it happens, at the time that 1970 study was being done, I personally knew both the researcher and the research subject, perceiving them both to be both intelligent and respectable people. Whatever errors might have occurred during that particular research, clearly people do differ in their memory abilities, and therefore one might expect that a few individuals have exceptional abilities, if not perfect or supernatural ones.

A very different issue, but one that connected indirectly to the research subject in the 1970 study, was a common belief that people with unusual mental abilities are idiot savants, whose unusual abilities are more than compensated for by mental defects in other areas. To be sure, some people with significant problems may have unusual abilities as well, but I see no reason to believe normal people cannot have unusual memories as well. Sharp, for example, is a completely successful person holding a doctoral degree. I recall an evening years ago when I challenged a perfectly normal Harvard student with long-digit multiplication and division problems, all of which he solved instantly without use of paper, pencil, or calculator. Truth to tell, we just don't know how the different dimensions of human mental variation fit together, and it is unfortunate that many people with superior abilities suffer a degree of stigmatization because of the popular stereotype that there must be something wrong with them.

One of the design features of Sternberg's experiment, flashing the sequence of digits one at a time rather than showing all at once, was intended to prevent people with eidetic imagery from simply holding a picture of all the numbers in their minds. Indeed, if some people really do have somewhat eidetic memories, do they function by means of visual pictures as the metaphor of photographic memory suggests? Or, indeed, could there be several different kinds of superior short-term memory, storing the information in different ways? Thus it was very interesting, frankly bordering on a shock, when I compared the error rates for Sharp and Dull, as shown in Table 5.1

Sternberg reported his subjects tended to make few errors, between one and two percent, whereas Dull made nearly 7% errors, despite like Sharp holding a doctorate in a similar field. Sharp, however, made zero errors, despite the experiment's attempt to exclude mental photography by presenting the digits in sequence. In an interview, Dull admitted finding the experiment confusing, struggling to remember the names of the digits as a word sequence, and not aware of using any visual imagery. Clearly, Table 5.1 presents evidence that normal people vary very significantly in how their short-term memory functions, and Table 5.2 offers a mix of similarities and differences in the response delay, measured in milliseconds.

On average, over the 720 trials, Dull delayed 765 ms in responding (3/4 of a second), while Sharp delayed slightly longer, 926 ms. Sharp seemed perfectly calm while participating in the study, while Dull was slightly frantic, which may account for Dull's quicker response as well as high error rate. But when we compare the delay, called *latency of response*, across sequences with different numbers of digits, Dull exactly replicates Sternberg's findings, while Sharp does not.

Across the 120 trials involving just one digit, Dull's average latency was 696 ms, while for sequences of 6 digits the latency was 843 ms. Going down the column for Total mean latencies shows a smooth increase from 1 to 6 digits. For Sharp, the

Table 5.1 Memory errors in number strings by two research subjects

Digits	Dull			Sharp		
	Yes	No	Total	Yes	No	Total
1	0	2	2	0	0	0
2	0	0	0	0	0	0
3	0	0	0	0	0	0
4	5	4	9	0	0	0
5	9	10	19	0	0	0
6	14	5	19	0	0	0
Total	28	21	49	0	0	0

Table 5.2 Response latencies in milliseconds by two research subjects

Digits	Dull			Sharp		
	Yes	No	Total	Yes	No	Total
1	682	710	696	866	942	904
2	696	737	717	917	911	914
3	716	765	741	927	964	946
4	769	790	780	894	969	932
5	805	824	815	903	926	915
6	858	827	843	954	935	945
Total	754	775	765	910	941	926

first three figures show a similar pattern of increase: 904, 914, 946. But then Sharp's numbers decrease: 932, 915, before increasing again to 945. This could, of course, be chance variation, although the sequences of different lengths were presented at random and we are looking at rather large numbers of trials. The distorting effect of random factors is one reason researchers tend to use large numbers of research subjects, so random factors will even out. But if our aim is to capture individual personalities, and study variation across individuals, this tactic can be counter-productive.

Both research subjects showed similar but complex patterns of latency differences between YES and NO sequences of digits, those that did or did not include the target. Over all 720 trials, the YES responses were slightly quicker than the NO responses, which suggests both subjects were about equally able to stop the scan when finding the target in the memorized sequence. But this was true for 1-digit sequences, where YES and NO should have shown no difference, and the opposite was true for 6-digit sequences where the stop-scan phenomenon should have been most obvious. Perhaps these patterns are meaningless, and again they might vanish in a study combining data from many subjects. However, one might expect individuals to have somewhat idiosyncratic patterns of response latency, if they reflect the complexity of the mental task for that individual, who may structure tasks in a unique manner.

An especially promising adaptation of latency measurement in a way that could capture personality characteristics is the Implicit Association Test developed by psychologists Tony Greenwald, Mahzarin Banaji, and Brian Nosek, who currently offer a version online through Project Implicit [13, 14]. Two important ambiguities run throughout this tradition of research. First, it is not clear whether a bias is subconscious or responses are consciously withheld from the researcher by the subject. Social desirability bias may motivate the subject to deceive the researcher. The developers of the Implicit Association Test recognize this problem. The general tenor of the debate suggests that the degree to which a bias is implicit, rather than fully conscious, or is mentally encoded in some third or fourth way, is yet another kind of individual variation that needs to be measured in its own right. Unfortunately, much of the literature about the test, and its current online version, use the example of racial prejudice, which taints the explanations with politics. As illustrated by Sternberg's study, latency of response may be an important clue about many kind of mental behavior, quite unrelated to current public ideologies.

Second, there exist several competing explanations for latency, which may correctly fit different cases. Latency of response entered personality psychology a century ago, through the word-association tests developed by Freud's disciple, Carl Gustav Jung, who believed that delays tended to indicate psychological repression of feelings associated with subconscious conflicts [15]. However, the act of conscious deception takes mental effort and thus perhaps increases latency. One of the classic psychological theories of prejudice, proposed by Gordon Allport, said that stereotypes tend to reduce the cognitive effort to make decisions, which implies that working against a stereotype consumes effort and therefore time [16]. The Implicit Association Test is to a great extent a further development of Allport's ideas, and the following section of this chapter builds on Allport as well, by constructing neural net computer models of stereotypes.

5.2 Neural Nets

Throughout this book we tend to find that personality capture is easier than personality emulation, although until we master both we will not really be sure how to accomplish either. Emulating intellectual skills might be one of the easier areas to achieve this convergence, for two reasons. First of all, whether expressed through an IQ test or the ability to perform as a competent technical professional, these skills tend to be rather systematized and logical. Second, solving puzzles like those on IQ tests or machine maintenance were among the original goals of artificial intelligence researchers, and indeed AI specialists tended to define human intelligence more in terms of artificial puzzle-solving than in terms of abilities to thrive within a complex, natural environment. In any case, in this chapter we can consider AI methods for fairly near-term success in personality emulation.

It would be trivially easy to write a computer program to emulate the behavior of Dull and Sharp in Sternberg's memory experiment. First, the program would take in the digits displayed, and record them in its memory registers. As Sternberg himself would have realized, there are several ways a computer can store this information. One way would be to save the digits as a text string in the order they were presented, like 34125, and scan through the string when the target digit was presented. Another way would be to have an array set up with one register for each digit—0, 1, 2, 3, 4,

5, 6, 7, 8, 9—and check off each digit as it appeared. Then the computer would look only in the memory register representing the target digit, to see if it has already been marked. Either way, the computer like Sharp would always get the right answer. Perhaps a time-delay loop would be added to the program, set to give the same distribution of latencies Sharp had exhibited during the experiment, but having no connection to the actual determination about the target digit, because that would be instantaneous. Indeed, Sharp's latencies could simply reflect habitual time to move a hand when in a relaxed mood, rather than anything really cognitive.

To emulate Dull, an additional routine could be added to Sharp's program, modeling Dull's error propensities. The computer would count how many digits were in the string, let's say 6 in one particular example. The computer would then determine the correct response, YES or NO, let's say YES because the target was in the string of digits. Dull responded 60 times to 6-digit strings that did include the target digit, but in fully 14 of these cases gave the wrong answer, NO. This is an error rate of about 23 %, so the computer program would have a routine that switched the answer 23 % of the time under these conditions. Built into the program would be all of Dull's error rates, specific to length of digit string and correct answer. Similarly, unlike the simpler case of Sharp, the program would need a dozen separate latency distributions, based on how quickly Dull had responded in each of the 720 trials. Note that if we integrated the testing program with the emulation program, no human being might ever have access to all of Dull's detailed response data, but the simulation would behave exactly like the real person, in this limited context.

There are many forms of AI, but among the most suitable for an integrated capture-emulation program are neural networks, which in the computational context we can call *NNs*. This approach was inspired by how the human brain works, where a very large number of neurons interact through their connections with each other, but today we realize very well that the specific designs of computerized neural nets are very different from the nets of neurons. Some researchers attempt to emulate biological neural pathways more closely than others, but only in the most abstract sense do most NNs really emulate the brain. Here I will describe two types I have worked with extensively, because they convey general principles, most notably the unresolved issue of how complex and hierarchical in structure NNs need to be to emulate human cognitive processes.

Figure 5.2 shows a form of NN I called MIND (Minimum Intelligent Neural Device) for an article published in *Journal of Mathematical Sociology* [17]. This is actually a rather conventional design, noteworthy only because I removed one feature that many NNs of its type have, in order to emulate human error exemplified by ethnic prejudice as conceptualized in Allport's stereotype theory. To set the stage for the simulation I imagined a real situation in which ethnic stereotypes were significant, but not one that would offend many readers, namely the division of Belgium into Dutch-speaking Flemish and French-speaking Walloons. The person simulated by the NN would meet various people, each of whom was either poor or rich, young or old, male or female, and Flemish or Walloon. So, the NN interacts repeatedly with a variety of strangers, each represented simply by four binary numbers. Each time the interaction turns out either well or poorly. If the NN interacts positively with a stranger, nothing is changed, representing the idea that the net is already

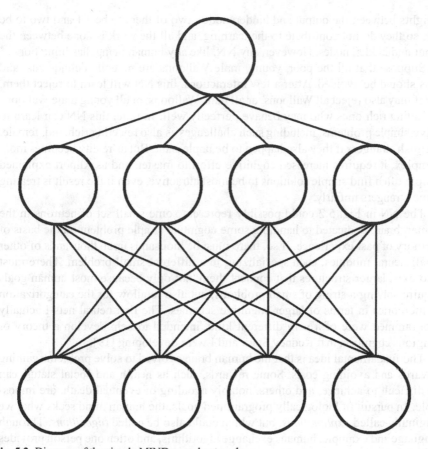

Fig. 5.2 Diagram of the simple MIND neural network

well-tuned to provide proper advice to the simulated person. But if the interaction turns out poorly, the NN uses a procedure called *back propagation* to adjust itself to be more likely to reject interaction with a similar stranger in the future.

In Fig. 5.2, the four circles at the bottom are input nodes, one for each of the four binary characteristics of a stranger. The one circle at the top is the output node, producing a 1 to represent willingness to interact with the latest stranger the person met, and a 0 to represent defensive rejection of the stranger. The four circles between the inputs and the output are hidden nodes, and the connections linking them with input and output are where the work of the NN is done. Each of those connections is represented by a real-number register in the computer's memory, called a connection weight. When the NN makes a decision, it performs somewhat complex sets of multiplications and sums, involving the input binary numbers and the weights, to decide whether the output should be 1 or 0. The exact details of the algorithm, and indeed some of the exact programming code, were given in the original article, while extensive consideration of the meaning of results is given in my book, *God from the Machine* [18]. I had limited the flexibility of this NN somewhat, by freezing the weights between the output and hidden nodes, two of them to be $+1$ and two to be -1, so they do not contribute to the learning, and all the work is done between the input and hidden nodes. However, any NN, like any human being, has limitations.

Suppose that all the poor, young, male Walloons are juvenile delinquents, and thus should be avoided. After a few interactions, this NN will learn to reject them, but it may also reject all Walloons, or all male Walloons, or all young male Walloons including rich ones who may behave perfectly well. In time, this NN can learn to solve simple problems, including such challenges as also rejecting rich, old, female, Flemish strangers if they also happen to be unpleasant. But as reality becomes more complex, it requires increased cognitive effort to master, and as Allport explained people often find simple solutions to be most attractive, even if the result is treating some strangers unfairly.

The NN in Fig. 5.2 could possibly represent some small set of neurons in the human brain, dedicated to handling some cognitive simple problem on the basis of memory of past experience. If so, there must be thousands upon thousands of other small neural modules, each specializing in a different small problem. There must also exist larger structures that connect them, not only because most human goals require solving a string of small problems, but also to allow for the categorization of memories in terms of larger cognitive schemes. The first neural nets I actually programmed were of a very different kind, intended to help develop a theory of religious cognition that Rodney Stark and I were developing [19].

The fundamental idea is that the human brain evolved to solve problems gaining rewards and avoiding costs. Some rewards, such as health and social status, can be difficult to achieve, and others, notably avoiding of eventual death, are impossible. In pursuit of biologically programmed goals, the human mind seeks what we originally called *explanations*, but which could also be called *algorithms*. Through language and example, humans exchange algorithms, and often one person provides a useful algorithm to another in exchange for a material reward, such as food or help in accomplishing a physical task. The lack of adequate algorithms for achievement of some goals, plus the benefits that can accrue to algorithm-providers, gave rise to shamans who pretend that their magic can cure diseases, and priests who pretend that they can open the doors to a happy afterlife [20].

The first program I wrote in late 1983 to model this theory imagined that very simple AI agents were seeking exchange partners from whom to obtain a variety of desired rewards, putting an ID number representing the name of another agent into a memory register prior to beginning an interaction with that agent. If the exchange worked out well, in trading some available rewards such as food, the name remained in the register, but if the exchange worked out poorly the name was removed. When an agent was seeking eternal life, the exchange with another agent always ended badly, and that agent's name was removed from the list of potential eternal-life provider. However, the list of names included some that did not belong to agents represented in the system, a metaphor for supernatural beings who could not actually be met. Their names would remain in the list, because their ability to provide eternal life could not be disproven. While the results of running this simulation—on an antique Apple IIe computer—fit our theory, I did not publish them, feeling that a more sophisticated cognitive model was needed.

Table 5.3 The structure of the direct reinforcement neural net

Output	Variance across 2-group registers	Group 1 of 2	Group 2 of 2	Group 3 of 2	Group 4 of 2
	Variance across 3-group registers	Group 1 of 3	Group 2 of 3	Group 3 of 3	Group 4 of 3
	Variance across 4-group registers	Group 1 of 4	Group 2 of 4	Group 3 of 4	Group 4 of 4

A minimum version of a new idea was published in *Experiments in Psychology*, modeling the behavior of a mouse in a simple T-maze, programmed for both Apple II and the IBM personal computers. On each of many trials, the mouse would scamper up the vertical path of the T and come to a decision whether to go left or right. The correct path led to cheese, and the wrong path to an electric shock. This decision was represented simply by two real-number memory registers, one representing left, and the other, right. Getting cheese would add a fraction to the corresponding register, and a shock would subtract a fraction. Over a series of trials, the mouse would learn to go the correct way most of the time, but not always. The number in a register had lower and upper limits, to permit the mouse to learn new behavior quickly if the experimenter changed the reward and punishment contingencies in the middle of an experiment.

The plot thickened when I added a second clue about the location of the cheese and shock: a light that made one path bright and the other dark, randomly switching the light between left and right between trials, so the two clues were independent. Perhaps the bright path led to cheese, and the dark path to the electric shock—or vice versa if the experimenter wished. This required not only adding two more memory registers to remember the results of taking the bright or dark path, but a system by which the mouse could learn whether to pay attention to left-right or to bright-dark. An easy way to do this is have the computer compare the variance in the left-right versus in the bright-dark registers, or any other measure expressing how the two variables distinguished reward from punishment. This is a *minimum hierarchical model* of cognition. First decide which theory or ontology applies best to the situation. Then, within the best framework select an action.

In my 1987 book and software package, *Sociology Laboratory*, I simulated a small society of 24 people—imagined as the first wave of colonists on Mars—who specialized in providing different rewards to each other, food, water, energy, and oxygen—but who also might seek a nonexistent reward such as eternal life [21]. A more technical article was published in 1995, and results of a vastly expanded version with 44,100 simulated agents was the basis for *God from the Machine* in 2006 [18, 22]. For each desired reward, each agent had an NN like that shown in Table 5.3. As with the mouse simulation, this NN did not use back propagation but *direct reinforcement*, learning not only to avoid error but to also seek positive reinforcement. The boxes in this diagram represent memory registers, rather than links between registers as in Fig. 5.2, and the complex NN connections between them are implied rather than shown. In the brain, a memory register would consist of several neurons, rather than just one as with each node in the MIND net.

The computer program permitted more complex options, but here we model three general theories of where to obtain a reward, whether it be water or eternal life: (1) The population is divided into two groups, and one of those two can provide the reward. (2) The population is divided into three groups, and one of those three can provide the reward. (3) The population is divided into four groups, and one of those four can provide the reward. The central metaphor was that the 44,100 agents were identified by ID numbers, and dividing by 2, 3 or 4 could identify which group a potential exchange partner belonged to under each of the three theories. The program saved the data in a 3×4 matrix of 12 real-number memory registers, a different set for each desired reward. After each interaction with another agent, the corresponding memory register would be updated—for each theory not just the one the agent applied—its contents increased if the interaction were profitable, and reduced if it were costly, within a set range so the agent could re-learn if contingencies changed. Each update ended by recalculating the variance across the registers for each theory, and placing that number in the variance register.

Each time one agent encountered another, the first agent would go through a two-step decision process: (1) Select a theory about the number of groups, with a probability of selecting one based on its variance. (2) Once a theory had been selected, select which group to accept interaction with, proportional to the numbers in the four memory registers for that theory. As in the original 1983 program, the agents could conceptualize but not interact with supernatural beings—now represented by the 3rd and 4th groups of 2 and the 4th group of 3—thus not altering the original numbers placed in those registers at the beginning of the simulation run. The net result was that the 44,100 agents, interacting under whatever conditions the experimenters set up at the beginning, would learn most of the time to seek material rewards from each other, following reasonably efficient theories about how their world was structured, and would tend to seek the unobtainable reward of eternal life primarily from beings that did not exist inside the world.

The specific theoretical and methodological implications are considered at some length in the original publications, but here the question is: How can this general approach be used to capture and emulate the behavior of real human beings? Whatever puzzle-solving or gamelike behavior one wants to emulate, one writes a program that will have the person repeatedly encounter a series of varied conditions, learning to respond ever more effectively but conditioned in some way by their personal assumptions and cognitive habits. All the data would be saved, and then used as a set of training data for an NN. It is standard practice with machine learning, not merely with the neural net variety, to use a set of training data that had already been characterized by some other, prior method.

5.3   A Personalized Expert System

A traditional form of artificial intelligence very different from NNs is expert systems, databases providing rule-based instructions for the accomplishment of complex practical tasks, based on the archived expertise of human beings. This section of the chapter will use an ordinary spreadsheet system to show how non-programmers with little database experience could create an expert system in an area of their own particular areas of skill, or the expertise of someone they might interview. The pilot study example was chosen because it has instructive qualities and because as a practical matter I happen to have the necessary background. We will imagine we can interview an expert piano tuner, Louis J. Sombaty, who not only knew this cognitive craft extremely well, but was well-prepared to communicate about it, because he taught a class in piano tuning and repair at the Oberlin Conservatory in Ohio for many years. We can only imagine doing these interviews with Sombaty, because he died in 1992, but as a student in his class I can represent him with some degree of fidelity.

Active people learn many skills, often concentrated in different areas in different years of their lives. Some skills are professional, but others are hobbies, sports, and tasks of daily life that could be either professional or amateur, such as cooking. People who play musical instruments typically learn how to do some of the maintenance themselves, such as replacing a broken string on a guitar or violin, but pianos are very complex and require special tools, not to mention a collection of replacement parts. Piano tuning is a rare profession, but with a very well developed skill set, and pianos are common enough that all cities and many suburbs can provide enough work for one or more tuners. In their standard work performance, they visit a customer's home every six months to tune the piano, using each visit to check for adjustments or other maintenance issues that might need attention. Only on rare occasions is a major repair needed, for example taking the mechanism to the tuner's workshop to replace a worn set of the hammers that strike the strings to produce the sounds.

There are many ways to prepare for and to organize interviews for an expert system, and here the strategy will be to emphasize information technology by starting with information available on the World Wide Web. If Sombaty were alive today, we would hold a preliminary interview, asking him about his life and professional experience. He would mention that he had worked for Halle Brothers, a dealer for the prestigious Steinway Piano Company, and tuned for the Cleveland Orchestra, prior to joining the staff at Oberlin [23]. Noticing his extensive collection of tools and supplies, we ask him where he gets them, and he replies the Schaff Piano Supply Company in Illinois [24]. Prior to our second interview, we would consult the online version of Schaff's catalog, perhaps focusing on the pages for toolkits. These are relatively inexpensive sets of specialized tools that a beginner would buy, while a professional would purchase additional or replacement tools separately over the years. Table 5.4 lists the tools in the two most basic kits, along with explanations that Sombaty might give in the interview, when we asked about each tool.

Table 5.4 is a small area of a spreadsheet that could be filled with all the products listed in the Schaff catalog, with Sombaty's comments about each. If this were a relational database, like Microsoft Access, or a wiki, it would be easy to link concepts, but a spreadsheet can do this, too. One way is to insert a web link, for example allowing a click on "tuning fork" to jump to the Wikipedia page for that tool [25]. Another way is to add columns to the spreadsheet, inserting in them words or numbers that place the term for each row into a category, following numerous inde-

Table 5.4 Two sets of piano tuning and regulation tools

Product	Sombaty's explanation	Procedure	Requires
Tuning lever	Sombaty calls it a "tuning hammer," a wrench for adjusting the tuning pins attached to one end of each string, to set the correct pitch. Its length is adjustable, and he suggest a fairly short length which requires greater strength from the tuner but gives better control. It comes with a standard head that fits the tapered tops of most tuning pins, but specialized heads are available and can be bought separately	Tuning	Mutes
Tuning fork C-523.3	The light, two-pronged vibrating fork used to set the pitch of the "middle C" string in the temperament octave, for American pianos that are tuned so that the A string in that octave vibrates at 440 times a second which requires 523.3 for the C. European pianos are often tuned so that A=435 and C=517.3	Tuning	
Temperament strip	A felt strip temporarily woven between the strings near the middle of the 88 notes of a piano, to mute the outer two strings on each three-string set belonging to each note of the temperament octave	Tuning	Tuning lever
2 #202 Mutes	Long, thin rubber wedges to be placed between strings on any kind of piano to mute them while tuning other strings. Sombaty would recommend using instead the two more specialized kinds of mutes in this tool kit	Tuning	Tuning lever
2 #203 Mutes	Thin rubber wedges with a wire handle inserted into the back end, so they can easily be placed in position for tuning an upright or spinet piano, in which it is difficult to use mutes lacking handles because the piano action is in the way	Tuning	Tuning lever
4 #205 Mutes	Wide rubber wedges used for muting strings on a grand piano while tuning another string in the set for that tone	Tuning	Tuning lever
Combination tool handle	A plastic and metal handle into which other tools are placed for use, avoiding the necessity of having a heavy handle dedicated to each tool, in the tuner's tool box. A professional carries two of these handles rather than just one, for greater convenience switching back and forth between two tools while doing a big, repetitive job	Regulating	A tool with the correct shaft for the handle's compressing nut
#31C Screw driver	Ordinary flat-blade screwdriver with 1/4″ diameter shank and 5/16″ wide blade	Regulating	Tool handle
#32C Screw driver	Ordinary flat-blade screwdriver with 3/16″ diameter shank and 1/4″ wide blade	Regulating	Tool handle

Table 5.4 (continued)

Product	Sombaty's explanation	Procedure	Requires
Regulating screwdriver	Has 5/16″ wide opening for turning large regulating screws, shaped like eyelets, rather than a blade	Regulating	Tool handle
Damper regulator, offset angle	Bends the stiff wire holding the damper on an upright piano, so it will properly mute the strings when the key is released. The more general of three sold by Schaff	Regulating	Tool handle
Spoon bender	Like the damper regulator but with shaft bent at two right angles to reach the spoon-shaped part of action	Regulating	Tool handle
Offset key spacer	Turns the oval pins in the keybed that guide the fronts of keys, with an offset to reach the pins for the sharps	Regulating	Tool handle
Bent back check regulator	Has two slots in its head for bending the short, stiff wires in the piano action that hold the back check or bridle tape	Regulating	Tool handle

pendent category schemes. For example, one column could be parts of speech, with "noun" on the row for *tuning fork*, and verb on the row for *tuning*. Tools can usually (but not always) be distinguished from supplies, so a tuning lever is a tool, while a tuning pin is a supply. Figure 5.4 has columns for the procedure (tuning versus regulating) and what other tool absolutely must be used in conjunction. Depending upon one's purpose at the moment, the spreadsheet can be sorted to bring together all rows relating to the topic at hand, which may, as in the case of the tuning lever and tool handle, require an additional column not shown here.

Another interview could ask Sombaty to explain tuning, which could be saved as a video demonstration, and a section of spreadsheet rows expressing concepts like middle C and A440 assigned to the process category *tuning*. Sombaty would open the lid of a grand piano, remove the desk that holds musical scores, and weave the temperament strip into the octave from F to F around A=440 and C=523.3. For the middle and higher range of a piano, there are three strings to each tone, hit by the same hammer after pressing one key to sound the tone defined by the note on a musical score. By muting the two outer strings from each tone in the tuning octave, it is possible for the tuner to adjust a single string with the tuning hammer, without confusing sounds from the other strings hit by the same hammer. Sombaty would then strike the tuning fork on his knee—or perhaps even his head right above his ear—press the C key, and listen to determine whether the C string was at the proper pitch. Here, a number of simple words make subtle distinctions—note, tone, pitch—that a non-expert might confound.

In terms of perceptual skills, a trained piano tuner hears very differently from the way a trained musician or untrained person hears, although depending upon their instruments musicians may have hearing skills that overlap those of a piano tuner. Piano tuners do not have perfect pitch, the ability to sing or select a tone at a specified pitch, such as middle C, without any reference sound [26]. Rather, a tuner can tell if the piano string is higher or lower than the tuning fork—usually it is lower because the tension of strings tends to drop over the months. Sombaty would then using his tuning hammer, holding in a specific way and perhaps wiggling it, to raise the C string slightly above the pitch of the tuning fork, then gently ease the string down to the exact pitch of the fork. Now comes the hard part.

Using middle C as the reference, the 12 other strings of the tuning octave—including the two Fs that frame the octave—must be tuned through a cycle of fifths and fourths, for example going down from C to F, up from F to B-flat, and down from C to G. A perfect fifth is a ratio of pitches exactly 3/2, and a perfect fourth is 4/3, but cycling through perfect fifth and fourth ratios does not return one to the exact ratio of an octave which is 2/1. So the tuner must create a tempered scale in which the mathematical error is spread equally across the cycle of 12 t. To do this, the tuner must be able to hear the beats—slight wavering in the sound that occurs when two piano strings are tuned near but not exactly to one of these ratios—and to instinctively estimate the speed of the beats. Remarkably, the Wikipedia page for piano tuning has two dynamic graphs showing visually how beats arise [27].

Once the temperament octave is set, the tuner uses the rubber mutes to walk up the scale to the top setting one as-yet untuned string in a set of three an octave above the corresponding already-tuned string, and then the other two strings in the set to be free of beats with the already-tuned string at that pitch. Then the same is done working downward from the tuning octave to the bottom of the range, after which the temperament strip is removed and the remaining strings of the temperament octave are set. A subtle point, surrounded by minor controversy, is the extent to which pianos sound better if the octaves are tuned slightly wide, rather than exact.

Piano tuners do not need the deep theoretical understanding of scales and all the alternatives to temperament that musicologists might have, but they do have a cognitive map of their very complex job. Sombaty's students were required in their final exam to complete a concert-quality tuning of a Steinway grand piano inside of 2 h, although in the field a practiced professional can do the job in just under 1 h. This requires physical skill in moving the right arm to use the tuning hammer, and the left hand to press the piano keys and quickly test fifths while setting octaves. And, as the previous paragraph demonstrated, the tuner also needed a trained ear, which means that many hours were spent listening, perceiving ever more subtle effects, and remembering them in a manner that no scientific research has yet to specify in terms of connections between neurons in the brain.

Near the end of Sombaty's career, two kinds of electronic tuning device existed that could substitute to some extent for the tuner's ear, one electronically producing sounds the tuner would use like a set of 88 tuning forks, and the other displaying a strobe representation of a tone, visually but silently. He was rather scornful of them, because a skilled tuner did not need them, and switching the dials on them merely wasted time. The current Schaff catalog lists contemporary versions of tuning devices using more precise digital technology and improving upon both of these methods [28]. We could capture Sombaty's conceptual knowledge through the interviews, and some outlines of his skill in physical movements videoing demonstrations of his work. Then, we could ask him to do his best possible tuning, exactly measure the pitches of the strings, and use those numbers as the criterion for one of these digital devices to emulate his tuning style.

The lower half of Table 5.4 lists the elements of a beginner's regulating tool kit. The mechanism of a piano is called the *action*, and adjusting it is called *regulating*. Or rather, the mechanism is in two parts, the keyboard and the action. In upright pianos the two can be removed separately, while they are screwed together in a grand piano and can be slid out as a unit. Sombaty loved to talk about the complex mechanism between the key and the string, duplicated 88 times in the typical piano, especially the wippen. An excellent online source, The Piano Deconstructed, defines the word thus: "The wippen is the part of the action that comes into direct contact with the key. It is responsible for transmitting the motion of the key to the hammer." [29] When I first looked at the wippen page of The Piano Deconstructed, I was immediately stuck by the fact that the diagram highlighted only part of what I call a wippen, covering the jack that pushes up the hammer and the repetition mechanism on two separate pages.

Some pianos lack wippens, but all except a few antique Austrian models have jacks, so the two must be conceptualized separately at least on occasion. When creating a personalized database, it is worth recording such points of debate, and the interviewer may wish to consult other resources to put the expert's opinions in a wider context. The Wikipedia page diagramming a grand piano action names fully 20 of its parts, wippen being just one, but leaves many parts unnamed, such as the important barrel on the hammer shank that the jack pushes on, but it does name the rather less interesting hammer shank flange screw [30]. Sombaty tended to use the term wippen for the entire mechanism between the key and the hammer of a grand piano. Schaff also uses the term for the entire intermediate mechanism, but spelling it *whippen* [31]. Furthermore, Schaff uses the term for the central part of the mechanism in both grand and upright pianos, even though the mechanism is quite different in several respects.

Whether using a spreadsheet or some more sophisticated data management software, one might want to package the information from one expert separately from other information, while linking across. As we have found throughout this book, capture of a specific individual's personality and mentality requires some connection to a wider culture. In addition to companies like Schaff and Steinway, or musical organizations like the Oberlin Conservatory and Cleveland Orchestra, professional organizations exist in the world of music. For tuners, the reference organization is the Piano Technicians Guild, "the world's premier source of expertise in piano service and technology." [32] Other keyboard instruments share some of the same features with traditional pianos, but require expertise of other kinds, notably: church organs, electric pianos, harpsichords and clavichords. Thus, an individual piano tuner will share many of the same skills as other members of the Guild, may have idiosyncrasies and opinions that differ from the majority without signifying incompetence, and may add expertise in adjacent fields. The final example for this chapter will illustrate a case in which one of the world's foremost experts had beliefs and practices now totally rejected by the majority of colleagues.

5.4   Chronic Intestinal Stasis

A second pilot study examining the professional cognitive skills of a highly-experienced individual will illustrate a range of other issues and methods of documentation. The case in question is my grandfather, Dr. William Seaman Bainbridge—whom I will call by his very appropriate nickname, Will—and a surgical approach to treatment of a range of diseases which he did not personally develop but was instrumental in popularizing in the United States a century ago.

There are three reasons why this case is appropriate here. First, by examining the cognition of my own grandfather, I illustrate how people may use documentary evidence to understand and thus mentally emulate the personalities of deceased persons about whom they care personally. Second, by using the web and a private wiki to do some of the work, I illustrate how commonly available information technologies can be adapted to new uses. Third, by selecting a very controversial aspect of Will's expertise, I illustrate the relativism that hovers around any intellectual skill, because the quality of the cognitive results is judged in terms of the cognitions of other people, before it is compared with anything that might be called *objective truth*.

On one of his early trips to London, Will met Dr. William Arbuthnot Lane, a vastly influential British surgeon who pioneered the use of metal plates to mend broken bones, and earned a knighthood [33][1]. Lane was controversial; Will said Lane was the inventor of injecting saline solution into the body, but nearly lost the right to practice because other physicians considered this so harmful [34]. Lane's obsession was the conviction that food should move swiftly through the intestines, lest it sit, rot and poison the entire system with its toxins [35]. He had devised a "cocktail" to speed dinner on its way, consisting primarily of liquid paraffin which he took daily and gave to his family, servants, parrot and monkey [36]. Slow digestion, he believed, unleashed toxins that could travel to any part of the body and trigger any manner of illnesses, including lumpy breasts, poor circulation, "lassitude, inability to perform ordinary duties, mental distress, migraine headaches, laziness, and poor temper control" [37].

Surgery could free the intestines to move to their proper positions, and removal of sections of intestine shortened the food's route. Even tuberculosis, Lane felt, could be the result of chronic intestinal stasis, and he operated when other doctors saw no role for surgery. One child was in the final stages of tubercular joint disease, until Lane excised all but nine inches of the lower intestine, supposedly causing a great improvement [38]. Will saw Lane's work in London on five trips between 1907 and 1913, operated with him, and became very enthusiastic about his theories and methods [39].

Professional practice is not merely a matter of individual skill, and technical realities, but also reflects the development of subcultures of interacting people who share the same views and support each other's social status. In the United States, there is one main subculture of piano tuners, represented in the Piano Technician's

---

[1] "Memo Concerning Dr. William Seaman Bainbridge," December 1942, typescript on yellow paper undoubtedly dictated by himself.

Guild, but there exist a vast number of medical subcultures, a situation that was more obvious in the nineteenth century but is still the case today despite the existence of the American Medical Association. Beyond that, medical subcultures exist in competition with other subcultures, often seeking to medicalize problems that might have very different real origins, so that they can benefit financially and socially from offering supposed cures [40, 41].

Skeptical doctors denounced the theory of chronic intestinal stasis, and in New York City, where many colleagues were already hostile to him, a group of physicians threatened to have Will's medical license yanked if he persisted. His response to the accusations was not to quit but to hire a medical artist to make accurate drawings of the intestines of 500 of his patients during operations and to project photographs of twisted intestines in public lectures. In St. Louis he showed pictures of stasis operations in exchange for an honorary degree, Master of Surgery [42]. Will never accepted Lane's contention that stasis caused all cancer, but he never quite abandoned belief in Lane's general theory, even as the fad faded from American medicine over the following decades [43–45].[2]

I inherited paper copies of a dozen of Will's century-old publications about chronic intestinal stasis, but used a modern tool, an online wiki, to organize information about the cognitive skills and assumptions that guided him in his work. We normally think of wikis as shared knowledge resources, but the technology works perfectly well for single users, as well. Anywhere I had Internet access, I could log in and add material, for example at home, office, or even a public library. As it happened, the wiki used the system offered by PBworks, an online collaboration company whose original product was PeanutButterWiki, so named to proclaim that making a wiki should be as easy as making a peanut butter sandwich [46]. I set the permissions such that only I could edit the wiki, even as it was available for anybody else to see, although I could have closed it from public view had I wished to do so.

Indeed, wikis like this are very easy to use. For example, one page referred to Dr. Eliza Mosher, a woman doctor who had been instrumental in tutoring Will in surgical methods when he was a teenager, and assisted him much later in promoting the stasis idea in America. I wanted to add another page entirely about this important figure in the story, so I simply went into editing mode, selected her name with the computer's mouse, and clicked a "link" icon. Two more clicks and a page with the title Eliza Mosher existed. In editing mode I wrote the phrase "Her Wikipedia page," selected that phrase and hit the link icon. This time I inserted the URL of her Wikipedia page, and clicking a save button took me out of editing mode. Clicking the phrase naturally opened Mosher's Wikipedia page [47].

Only a few minutes were required to find and add links to *The Woman's Medical Journal* indicating she was its editor for several years, the text of an article she contributed to that journal about chronic intestinal stasis, the full text of her book *Health and Happiness: A Message to Girls* which does not happen to emphasize the

---

[2] Some hint of the theory appears among Will's last publications, such as William Seaman Bainbridge, "Intra-Abdominal Surgical Technic," *The Military Surgeon*, July 1946.

stasis idea, a list of her papers at the University of Michigan which themselves are not yet online, a news article about a 1925 tribute to her at age 75 on the website of the Faculty History Project of the University of Michigan, and a photograph of her as a young woman when she was the chief physician of Vassar College [48–50]. I wanted a picture of her later in her career for the wiki page, and could have scanned in a paper one I possessed, but to keep in the online spirit of this demonstration project, I found that the collectables part of Amazon.com was offering for sale three copies of the same photo I had from the 1925 tribute at prices of $ 7.75, $ 8.99 and fully $ 67.00. Rather than buying one, I simply copied the image. For the main page of the wiki, I similarly cribbed a portrait of Will that was for sale at eBay.

To be sure, few people are as amply represented on the Web today as Will and his mentor, Eliza Mosher, and few people have published many articles revealing their thought processes. That situation is changing, as more and more people express themselves in social media sites, and professionals develop multiple equivalents of personal websites. Furthermore, the work involved in actively capturing a personality can result in much more electronic material, whether or not it is available to the general public online. Interviewing a person repeatedly about various topics can substitute for publications the individual might have written. Examining Will's stasis publications suggested some kinds of information that would be important in capture, even outside the medical field, as the following example shows.

The January 1914 issue of *The Woman's Medical Journal* carried an article by Will titled "Chronic Intestinal Stasis: A. Types of Cases. B. Preventative and Medical Treatment Outlined." I have not found an online version, nor that issue of the original journal, but have a reprint, which illustrates the fact that information documenting a personality may be in many forms and come from diverse sources. It is a printed version of a talk Will gave in a symposium about stasis at the Woman's Medical Association of New York City, November 19, 1913, thus representing an episode in Will's life, and capturing episodes will be considered in the following chapter. The symposium and the journal were dominated by Mosher, so there is also a social connection linking two people. We have already seen that Will was influenced by Lane and in turn influenced Mosher.

People who collaborate combine their separate expertise, and another example was radiologist A. Judson Quimby, who collaborated with Will in a study of 11 supposed cases of chronic intestinal stasis, in which Quimby took X-rays of the patients, and Will cut them open for an artist to sketch their intestines, comparing how the 2 methods identified bands, adhesions, and swellings. They gave parallel papers at the September 1914 meeting of the American Roentgen Ray Society in Cleveland, Ohio, that were published together in a booklet, but apparently do not exist in any other form. These examples show both the ephemeral nature of even well-organized human communications, and their fundamental basis in social dyads and groups.

Another group relevant for Will's article in *The Woman's Medical Journal* was the readership, who may have included some patients, a few women doctors, but also nurses and other female medical professionals. Thus it is revealing that this article includes four photographs showing how a woman could wear a contraption

Table 5.5 Captions of abdominal surgery illustrations, representing picture documentation

Patient	Context	Description of Points Marked in the Drawing
M. W., female, 29 single	Referred by Dr. E. M. Mosher. Operation, New York Polyclinic Hospital, June 3, 1913	A. Mobile caput colii; B. Lane's band
A. L., female, 42, widow	Operation, New York Polyclinic Hospital, May 23, 1913	A. Strong bands to ascending colon; B. Mobile cecum; C. Appendix placed upwards on anterior surface of mesentery, and adherent; D. Right tube and ovary seat of inflammation; E. Long redundant sigmoid adherent to right adnexa
E. B. female, 30, single	Referred by Dr. E. M. Mosher. Operation, Alston's Private Hospital, February 11, 1913	A. Lane's band; B. Ileal stasis; C. Appendix and ovary caught in band; D. Caecum dilated
C. S., female, 20, single	Referred by Dr. Wm. T. Scovil. Operation, New York Polyclinic Hospital, July 1, 1913	A. Ileal band; B. Appendix caught in band and adherent to ileum; C. Bands to caecum; D. Bands to ascending colon; E. Band from gallbladder across duodenum and over transverse colon causing much obstruction; F. Enteroptotic transverse colon
E. N., female, 46, married	Operation, New York Polyclinic Hospital, March 22, 1913	A. Omentum adherent to abdominal wall; B. Dilated duodenum and ulcer of stomach. Second drawing: A. Lane's band; C. "Jackson's membrane;" D. Intercolonic adhesions
C. B., female, 46, widow	Operation Skin and Cancer Hospital, June 2, 1913	A. Dilated stomach; B. Veins around congested pylorus; C. An ulcer size of dried pea found, with a varix of one of the veins; D. Duodenum angulated at duodenal-jejunal junction—duodenum in consequence dilated—dilated duodenum seen in picture
A. S., female, age unknown, single	Referred by Dr. Herman Eichorn. Operation, New York Polyclinic Hospital, June 7, 1913. Cancer and stasis	A. Carcinomatous mass found in ascending colon, near ileo-cecal valve. Great omentum adherent to mass, thus fastening greater curvature of stomach to ascending colon; B. Jackson's membrane; C. Marked ileal stasis

called the Curtis Abdominal Belt under her tight corset, to hold her internal organs in what was believed to be the correct position. The article also includes high resolution drawings of the intestines of seven women, exposed for the artist's convenience in sketching, during major stasis-related surgery by Will. Table 5.5 organizes information from the captions of these illustrations, as one might do for any pictures used in the capture of an individual's expertise or interests. A similar article is currently available at Google Books, if the reader wants to see how completely Will opened his patients' abdomens for the illustrator [51, 52].

By modern standards, only the last of these seven cases really required surgery, and Will unnecessarily risked many lives during his Lane discipleship, in the years before the introduction of antibiotics. While extreme, this example makes a general point. Personality capture must first and foremost record the people of interest as they were, not as we might wish them to be. Judgment of the person plays two secondary roles, first to understand the person better in comparison with others, and second to implement the emulation in a manner consistent with our own goals.

Table 5.5 lists seven women patients, with their correct initials but without revealing their full names, plus the full names of three referring physicians and three hospitals. Again, technical expertise is embedded in social relationships, rather than being entirely abstract. The descriptions from the captions refer to points marked in the drawings, and the technical terms can now all be looked up online. These are examples of the kinds of metadata that might be associated with any pictures used in connection with personality capture, although of course today we might use digital photographs with the textual information directly linked to areas of the image and automatically connected to definitions and even to other images for purposes of comparison.

Will used both a stenographer and a medical illustrator artist, during his research operations, but documenting activities can be handled differently today. Imagine we are not observing surgery, but any expert going about a technical job. As appropriate for the circumstances, the expert may be interviewed while working, or spontaneously describe the work while doing it. Not only can the person's voice be recorded, but speech recognition software trained to the person's voice can provide text including image captions, synchronized with a video record plus any other relevant data.

The question then becomes how we can extract more general principles about the expert's cognitions and skills from such a complex record. Despite much work on text summarization in natural language processing, we are far from good answers. Using human intellectual effort, and the online wiki system applied to this pilot project, I sought to extract general principles from all of Will's publications about chronic intestinal stasis. Without going into unnecessary procedural details, here are his four cognitive principles, as best I can determine them, arranged in a logical order:

1. Chronic intestinal stasis is ultimately the result of the incomplete status of human biological evolution, as we evolved from four-footed animals to an upright posture that put great stress on our internal organs.
2. The goal of scientific medicine should be to discover a small number of causes for the great variety of symptoms patients bring to doctors' offices.
3. Each disease has a natural course, running through a set series of stages.
4. Despite the single origin of many diseases, there is no one best treatment, because different stages in the development of a progressive degeneration could be cured by different remedies.

General principles like these may organize the thinking of most people, including in professional areas, although individuals may differ precisely in how systematized their cognitions tend to be. Twenty years ago, there was much enthusiasm for the idea that expert systems could be constructed, based on the expertise of specific people in a particular profession, and organized according to definitive, rule-based, "if-then" principles [53]. There were also debates about whether information was best expressed in this manner, or in the more probabilistic manner of neural networks [54]. Today, whatever technical approaches we use, we must be aware that expertise is problematic, subculturally-based, and will manifest somewhat differently from one individual expert to another.

5.5 Conclusion

The variety of examples and pilot studies presented in this chapter suggests the huge array of tasks before us. Each form of skillful cognition demands appropriate theories, research methods, and emulation technologies. But they function together during the course of a day in the person's life, so how are they integrated and differentiated? If Sombaty had learned surgery, or Will had learned piano tuning, how would the possession of one skill set have affected the other? As it happens, both professions employed hypodermic needles, piano tuners using this medical tool to inject tightening solution around tuning pins when these loosen and cause a piano to go quickly out of tune. What other cognitive commonalities could there be? How do short-term memory and long-term classification occur in the human brain? What are the roots of very general cognitive characteristics, such as the dogmatism found in classification of ethnic groups or intestinal structures? Answering such questions is itself an exercise of cognitive skills, even as it concerns such skills, suggesting that the answers will come only during an extensive campaign of iterative research and development.

References

1. Edgerton, R. B. (1967). *The cloak of competence*. Berkeley: University of California Press.
2. Mercer, J. R. (1973). *Labeling the mentally retarded*. Berkeley: University of California Press.
3. Gould, S. J. (1981). *The mismeasure of man*. New York: Norton.
4. Bainbridge, W. S. (1992). *Social research methods and statistics: A computer-assisted introduction* (pp. 335–338). Belmont: Wadsworth.
5. Miller, G. A. (1956). The magical number seven, plus or minus two: Some limits on our capacity for processing information. *Psychological Review, 63*(2), 81–97.
6. Newell, A. (1990). *Unified theories of cognition*. Cambridge: Harvard University Press.
7. Bainbridge, W. S. (1986). *Experiments in psychology*. Belmont: Wadsworth.
8. Kalat, J. W. (1986). *Introduction to psychology*. Belmont: Wadsworth.
9. http://en.wikipedia.org/wiki/Eidetic_memory. Accessed 24 Feb 2013.
10. Stromeyer, C. F., & Psotka, J. (1970). The detailed texture of eidetic images. *Nature, 225,* 346–349.
11. Blakemore, C., Braddick, O., & Gregory, R. L. (1970). Detailed texture of eidetic images: a discussion. *Nature, 226,* 1267–1268.
12. Stromeyer, III, C., F. (1970, November). An adult eidetiker. *Psychology Today*, 76–80.
13. https://implicit.harvard.edu/implicit/. Accessed 26 May 2013.

14. Banaji, M. R., Nosek, B. A., & Greenwald, A. G. (2004). No place for nostalgia in science: a response to Arkes and Tetlock. *Psychological Inquiry, 15*(4), 279–289.
15. Jung, C. G. (1919). *Studies in word-association*. New York: Moffat, Yard.
16. Allport, G. W. (1954). *The nature of Prejudice*. Cambridge: Addison-Wesley.
17. Bainbridge, W. S. (1995). Minimum intelligent neural device: a tool for social simulation. *The Journal of Mathematical Sociology, 20,* 179–192.
18. Bainbridge, W. S. (2006). *God from the machine: artificial intelligence models of religious cognition*. Walnut Grove: AltaMira.
19. Stark, R., & Bainbridge, W. S. (1987). *A theory of religion*. New York: Toronto/Lang.
20. Bainbridge, W. S. (2002). A prophet's reward: dynamics of religious exchange. In T. G. Jelen (Ed.), *Sacred markets, sacred canopies* (pp. 63–89. Lanham: Rowman and Littlefield.
21. Bainbridge, W. S. (1987). *Sociology laboratory*. Belmont: Wadsworth.
22. Bainbridge, W. S. (1995). Neural network models of religious belief. *Sociological Perspectives, 38,* 483–495.
23. Kehl, R. F., & Kirkland, D. R. (2011). *The official guide to Steinway Pianos* (p. xiii). Milwaukee: Amadeus.
24. http://schaffpiano.com/. Accessed 5 Aug 2013.
25. http://en.wikipedia.org/wiki/Tuning_fork. Accessed 25 May 2013.
26. http://en.wikipedia.org/wiki/Perfect_pitch. Accessed 25 May 2013.
27. http://en.wikipedia.org/wiki/Piano_tuning. Accessed 25 May 2013.
28. http://schaffpiano.com/catalog/electronic_tuning_devices.pdf. Accessed 25 May 2013.
29. http://www.piano.christophersmit.com/wippen.html. Accessed 30 Mar 2013.
30. http://en.wikipedia.org/wiki/Action_(piano). Accessed 30 Mar 2013.
31. http://schaffpiano.com/catalog/action_parts_-_grand.pdf. Accessed 30 Mar. 2013
32. https://www.ptg.org. Accessed 25 May 2013.
33. Meade, R. H. (1968). *An introduction to the history of general surgery* (pp. 68–69). Philadelphia: Saunders.
34. Bainbridge, W. S. (1938). Notes from a speech, New Haven School of Physical Therapy, New Haven, Connecticut. June, 18, 1938.
35. Dally, A. (1996). *Fantasy surgery 1880–1930* (pp. 112–112). Amsterdam: Rodoppi.
36. de Forest, L. E. (1950). *Ancestry of William Seaman Bainbridge* (p. 28). Oxford: Scrivener.
37. Barnes, B. A. (1977). Discarded operations: Surgical innovation by trial and error. In J. P. Bunker, B. A. Barnes, & F. Mosteller (pp. 109–123) *Costs, risks, and benefits of surgery*. New York: Oxford University Press.
38. New Tuberculosis Cure. New York Times, January 14, 1914, p. 4.
39. Bainbridge, W. S. (1913, November 1) Remarks on chronic intestinal stasis, with reference to conditions found at operation and the mortality. *British Medical Journal, 2,* 1128–1130.
40. Conrad, P. (1976). *Identifying hyperactive children: the medicalization of deviant behavior*. Lexington: Lexington.
41. Conrad, P., & Schneider, J. W. (1980). *Deviance and medicalization: From badness to sickness*. St. Louis: Mosby.
42. Bainbridge, W. S. (1914). Notes from a speech, National University of Arts and Sciences, St. Louis, Missouri. October, 27, 1914.
43. King's Surgeon on Man's Worst Peril. New York Times, November 26, 1925, p. 17.
44. Health and Civilization. New York Times, December 6, 1925, p. 14.
45. Lane, W. A. (1927). *Secrets of good health*. Garden City: Doubleday, Page and Company.
46. http://en.wikipedia.org/wiki/PBworks. Accessed 30 Apr 2013.
47. http://en.wikipedia.org/wiki/Eliza_Maria_Mosher. Accessed 20 July 2013.
48. Mosher, E. (1916). Intestinal stasis: Its causes, prevention and treatment. *Woman's Medical Journal, 26*(12), 283–285.
49. Mosher, E. (1912). *Health and happiness: A message to girls*. New York: Funk &\and Wagnalls.

50. http://xdl.drexelmed.edu/viewer.php?object_id=2996, http://um2017.org/faculty-history/faculty/eliza-maria-mosher/commemorate-fifty-years-service, http://digitallibrary.vassar.edu/fedora/repository/vassar%3A30578, http://quod.lib.umich.edu/b/bhlead/umich-bhl-852016. Accessed 20 July 2013.
51. Bainbridge, W. S. (1916). Chronic intestinal stasis: Report of twelve cases, with points of special interest illustrated. *American Journal of Obstetrics and Diseases of Women and Children, 73*(2), 193–227.
52. http://books.google.com/books?id=LehXAAAAMAAJ. Accessed 20 July 2013.
53. Benfer, R. A., Brent. E. E., & Furbee, L. (1991). *Expert systems*. Newbury Park: Sage.
54. Garson, G. D. (1991). A comparison of neural network and expert systems algorithms with common multivariate procedures for analysis of social science data. Social Science Computer Review, 9, 399–434.

Chapter 6
Autobiographical Memories

This chapter will introduce a remarkable questionnaire dataset consisting of auto-biographical memories of thousands of people, in a pilot project to begin to derive principles for capturing these crucial aspects of individual personality, with some suggestions about how the technology of capture and emulation could be advanced through future research. But before we launch a brief reconnaissance into an ocean of text, we should note that several other approaches are being explored by computer and information scientists, and should be part of the comprehensive capture approach.

While Julius Caesar is reputed to have had a remarkable memory, in writing his books he probably relied upon a trunk full of documents he had written and collected during his military campaigns. Thus, a few rare humans were documenting their lives even thousands of years ago. We know that some of Caesar's messages were encrypted, and we even know the form of code he used [1]. This is a nice metaphor, because there is a sense in which every written document is encrypted to some degree, because it relies upon unwritten assumptions that the author had in mind but does not fully explain to the reader. Providing context and achieving translation into terms satisfactory for the audience—a main dimension of emulation—can be conceptualized as computerized decryption.

Over the centuries, human culture developed additional means of recording events, and perhaps even before writing was invented some of the animal pictures drawn on the walls of a cave 20,000 years ago may have depicted a specific hunt. By the end of the nineteenth century, photography, motion pictures, and sound recording had been invented, and they were perfected and integrated during the twentieth century. On the website of the Library of Congress, I can listen to the voice of my grandfather Will's favorite first cousin, Bainbridge Colby, speak these words in about 1920: "It is important that we should constantly keep before us the duty of inculcating in the minds of our citizens from overseas, the true meaning and significance of America, and the high duty that rests upon every generation to sustain our blessed institutions, and to transmit them to posterity strengthened and unimpaired." [2] I used to possess recordings of two speeches by my grandfather, himself, but their loss in an accidental fire, and the loss of tape recorded copies in a flood, highlight the point about preservation made by Colby. Because long-term

W. S. Bainbridge, *Personality Capture and Emulation,* Human-Computer Interaction Series,   127
DOI 10.1007/978-1-4471-5604-8_6, © Springer-Verlag London 2014

personality emulation relies upon durable archiving, some institutions of society will also need to endure.

In 2006, I attended the third CARPE workshop in connection with the multimedia conference of the Association of Computing Machinery, in Santa Barbara, California. CARPE stands for "Capture, Archival and Retrieval of Personal Experiences," and presumably derives from *carpe diem*, the Latin proverb for *seize the day*. The workshop's website still describes the scope:

> Personal storage of all one's media throughout a lifetime has been desired and discussed since at least 1945, when Vannevar Bush published As We May Think, positing the "Memex" device "in which an individual stores all his books, records, and communications, and which is mechanized so that it may be consulted with exceeding speed and flexibility." His vision was astonishingly broad for the time, including full-text search, annotations, hyperlinks, virtually unlimited storage and even stereo cameras mounted on eyeglasses. Storage, sensor, and computing technology have progressed today to the point of making Memex feasible and even affordable. Indeed, we can now look beyond Memex at new possibilities. In particular, while media capture has typically been sparse throughout a lifetime, we can now consider continuous archival and retrieval of all media relating to personal experiences [3, 4].

Among the most influential contributors to the CARPE conferences was Gordon Bell, which the first chapter of this book identified as a leader of this field. At the first CARPE workshop in New York in 2004, he and four colleagues had presented a paper about SenseCam, a wearable camera with sensors that could automatically capture pictures of meaningful moments in every day of a person's life [5]. By the time of the third CARPE workshop, SenseCam and the wider MyLifeBits project Bell led at Microsoft had received considerable attention, and the cover of the November 2005 issue of *IEEE Spectrum* had proclaimed, "With new database software and a wearable camera, computer pioneer Gordon Bell is helping Microsoft reinvent the PC as a personal mainframe for storing all your daily transactions." [6] Yet when I asked Bell if Microsoft planned to market a new kind of software, comparable to a personal digital library, he said that it did not. Since then, many individuals have advanced the technology for capturing personal experiences in realtime, notably Deb Roy at the MIT Media Lab who has been recording the entire childhood of his son [7]. A coordinated CARPE movement seems not to exist, but an occasional special issue of a journal or review essay indicates the potential for one [8–10].

Automatic recording of the incidents in a person's life can contribute to personality capture and emulation, but chiefly by documenting the context in which memories are formed in the mind of the person. It is the person, after all, not the environment, that this book is about. Here we will focus on text-based descriptions of autobiographical memories, chiefly episodic memories although many autobiographical memories may be more general, such as recalling the arrangement of rooms in a former home, which related to a particular period of the individual's life, but not to a single moment in time. There are three reasons for this focus. First, we do possess a marvelous set of data that can contribute to developing strategies for autobiographic memory retrieval. Second, the methodology described here connects one major methodology of this book, written questionnaires, to another important social science methodology, interviews. Third, while decades of research and development may be required to perfect this approach, we can already achieve significant success even with very primitive methods.

6.1   Views and Interviews

Fixed-choice questionnaire items allow us to place the responses of any one individual exactly in the context of responses from other individuals, and this is important for personal capture. However, much of the uniqueness of each person cannot be detected in this way, and in my own work I have often found value in conducting open-ended interviews, including but not limited to questions about a person's life experiences. How can we add information technology to the interview toolkit? One way to imagine our future goal is as a robot servant named Boswell, one for each individual human being, serving as the archive for all personal records, but also interviewing the person to construct a dynamic biography that expands and evolves with the passage of the years and will be available to survivors after the person's death.

Boswell will contain far more information than anyone will ever want to read, but can distill that information in at least three forms: (1) Boswell will compose a written biography of conventional length that friends and relatives of the person will want to read, and perhaps also an occasional student of history selecting the deceased person at random from all those of the given time and place. (2) Boswell will be able to answer any question about the person's life, as briefly or extensively as the person asking the question wants, even to enter into a dialogue representing the deceased person, if the survivor so wishes. (3) Boswell will be a member of a team of similar intelligent agents who collaborate to perform those two functions on the collective level, for example in constructing the history of a city the person dwelled within, or to answer questions that go beyond the ability of any one person's memories to answer.

I used interviews extensively in the research for my second book, *Satan's Power*, a study of a remarkable communal religious group called The Process Church of the Final Judgement that in part was an offshoot of Scientology, and also drew upon the Psychoanalysis and Golden Dawn traditions. My primary research method was ethnographic participant observation, and I was present for hundreds of the group's activities, in the 1971–1975 period, as well as collecting all possible written documents. My initial reason for undertaking the interviews was to learn the history of the group, but I soon discovered two other valuable themes: First, I wound up learning much about the sequence of events that caused each individual to join the group, which prepared me to do research and theory development subsequently about the processes of recruitment to deviant subcultures. Second, I learned a good deal about the personality of each individual I interviewed, which was especially relevant to that study because the group had its own personality theory which categorized people in terms of their subconscious relations to four co-equal gods: Lucifer, Jehovah, Christ, and Satan.

Several chapters of the book contain brief biographies of individual members, who often appeared in other sections that described group events, always identified with a pseudonym. The standard theories of cult recruitment at the time asserted that recruits suffered life problems when they encountered the group and thus were vulnerable to its radical appeals [11]. I found this was not true for many recruits to the Process, and that the old theories probably applied only to people who lived in societies that possessed a high degree of cultural consensus. If consensus did not exist, even the most able and mentally healthy people might join such a group. The three-page biosketch of a man I called Paul begins:

> Paul is a man of charm and ability who left science for the cult not because of failure, but because the cult gave much greater personal and social gratification than laboratory research work. His actual conversion involved some temporary strain and a tortured personal reevaluation, but was highly situational rather than the result of any longstanding problems [12].

I have kept in touch with Paul over the more than four decades since I first met him, when he was using the name Father Dominic in the Process, and under his real name (which I will not give here) he has written a good deal about his experiences then and afterward. He would definitely have much more to say about his life and personal characteristics than I shall ever know, but interviews with him did provide the basis for a reasonably accurate biosketch. After the book was published, one of my interviewees pointed out an error in my account of her steps to membership, a lesson to me that more complete inclusion of the person in the biography-writing process could reduce factual errors and improve the degree of emphasis given to various factors.

The interviews were done in two ways. First, after each visit to a Process activity, I would write extensive field notes from memory, which sometimes included my best recollection of what a member reported about an autobiographical incident. Second, at various points I was able to use a tape recorder in open-ended life-history interviews, focusing my mind on what question I should ask next, and letting the machine serve as my memory. This brings up a general point of importance for this chapter. While much of a life-history documentation can use pre-determined questions, it is essential to be able to frame new questions, most obviously to get clarification on what the interviewee has just said, but also to explore new themes that arise during the discussion.

Two decades after I started the Process research, I used it to illustrate interviewing in my software-textbook package, *Social Research Methods and Statistics: A Computer-Assisted Introduction* [13]. The section on life-history interviews referenced some of the classical sociological examples, including *The Professional Thief* by Edwin H. Sutherland, *The Jack-Roller* by Clifford Shaw, and Barbara Heyl's study of a Peoria, Illinois prostitute [14–17]. These were all sociological biographies of "deviant" individuals, as presumably were the members of the Process, but the methods are by no means limited to people we do not initially feel we understand. Indeed, the challenge in interviewing "normal" people is to avoid making too many assumptions from our own presumably normal perspective.

In the textbook, I included a verbatim transcript from a life-history interview I had done with a leader of the Process I called Mother Juliet. Today we could imagine a system for extracting answers to new questions from the full corpus of transcribed interviews I had done. But there was no way back in 1991 that I could write software for deep life history interviews, so I had to settle for something that at least would be educational. So I wrote a simple program that let the student select one of 20 Processeans I had interviewed and select among 25 predetermined questions, which would produce appropriate text I had manually extracted from the original transcripts.

Now I did not really ask these exact questions of all the members, but they covered the span of the ethnographic material and served to suggest how one may begin with questions about the episode of joining the group, which was a significant autobiographical memory, then branch out to descriptions of the cultural environment and its meaning for the person. The program was written for pre-Windows IBM-type personal computers, but I knew how to program my own windows, so the interface was divided into two parts which scrolled independently, one for questions and the other for answers. Here for example is part of an emulated interview of Juliet, if the user chose to ask her the particular questions from the list:

A. *When and where did you join the Process?* London in the early 1960s.
B. *Were you experiencing trouble of any kind when you joined?* Slightly. My career was going well, but personal relationships were strained.
C. *Had you participated in any other unusual religious groups before joining?* None. The Process was not a church, back then.
D. *Were many of your friends members of the Process when you joined?* I knew Bathsheba, one of the original group, and Cain who came in later.
E. *What was the Process like when you joined it?* The thing that struck me was the intensity at which everything was done.
F. *Did you travel much with the Process? If so, where did you go?* I was on all the trips. XTUL and MATTHEW TEN, you name it.
G. *How has the Process helped you?* Psychological intimacy was fascinating.
H. *State one of the basic beliefs of the Process.* Process means change.

A different virtual respondent would have provided different answers, all based on that individual's personality and the interviews I had done with him or her. But in such an antique simulation program as this one, it was difficult to include follow-up questions, so I mimicked them by having a large set of pre-written answers to questions of definitions, the same for all 20 respondents, and capitalized terms in the answers that could be asked about. Question Z, "Define a WORD or PHRASE," allowed the user to type in a short word or phrase that the respondent should define or explain, although the answers sometimes were intentionally cryptic. XTUL referred to the group's sojourn on a remote Mexican beach, while MATTHEW TEN referred to its wanderings across Western Europe. If the user typed in a term that was never completely capitalized in an answer, such as Process, the name of the group itself, the computer selected at random from enigmatic phrases that sometimes would seem to be valid answers. For example:

Z. What does XTUL mean?
The place we found GOD.
Z. What does GOD mean?
GOD is the coming together of the GODS.
Z. What does GODS mean?
The shattered fragments of GOD.
Z. What does GOD mean?
GOD is the coming together of the GODS.
Z. What does MATTHEW TEN mean?
A chapter of the Bible.
Z. What does PROCESS mean?
What did you say?
Z. What does PROCESS mean?
You should ask FATHER Dominic.
Z. What does PROCESS mean?
You sound like JOHN GRAY.
Z. What does JOHN GRAY mean?
A lifeless, conventional person.
Z. What does PROCESS mean?
May the WATER give me life.
Z. What does WATER mean?
Life, the gift of CHRIST.
Z. What does CHRIST mean?
The spirit of UNITY.
Z. What does UNITY mean?
CHRIST and SATAN joined.
Z. What does SATAN mean?
The principle of separation

This instructional computer program was a very crude representation of the Boswell idea introduced above, and it is high time to develop this concept further. Survey2000, which provided the data for our exploration of The Year 2100 in Chap. 2, included many questions about regional culture and the effect of residential migration [18]. The same section of the survey that offered my question about the future asked respondents to write a brief description of their most significant residential move. We can imagine that our Boswell would ask this same question, listen to the answer and use speech recognition techniques to produce a text-based record that could be searched for words that would become the basis for additional questions. For example, here is a fairly typical Survey2000 response to the question, selected because it succinctly illustrates several points:

> My husband and I were posted with the Canadian Military to London, England during the mid-60's. We had a small child at the time and the opportunity to visit with her so many of the famous places in Great Britain and Europe that I had read about was a dream come true.

If Boswell were fairly stupid, a system we could easily build today, it could ask follow-up questions such as these:

> Did you move again after that? If so, please describe that move.
> What famous places in Great Britain did you visit?
> What famous places in Europe did you visit?
> Can you recall an experience you had in London?
> Can you recall an experience you had with the Canadian Military?
> Can you recall when you met your husband?

Development of each of those questions would start with a word or phrase in the response quoted above, and look it up in a list of plausible question formats. "Husband" or "wife" would have been programmed to ask about the first meeting, because we know that is often a memorable experience. With somewhat more advanced artificial intelligence, Boswell could take "a small child" and "with her" to deduce that a daughter was being discussed, perhaps triggering questions like: "What is your most memorable experience involving your daughter?" "Can you recall a specific birthday celebration for your daughter?" "Can you recall a time your daughter made you feel proud?" "Can you recall a time your daughter made you feel ashamed?" If Boswell were very sophisticated, it could correlate information across answers to many different questions, assembling a complex picture of the person and asking questions about connections between themes that defined that person's life.

We are not really ready to build Boswell today, but this chapter is a step toward that possibility. We begin with a general discussion about a few of the many ways in which autobiographical memories can be conceptualized, then turn to the stories provided by Survey2000 respondents for a first attempt to catalogue the kinds of questions Boswell might be programmed to ask. Even before such a smart robot is built, we can use that perspective to assemble our own autobiographies, and consider what our life experiences really mean.

Of course, a Boswell has already existed, with the first name James. The author of a highly regarded biography of Samuel Johnson, James Boswell (1740–1795) worked very closely with his subject, conducting what amounted to interviews, and collected letters and other written records [19]. His Wikipedia page reports: "Boswell's surname has passed into the English language as a term (Boswell, Boswellian, Boswellism) for a constant companion and observer, especially one who records those observations in print. In *A Scandal in Bohemia*, Sir Arthur Conan Doyle's character Sherlock Holmes affectionately says of Dr. Watson, who narrates the tales, 'I am lost without my Boswell.'" [20] The word can be written *BOSwell*, to represent a Biographic Operating System that functions well, but from this point onward we shall simply use it as a common noun, *boswell*.

6.2 Cyrus the AI Boswell

The most significant early boswell prototype was a system called CYRUS created by Janet Kolodner in her doctoral dissertation research and reported in several 1983 publications [21–23]. She was a student of Roger Schank at Yale and today is considered one of the leaders in the case-based reasoning approach to artificial intelligence, which he pioneered. CYRUS was an artificial intelligence system for accessing autobiographical memories, using as its data many episodes in the careers of two American secretaries of state, Cyrus Vance and Edmund Muskie. CYRUS is recognized as a landmark for the field, for example being the central example in the authoritative 1997 review essay, "Representation of Autobiographical Memories," by Steven J. Anderson and Martin A. Conway. These authors summarized Janet's general approach thus:

In CYRUS, memory is organized in terms of categories of shared meaning, or so called conceptual categories. These categories represent both prototypical information or "norms" about the types of events contained within the category as well as other structures that organize the category-specific events by their differences. These normative event categories correspond to Schank's concept of scenes. Norms are connected to one another by indices based on the salient features of the categories. Indexing supports several tasks. For example, indexing allows categories to be subdivided into smaller, more easily manageable, subcategories, as well as allowing category members to be easily accessible through cross-indexing (the reference of an item in many different ways) and sub-indexing (an item is given a unique set of pointers that makes it more easily discriminable). [24]

In effect, CYRUS is a question-answer system. One might ask it, "Mr. Vance, when and where did you last meet the Russian foreign minister." The system could not only retrieve the date and place, but also the fact that the Russian's name was Andrei Gromyko. Indeed, that meeting was represented in the memory of CYRUS as a unit consisting of a collection of facts, logically connected to each other. Human autobiography is both a set of separate episodic memories, and also connections between them. For example, CYRUS could answer a question like, "On what other occasions did you meet Andrei Gromyko." Information retrieval is one challenge, but entering the information into the system in the first place is another. Kolodner's research succeeded because she used and to a great extent constructed compatible systems for data entry, structuring, and retrieval that were based on similar case-based reasoning principles. Thus, her research was an example of the need for integration as well as innovation in personality capture and emulation.

The procedural methods used to organize information in Cyrus were an important variant of the dominant approach when the work was done, based on collections and networks of well-defined concepts, and such methods of 30 years ago still play significant roles in artificial intelligence today. However, they may not in fact be the most important methods of organization and retrieval of information in the human mind, and many other well-defined concept models of human memory have been proposed. Most obviously, procedural methods are logical, while humans seem more intuitive. To put that point the other way around, procedural methods require there to be clear relationships between the relevant concepts, often arranged in the structure of a tree diagram in which each step in the branching is contingent upon the previous one. But the world, at least as the human mind perceives it, is far more ambiguous.

Artificial intelligence employs metaphors drawn from human intelligence, but usually has very different goals, most traditionally to solve well-specified problems that are sufficiently complex to pose challenges for human cognition. In its early days, computers had very little memory or power, so concepts were represented very abstractly. Computer programming followed the laws of formal logic, at the very least to avoid crashing the computer or locking it into endless loops. Programmers were trained in mathematics, so they naturally followed its principles of abstraction, deduction, and adherence to strict rules.

The chief alternative in computer programming was neural networks, which we briefly considered in the previous chapter. The programs need to be written just as carefully, and on low levels of programming they also follow procedural logic. But at the higher level where they store and process memories, they are far more fluid, concepts need not always be well-defined, and outcomes are probabilistic rather than fully pre-determined. In the history of artificial intelligence, neural nets arose quite early, but were largely abandoned for several years, and the explanation may be political rather than scientific. The pioneers of the artificial intelligence field found it effective to make extremely optimistic claims about how well their primitive methods could solve difficult problems, in order to obtain both financial support for their research and fame for their sometimes flamboyant personalities [25, 26].

As every history of AI reports, the field was born at a small conference held at Dartmouth College in 1956 [27]. To be sure, computers had been solving intellectual puzzles, arguably since Hollerith had used mechanical-electric tabulating machines to analyze the 1900 census, and science fiction writers had long imagined that robots or computers could be designed to mimic human behavior. But this meeting promulgated both the concept of artificial intelligence and a particular formulation of it. Notably, Allen Newell and Herbert A. Simon presented the early concepts of a system that they believed could solve any soluble problem, using logical deduction, often called *rule-based reasoning*. This approach could be conceptualized as linking together well-defined principles to find a route to the unique solution for a puzzle, or as searching a well-defined problem space for the mathematically optimal solution [28–30].

Very different approaches were possible, for example neural networks, but they seemed ill-designed to give definitive results. A dozen years after the conference, Dartmouth co-organizer Marvin Minsky co-authored a book with Seymour Papert arguing the neural networks were incapable of dealing even with very simple logical problems, and thus were a useless approach for artificial intelligence [31]. Their analysis was in fact wrong, based on a very simplistic model of how neural nets could be constructed, and two decades later neural nets were advancing rapidly in their capabilities [32].

My point is not to say which approach is best, because it seems likely that each will have a role to play in the advance of personality emulation. Rather, I note that several scientific social movements were competing against each other at the time, and the Dartmouth AI approach used rhetorical tactics not unlike those of a political movement, to gain temporary supremacy, and indeed to suppress government support for neural network research for the better part of two decades. The case-based reasoning approach pioneered by Schank and Kolodner could be described as a compromise theory, constructing memory models as networks and categories of well-defined concepts, but starting with the premise that these ultimately derived from specific episodes the individual experienced. This is similar to the *exemplar model* of cognition, that assumes people develop abstract concepts gradually, on the basis of experiences with specific examples, perhaps as few as one [33, 34].

6.3   Episodic Memories

In developing an initial set of design principles for boswells, we do not need to decide among the many competing models of human memory, and indeed we are not able to do so. Laboratory experiments have identified strengths and weakness of many models, and no one model seems best. Rather, different models seem to apply better to different kinds of memories and current situations of memory retrieval. One consequence has been the proliferation of labels for different "kinds" of memories, which may not really be different in how the brain handles them but only in terms of which theoretical models seem to fit them. It has not yet proved possible to integrate all the plausible models of memory into an over-arching theory, and one reason is that we lack good neuroscience research methods for studying what happens on the scale of the small groups of neurons in the brain that presumably encode and process specific memories.

For our present purposes, among the most relevant of the alternative approaches are *situational models* of memory, that may form the basis for case-based reasoning [35]. A common way cognitive scientists conceptualize them is in terms of a collection of perceptions and concepts that represent a particular situation, perhaps representing each of its components through a *token*, the neurological nature of which remains unknown. Situational memories include what has traditionally been called *episodic memories*, which are recollections of specific events in the person's past that were originally housed in working memory but were moved elsewhere in the brain—some researchers think from the hippocampus to the cortex, but I take no position on that—and were memorable enough to be recalled long afterward. As an example of an episodic or situational memory, and an example of how memory concepts have proliferated to the point that the field suffers from overspecialization, here are three of my own *flashbulb* memories.

> I am standing in the cafeteria on the second floor of William James Hall at Harvard University, holding a tray and going through the short line to purchase a snack from either Fay or Sid, resting the tray on the rack that trays can be slid along, perhaps 5 feet to the right of the cash register. To my immediate right is a tall man named Roger Brown, who is explaining flashbulb memories to me. The example of a flashbulb memory he cites is the answer people give to the question, "Where were you when you learned that Kennedy had been assassinated?"
>
> I am driving my gray-colored Rambler station wagon westward on Elm Street in Greenwich, Connecticut, with my wife in the passenger seat, having just turned onto Elm from Milbank Avenue. The radio is playing, and the announcer reports that Kennedy has been shot.
>
> I am standing with two other men, discussing flashbulb memories, and I raise the question, "Where were you when you learned that Kennedy had been assassinated?" Each of them reports having a clear memory of learning that news, but as we compare their memories we notice discrepancies. Then we discover that the one to my left is recalling the assassination of John Kennedy, while the younger man to my right is recalling the assassination of Bobby Kennedy.

All three of these are real episodic memories, reported as accurately as I can, although whether *flashbulb* is the right name for them is open to question. A longstanding concept in behavioral psychology is *one-trial learning*. Most learning, according to behaviorists like my late colleague B. F. Skinner, takes multiple trials. A pigeon pecks around and hits a lever in the Skinner box. A food pellet drops down and the bird eats it. More random pecking, until the bird again hits the lever and gets a second food pellet. Three or four more rewards, and the pigeon will have learned to peck that lever when hungry. Now suppose there is a second lever, clearly marked with a bright light. The pigeon pecks it and immediately receives an extremely painful electric shock. This trauma causes one-trial learning, and the pigeon will never peck that particular lever again.

Flashbulb memories are one-trial permanent records of an emotionally impressive event, so-named because it is as if the flashbulb of a camera had briefly illuminated the scene so the film could record it forever. However, we don't use film in our cameras anymore, and pictures are not only digital but ephemeral. So the metaphor is obsolete, and may always have been inappropriate. Of the three memories reported above, none were actually traumatic experiences for me personally, and only their content connects them to the concept of flashbulb memories.

Roger Brown was in fact the psychologist who proposed the concept of flashbulb memories, arguing that it really did apply to a very distinct form of memory, encoded somehow differently in the brain [36, 37]. One point he made is that flashbulb memories might be permanent but difficult to access, perhaps influenced in this idea by the psychoanalytic notion that forgotten traumatic events from childhood have great influence on our behavior today. So, let's decide that the three memories were not of the flashbulb type, but rather situational memories, and analyze their components.

I have often thought about that moment in the cafeteria, essentially rehearsing that memory, both soon after it occurred when I was reading about flashbulb memories, and at other times up to the present. Long-term memories are often preserved by rehearsal. What comes to my mind's eye is a visual impression of the particular spot in the cafeteria, and a sense of how the components of the memory are physically arranged around me. The cafeteria was run by a married couple, named Sid and Fay, so while neither of them is really present in my visual memory, I readily connect them to it, without recalling which of them was on duty at the moment. Thus, whatever forms the core of a situational memory, we attach other memories to it, some of which are other situations. Immediately I think of the farewell event for Sid and Fay months later, rather crudely represented by words on the poster advertising the party as if we wanted them served in a bag: "Sid and Fay to go."

In the memory of learning about President Kennedy's assassination, I recalled the name of the street because that was where we lived and we were driving home. Thus the words "Elm Street" did not really belong to the core situational memory, but naturally attached themselves as I began to. I sense I had just turned right onto Elm, but that also may not belong really to the situation, because the way we generally returned home was by going south on Milbank from the Boston Post Road, which would require turning right. Indeed, I must admit I cheated, because while I recall that the big street west of Elm is Greenwich Avenue, I did not recall the name of the big street east of Elm. So I consulted an online map to remind myself it was

Milbank—a name that indeed was familiar once I saw it on the map after so many years. This cheat illustrates how our memory can reach further and further from the core of a situational memory, until it leaves the brain altogether.

For some weeks after the third situation described above, I could have named the two other men, and I do have vague candidates in mind, although their definite identities are lost. Indeed, the memory has morphed into what we might call a *proverb memory*, presumably a newly discovered subcategory of semantic memory, in which only enough is recalled to make a clear philosophical point. Each person recognizes a situation in terms of their own prior experiences, which differ even when they fail to recognize that fact.

All three of these particular memories are framed in spatial terms. I have a sense of rather exactly where I was, or at least of the spatial relations among the components of the memory. People may differ in the extent to which their episodic memories have this degree of spatial orientation, and of course there are other components, in each of these cases a verbal communication that may be remembered as the general sense of what was spoken, or perhaps even some of the exact words. These particular memories include other people, but other memories may lack people—for example the time I was walking toward our family barn eating an apple when my tongue was stung by a bee.

It is worth noting that by their very nature, episodic memories have some conception of the duration the event took or about when in our personal histories they occurred, but hour and date are almost never part of an autobiographical memory, so it is difficult to arrange them correctly over time without the use of external documentation, which often is not available. Wikipedia tells me that I heard the radio news that Kennedy had been shot on November 22, 1963, but that detail is not included in my memory itself. I presented the three memories above in a logical order, but not the chronological order, because Kennedy was shot before Brown invented flashbulb memories.

Clearly, I am skeptical about Brown's claim that flashbulb memories are a distinct kind, and indeed that many of the other types and models really are distinct from each other, even though laboratory experiments do show fairly consistent patterns, such as relatively long delays recalling autobiographical memories compared with other kinds of situational memories that refer to repeatable events (like buying a donut and hot chocolate from Fay or Sid) rather than one-time episodes (like talking with Roger Brown while doing so) [38]. However, this does not mean I am pessimistic about capture of a person's memories, and the possibility of using them as the basis for emulation.

Our two saving graces are fidelity and utility. When Thomas Alva Edison recited "Mary had a little lamb" into his first tinfoil phonograph, the fidelity was exceedingly low, but the nursery rhyme was recognizable. When Peter Carl Goldmark's team developed the 33 1/3 RPM long-playing phonograph record, they improved the fidelity of the existing 78 RPM records that then dominated the industry, as one among many steps in the history of ever more accurate recording. With respect to personality capture, we are still at Edison's stage, and when we reach Goldmark's we will still be just beginning. But as with many of his inventions, Edison was able rather quickly to produce workable versions that found favor in the marketplace.

Autobiographical memories are already useful for us as human beings, the moment they have been written down, or as in the case of Edison's famous nursery rhyme, spoken into a recording machine. Most obviously, they become paragraphs that can be assembled along with other kinds of information to create a book-length autobiography. For commercial and scholarly purposes, only books about famous people tend to be considered successes, yet the new information technologies, applied to new purposes, may change that. Already some archives preserve life histories of obscure people. When I taught at the University of Washington, one of my students shared with me her translation from German into English of her mother's autobiography, which was preserved in a local archive dedicated to the European Holocaust. My student's mother was a Jewish women who had been locked into a urban slave-labor factory until, late in the war, she was sent to a concentration camp, and with others was able to escape while being transported. Yes, hers was an interesting life, if an obscure one. Yet the motto of Holocaust archives might well be applied more broadly to the life experiences of all people: Never forget!

6.4 Migration Memories in Survey2000

Several questions in Survey2000 asked where the respondent had lived at various points in life, so the open-ended question about a significant residential move was well-prepared in the respondent's mind. The reconnaissance reported here is based on the first 4,000 valid responses in the smaller of two massive data files. We begin without a pre-conceived theory, nor having an analytical methodology in place. Thus we must start with common-sense notions and reach scientific concepts only after wandering.

First, let us imagine a standard model for describing a residential move, and some of the questions about details that may distinguish the personalities or the perspectives of the people writing the answers. Logically, a person might both name and describe the original location and the destination, mention the experience of moving including perhaps problems that arose, and then contrast the two environments. Many respondents did in fact do this, in finer or coarser detail. Many respondents went further, suggested how they themselves changed in connection with their migration. Of course, exactly what they wrote resulted from a combination of personal characteristics and the actual facts of the particular move, the character-context distinction we identified earlier. Some examples of details can get us ready to consider broader issues.

The corpus of data includes a huge number and variety of place names. A name anchors the place in the person's own memory, potentially associating many other memories in the person's mind, but it also serves communication functions. We, reading what the respondent wrote, will have our own mental associations with the names. However, people differ in the names they use for the same places, largely on the basis of familiarity. For example, where are Nfld and NWT? They are in Canada, and people familiar with Canada will immediately recognize that respondents referred to Newfoundland and Northwest Territories. Sometimes respondents provide extra specification beyond the name itself, as in, "from Columbus OH to Evanston IL," on the assumption that most readers will recognize the abbreviations of two prominent American states. Others limit the information to that code: "from NJ to WV," "from CT to WI," "from NY to MA."

One person went to Cambridge for "postgraduate study," and an American boswell might assume that meant either MIT or Harvard in Cambridge, Massachusetts. But no, it meant Cambridge in England, as indicated by the names of the Cambridge University faculty mentioned: "I met up with Paul Dirac and switched from engineering to physics, and with Thurston Dart and switched from piano to harpsichord." Another experienced a "move to LA," which we might guess means Los Angeles but could mean Louisiana. Other names would be unfamiliar to most readers, but could be located with some confidence via Wikipedia—Yellowknife, Yosemite, Poughkeepsie, Wallaceburg, Nanaimo, or Krugersdorp.

Some location descriptions are rather abstract, such as "Returning to hometown after living on East Coast and then West coast." Readers might assume this person lives in the United States, but Canada, Australia and many other English speaking nations have coasts on both east and west. Yet even vague references can provide a meaningful context for understanding the person's experience. "Moving from the country to the city to obtain work." Immigrants from one nation to another often name the nations, rather than the cities: "my move to the United States from India," "from Poland to Australia," "from Malaysia to Singapore."

The portion of a boswell system devoted to the person's travels could easily have a list of standard information required for each location, which could be framed in realtime as follow-up questions: "By LA, do you mean Los Angeles, Louisiana, or someplace else?" "Was that the Yellowknife in the Northwest Territories of Canada?" "Where in Malaysia did you live before moving to Singapore?" This last example focused on Malaysia alone, because Singapore is a city and thus the name provides more specificity than the reference to the nation of Malaysia. Subsequent questions might seek the specific addresses in both places.

One possible format that seeks to maximize communication with the reader was to begin with a simple factual framework, then add a comment about the meaning of the event. For example, here is my own response to the question, case 2693 in the smaller of the two datasets: "In 1950, leaving Bethel, Connecticut, and moving to Greenwich, Connecticut. I was 9 years old. It was significant because we moved from an isolated rural area to an intensely social upper-class suburb." This is a very common narrative strategy, defining the context early in the description then expressing its meaning. Here are four people's responses, consecutive cases only slightly later in the same dataset:

Travelling to India to do anthropological research along Himalayan pilgrimage routes. The richness of experiences and interactions with people of different cultures.

The most significant move of my life was moving away from my parents' home at 19 to go to university. This was the most important for me because it represents the first time I was able to assert my independence.

Moving to Utah at age ten with my family. Utah made me what I am today. If I had grown up in Cody, Wyoming (between the Seattle and Utah moves, but not asked about in the survey) I would probably be religious and a cowboy.

I moved to Odessa, TX in 1990, it was significant in that it was a major lifestyle change for my (ex) husband and myself, we were trying to improve our lives.

Some respondents followed a narrative model that was not framed in terms of migration from one precise location to another, describing a time of wandering:

I spent a year traveling around Asia including months in India, Vietnam, Laos, Indonesia, and several other countries. This experience gave me the maturity and perspective to appreciate and enjoy people, culture, and habits vastly different than my own.

Most significant was moving: Not any single move, but the opportunity to live on five continents and visit more than 50 countries!

Between the ages of 23 and 33, I moved all my personal belongings, dog in my van. During this time, I moved a total of 43 times. I was single and in a career path that required moving if I wanted to advance professionally. I also moved to take advantage of cheaper housing or finding a roommate. Employment changes required moving distances of up to 100 or more miles. This transient period was the most significant move for me.

Many of the reports connected a residential move to a life transition experienced by many people which therefore could become the basis of standard questions in the boswell's prepared list:

Moving out of my parent's home established me as an adult.

The most significant move was not one of distance but one of great change: our first house. My husband and I bought our house 3 years ago and I finally felt more "adult" than I did when I finished college or got married.

The most significant move of my life was to get married. It led to my children (good!) and my divorce (bad!). It also caused me to miss out on developing a more independent lifestyle when I was younger.

To Texas after my first wife got a job at Texas Tech. Significant because I met my second wife there!

Retiring from the U. S. Navy and also Retiring after 20 years as a Correctional Lieutenant in the local county Jail.

Examples such as these naturally suggest simple but often relevant questions: "What happened when you finished school?" "What happened when you left your childhood home?" "What happened when you got your first job?" "What happened when you got married?" Of course, some people will not have experienced one of these transitions, despite the fact they are all very common, so even questions on a standard list will need to be contingent. "Have you finished school?" "What happened when you did." "Did you move immediately after finishing school?" "How would you describe that move?" "Are you single, married, divorced, separated, or widowed?" "What happened when you got divorced?"

A detailed study of the full Survey2000 data could identify some set of very common and easily described life transitions that might involve a residential move:

going to a school, leaving school, leaving the childhood home, buying a house, marriage, divorce, getting a job, leaving a job. Each of these might have subcategories that would trigger different follow-up questions, for example: leaving one job to take a better one, being fired from a job, retiring from employment altogether. Once the person had answered many questions, connecting the answers could lead to more questions that would need to be framed in realtime, rather than taken from a pre-existing list. For example, a move is often one stage in a series of transitions that need to be connected in the growing data archive, often involving issues of personality evolution versus preservation as well as simply a chain of logistical changes:

> Marriage and birth of my 1st child required a move to New Hampshire which opened up a new career opportunity that changed my life forever.
>
> In 1983 I came to the United States by accident (I was drunk and on the way to New Zealand). Although my travelling partner was eventually deported, I stayed. Since then I have made my home in Washington DC although eventually I may move to Northern California. In 1997 I became an American citizen.
>
> The most life changing move in my life was from Germany to the US. Even though I came here with lots of promises (none kept!), very happily married, but the happiness did not last too long. Unfortunately, the man I was married to loves being married: The more often, the better (he presently is married for the 8th time—and he is American!) I would have had another important move when I got remarried to a wonderful and very special man after raising my son pretty much alone for 13 years. But it was easier to remain in the residence that my son had lived in all his life until then.
>
> The most significant move of my life was one that did not happen. I interviewed for a job in Florida and was a final candidate but did not receive a job offer. Within a few weeks I interviewed for a job in Massachusetts that was only 30 miles from my home. I was offered the job and accepted it. About a year later I met my wife at work. We have been together for seven wonderful years and have a great little boy. If I had been offered the job in Florida I never would have met my wife or had my son.
>
> When we sold our farm and bought an old touring bus to travel in. We lived in it for 6 months, traveling through Tennessee, preaching the gospel and leading people we met into a relationship with God through his son Jesus Christ. This came after I had been a Christian for 25 years, and when we made that move, God began revealing himself to me and answering my prayers whenever I prayed. It has been an awesome time in my life. It was this past year.
>
> I moved from California to Denver in 1995. From the get go I found it to be a mistake. It was hard to create community. I felt judged on the basis of everything, my skin color is slightly darker than white, the clothes I wore or my exuberant personality. I found a few good friends, but it took me at least 2 years to move back to California. I felt that financially I got stuck. The whole time period really made me realize the importance of following my heart and dreams.
>
> It seems funny… but I don't seem to find peaks in my life… just stepping stones. This stone represents the years I spent in college and this one would be my first years of marriage. There are stones for each child… even the mis-carriage. Stones for the buying of the bookstore and stones for the motorcycles… Sometimes the stones were a bit unstable and I had to move quickly… I don't see an end in sight… just more stones spreading like a fan.

One type of move mentioned by dozens of respondents, including myself, was one that occurred in childhood when the person had little ability to decide where to go or how to adapt to the new circumstances. Some of these respondents mentioned increased opportunities for growth at the new home, especially if it was economically more prosperous or more cultivated, but many mentioned the loss of friends and the difficulty of adjusting to an unfamiliar culture at the destination:

> Illinois to Pennsylvania, age 13, grade 9: all social cliques have been set in stone by 9th grade in a US high school. It took at least a year to fit in and find good friends. Very alienating.
> From England to Canada when I was 14. It was very traumatic for me because I was taken out of the British School system of a top quality all girls Grammar school and sent to school in Canada to a co-ed school that was very different socially. I was very shy in Canada and didn't like my accent because it was different to everyone else's. Therefore, I never said much and everyone thought I was a snob. Consequently, I never made any close friends at the time of my life when I should have been forming lifelong friendships. I swore I would never do that to my children and therefore I have stayed in one location during my children's high school years, even though I was not really happy there.
> In 1971 my family moved from Michigan back to Southern California, I was a junior in high school and had finally found my "niche", had a group of friends, doing well in school, and had an idea on what I wanted to do after high school. When we moved I basically had to start all over again, it was kind of late and so for years I felt like I was just lost with no clear idea of my future. It took me years to finally get back on track. Where could I have been now if we had not moved?
> The most significant move of my life happened just this past March. I had lived my whole life in Edmonton, Alberta, Canada. All of a sudden my father comes home from work one day and says we are moving down to Olympia, Washington USA. I have to leave my friends and everything familiar to me, behind. Our family split up. My older sister remains in Edmonton where she is going to school. My grandmother came with us, but she resides in an elder care facility very far from where we live. In August, we moved again to Newcastle, Washington USA so my mother could be closer to her new job. For the past months I have felt disconnected and isolated. It is not a pleasant feeling. Also, experiencing troubles with starting school and residency requirements do not make the situation any better. I miss my sister. My parents are off with their new jobs and friends. It is very lonely trying to fit in and not quite making it.
> When I moved when I was 10 because my family was killed in a plane crash.
> As a 15-year-old, I refused to move with widowed mother when she got married. I was truly on my own and stayed with friends in Simi Valley, CA until graduating from high school.
> Leaving my mother and step-father to live with my father at the age of 16. Significant because mom and step-dad were moving from Texas to Maryland and I didn't want to leave Texas at the time. I am now ready to leave.

The last two examples are cases in which the individual asserted some autonomy as a teenager, during what must have been troubling times. Two lines of questioning could follow responses like those above. One would begin by asking the names of friends who were lost or gained because of the move. After a list had been constructed, the person would be asked to recall one or more episodic memories concerning each friend. The second line of questioning would catalogue the feelings generated by the move. Then the person could be asked to describe several other incidents in life that had generated emotions like each feeling on the list.

This suggests that a list of common transitions could be cross-tabulated against lists of common characteristics of social environments, friendship relations, and distinctive emotions, allowing the boswell to frame many relevant questions in an efficient manner. But it is also clear, as in the last examples just quoted, that many people face unusual circumstances, do so occasionally in unique ways, and a sophisticated boswell will need methods for interviewing about them.

6.5 Sophisticated Issues

Much sociological research documents the fact that residential migration can disconnect people from the social bonds that enforce conventional behavior, and areas of high migration tend to be more tolerant of cultural and personal variation [39]. In both Canada and the United States, this is why many unusual lifestyles are more common in the high-migration areas near the west coast, than in older regions of the countries. But in any geographic location, some individuals have experiences that are not common in the general population, whether or not they can be said to have chosen those experiences:

Some years ago I was abducted and tortured by the Federal Police, and in that way, I got involved in Human Rights.

The most significant move of my life was when I moved away from an abusive spouse with two toddlers and no extra funds. Thank God I was employed.

My most significant move was when I was a B-52G Gunner and went to war over Iraq and had the love of my family. Although I haven't always agreed with the intent of war, the purpose and ideal nature is a necessity for our patriotic needs. I think therefore I am!!!!!! I will never forget coming home and having my Mother grab and hold me tighter than I can ever remember her holding me before! That was the most significant move in my Life!!

The most significant move of my life was moving in with my same sex partner. It was a big moment personally, becoming aware of being gay. We feel relatively safe in our community, the West Coast does tend to be very relaxed in attitudes. But at the same time we keep a very low profile as you are never 100% sure of anybody. The area we live in is predominantly very family oriented and leaning towards the right.

As a lesbian, I wanted to have a child, but was unable to adopt in California and did not want to carry my own child. I moved to Oregon, looked into adoption through the state system (special needs kids), and a year later we were the proud moms of a 6 year old wonderful boy!

Directly or indirectly, reports like these connect to social issues, and boswell could switch to some standard opinion poll questions, perhaps about political perspectives or conceptions of how families should be organized. Many respondents to Survey2000 reported significant cultural differences between the origin and destination of their significant move. Several say they learned from this contrast, others felt they personally fitted the new environment better, while others regretted the loss of their home culture. The first example below undoubtedly concerns a move from one part of Canada to another:

In 1980, my husband and I started a business and in 1983 moved to a small Anglophone town located about 250 miles from the small francophone town where we were both brought up. We discovered to our surprise that the values, ethics, and mentality of both towns were quite different and that it was very difficult for us to trust the people around us. Although it may not be the cause of the eventual failure of the company, it certainly contributed to it. We were very happy in 1990 when the company closed and in 1991 we got out of there!

Fig. 5.7 A few interfaces of a prototype of the toolbox. (**a**). Interfaces to simulate the effects of different diseases. (**b**). Interfaces to simulate the effects of different visual functions and hand strength metrics. (**c**). Interfaces to run image processing algorithms and set demographic detail of users

on hand strength and the system can show the effects of Cerebral Palsy or Parkinson's disease for different age group and gender. **A demonstration copy of the simulator can be downloaded from** http://www-edc.eng.cam.ac.uk/~pb400/ CambridgeSimulator.zip. The simulator works in the following three steps.

1. While a task is undertaken by participants, a monitor program records the interaction. This monitor program records

    (a) A list of key presses and mouse clicks (operations),
    (b) A sequence of bitmap images of the interfaces (low-level snapshot),
    (c) Locations of windows, icons, buttons and other controls in the screen (high-level snapshot).

2. Initially, the cognitive model analyzes the task and produces a list of atomic tasks (detailed task specification).

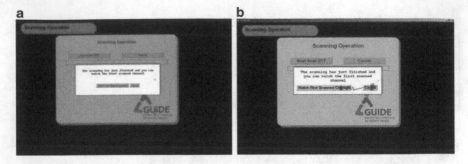

Fig. 5.8 Correcting interface layout. (**a**). Initial interface. (**b**). Changed interface with simulation of medium visual and motor impaired profile

3. If an atomic task involves perception, the perception model operates on the event list and the sequence of bitmap images. Similarly, if an atomic task involves movement, the motor behaviour model operates on the event list and the high-level snapshot.

Interface designers have used the simulator for improving their designs. Figure 5.8a, b demonstrate such an example. In Fig. 5.8a, the font size was smaller and the buttons were close enough to be missed clicked by a person with tremor in hand. The designer chose the appropriate font type (Tiresias in this case) and size and also the inter-button spacing through simulation. As Fig. 5.8b shows, the new interface remain legible even to moderate visually impaired users, the inter-button spacing is large enough to avoid missed-clicking by moderate motor impaired users. In Fig. 5.8b the purple lines show simulated cursor trajectories of users with tremor in hand.

5.4 Design Improvement & Adaptation

The simulator can show the effects of a particular disease on visual functions and hand strength metrics and in turn their effect on interaction. For example the simulator can predict how a person with visual acuity v and contrast sensitivity s will perceive an interface or a person with grip strength g and range of motion of wrist w will use a pointing device. We collected data from a set of intended users and clustered their objective assessment metrics. The clusters represent users with mild, moderate or severe visual, hearing and motor impairment with objective measurement of their functional abilities. We have used the simulator to customize interfaces for all applications for each cluster of users. So we have customized interfaces for a group of users with similar type of perceptual, cognitive and motor abilities. The process is depicted in Fig. 5.9.

We ran the simulator in Monte Carlo simulation and developed a set of rules relating users' range of abilities with interface parameters (Fig. 5.10). For example

> I spent a year in the South Pacific. It was the closest I've ever lived to another culture; getting to know the people, their history, how they lived their lives. I did a lot of study during that time and since, about the Polynesian people from earliest times. I felt I belonged there and didn't really want to return to the States but had to because of spouse's job. I actually mourned the loss of the place and the people.
>
> My move from Salt Lake City to Seattle was an important way for me to break away from an oppressive environment with family and the predominant Mormon religion. In Seattle, I came into my adulthood and discovered much about myself. Seattle is more home to me than Salt Lake ever was.
>
> My most significant move in my life was from Zimbabwe to Canada and the obvious difference was the weather, but there was a tremendous culture shock as well. I found the general population ignorant of anywhere other than North America. The colloquialisms are very different and therefore communication was a little challenge. Discipline of children is often non-existent in North America. But what freedom of speech and freedom to explore the wonders of nature here in Canada as it is so safe to wander the wilderness.
>
> My move from Hong Kong to Canada changed the whole course of my life. Now, instead of speaking Cantonese, as I would have in Hong Kong, I speak English most of the time. Instead of having primarily Cantonese-speaking friends, I hang out with people of different cultural backgrounds. I also think being in Canada, a Canadian, now has changed my views. People here are more forgiving, and give less value to money. I feel I am richer morally being a Canadian than I would have been had I left Hong Kong later.

The last of these examples reminds us that the point of boswell's interviews is not to compare Canada objectively with Hong Kong, but to learn how the particular respondent conceptualizes and feels about them. However, the examples given here all concern not only the individual, but his or her relations to other people, including the general population and culture of the locales that situated the move. In the chapters focusing on questionnaires, it was natural to measure one individual in the context of others, and that is true for biographical methods as well.

6.6 Citizen Social Science

There are three reasons why we cannot here provide a comprehensive theoretical and methodological approach to autobiographical memories. First, cognitive science is still working out how such memories operate in the human brain, and future discoveries might influence the direction our work would take. Second, as many of the examples cited above amply demonstrate, human lives vary greatly, influenced by culture, personality, actions of other people especially parents and spouses, and the often random events that shape a person's life. Third, means depend upon goals, and we cannot define now what purposes other people might in future have when they seek to collect and use memories. But there is a way around this impasse: encouraging future users to do the research themselves. A logical starting point would be the oral history projects that already exist.

Once upon a time, I rode through an honest-to-goodness wild-west town, to a set of prefab mobile trailers, where people were processing memories of the European Holocaust of the early 1940s, which happened to be the period but thankfully not the place where I was born. The site was on a back lot of Universal Studios near Los

Angeles, where the Survivors of the Shoah Visual History Foundation was processing oral history interviews with Holocaust survivors. Today, the project is centered
at the University of Southern California at the USC Shoah Foundation, which describes its institute thus:

> The Institute for Visual History and Education is dedicated to making audio-visual inter-
> views with survivors and witnesses of the Holocaust and other genocides a compelling
> voice for education and action.
> With a current collection of 51,696 eyewitness testimonies, the Institute's Visual History
> Archive preserves history as told by the people who lived it. Each testimony is a unique
> source of insight and knowledge offering powerful stories from history that demand to be
> explored and shared. In this way we will be able to see their faces and hear their voices,
> allowing them to teach, and inspire action against intolerance.
> The Visual History Archive is the largest digital collection of its kind in the world. Cur-
> rently encompassing 105,000 hours of video testimony, the archive is an invaluable
> resource for humanity, with nearly every testimony containing a complete personal history
> of life before, during and after the interviewee's firsthand experience with genocide. The
> Visual History Archive is digitized, fully searchable, and hyperlinked to the minute. This
> indexing allows students, professors, researchers, and others around the world to retrieve
> entire testimonies or search for specific sections within testimonies through a set of more
> than 60,000 keywords and key phrases, 1.2 million names, and 700,000 images.
> In the Spring of 2013, the Visual History Archive expanded to include testimonies from
> eyewitnesses of genocide from Rwanda, Cambodia and Armenia. [40]

Table 6.1 lists six oral history projects that have websites and illustrate the wide
range of possibilities, beginning with the Shoah project [41]. The Greenwich project suggests that every community could have an association dedicated to collecting
oral histories, although this particular town was a pioneer because it happened to
be a wealthy suburb of New York City where many prominent and literate people
lived. I lived there myself through the 1950s, and often wondered about a huge,
mysterious stone house that glowered over a tiny lake set in a small peninsula that
thrust out into Long Island Sound, within walking distance of our home. Called the
Tod Mansion, it had belonged to a rich person, but what was its story? Was there
any significance in the fact that in the middle of the lake an island the size of a table
supported a pillar decked with a bronze eagle? Years later I read one of the oral history books published by this project, and learned that the mansion had belonged to a
Scottish immigrant, J. Kennedy Tod, who became rich in banking [42].

Each of these six projects has a theme, which is a limitation because it excludes
the lives of people who were not involved in that theme, but is an advantage at this
point in the development of the genre because it provides both organization to the
work and an audience for the product. When I learned about the rich man, Tod, I did
so by reading the words of more ordinary people, often learning also about some
of their personal experiences. One obvious organizational structure for an archive
of oral histories is the *chronicle*, indexing the memories of individuals by time and
place, so that someone using the archive can fit memories together that belonged
to different people. Quite apart from any overarching theme the entire archive may
have, there can be lesser themes indexed by topic. Thus we can imagine a future
archive methodology in which individual boswells represent individual people who

Table 6.1 Six prominent oral history projects that illustrate the possibilities

Organization	Cases	Motivation
Shoah Foundation	51,696	Primarily Holocaust survivor memories, commemorating those who suffered and educating people to prevent such tragedies in the future
Greenwich Library	850+	Greenwich, Connecticut: "interviews with people who have helped to make or witnessed the history of Greenwich, Connecticut, since 1890," that contributed to 137 books.
Oberlin Heritage Center	100+	Oberlin, Ohio: "memories of downtown, college life, local industries, world events, politics, entertainment and daily life from the early 1900s to the present"
Cambridge Historical Commission	125	World War II and the Home Front in Cambridge, Massachusetts, one of four oral history projects: "These recollections are told by soldiers in combat, nurses in hospitals in Europe and the Pacific, women who worked at the Charlestown Navy Yard and other defense industries, and servicemen's families who waited for loved ones to come home."
National Aeronautics and Space Administration	675	Johnson Space Center Oral History Project: "Participants include managers, engineers, technicians, doctors, astronauts, and other employees of NASA and aerospace contractors who served in key roles during the Mercury, Gemini, Apollo, Skylab, and Shuttle programs."
British Library	200	Oral History of British Science: "a major archive for the study and public understanding of contemporary science in Britain."

contributed their data, and a broader information retrieval system unites all of the boswells into a virtual community.

The Oral History Association "seeks to bring together all persons interested in oral history as a way of collecting and interpreting human memories to foster knowledge and human dignity [43]." Two words in this brief quotation raise very serious questions, *interpreting* and *dignity*. For an historian, interpretation involves fitting facts together to make a consistent, correct narrative, but screening the facts through criteria based on a theme, such as the vast European Holocaust or the small transition of Tod's Point from a rich man's abode to a town park. A social scientist wants more, both linking the descriptive themes to general theories, and capturing the lives of the general population within some rigorous framework. Accomplishment of both tasks, the historical and the sociological, would transform the archive into an emulation of the people whose lives were its input.

Dignity is a challenge, because every life includes a measure of disgrace, some lives more than others. Should the Shoah project have interviewed unrepentant Nazis, to add their lives to the historical archive? As the works of Sutherland, Shaw and Heyl imply, the lives of deviants must be included—but how? Is dignity really compatible with truth? This, of course, is an issue that runs throughout this book, although seldom explicitly mentioned. To what extent should we "improve" a captured personality when we emulate it? I have no answer for such questions, but can suggest a way forward.

6.7   Conclusion

The integration of autobiographical memories into a community archive that emulates hundreds or thousands of people requires advances in cultural science, and the best way to achieve them may be through citizen science. Ordinary members of the community can collect documents and administer oral history interviews to each other, or much of the work can be offloaded onto boswells. In either case, human minds need to make sense of all the information, both linking individual records together into social networks, and identifying underling themes. That requires the participation of professionals. Consider the case of Oberlin, Ohio, a small town dominated by a college that came into existence originally as a utopian community. Faculty in history, psychology, and social science could work with students and townspeople to expand their archive into an online representation of the entire sweep of this community's evolution, unifying "town and gown" while preserving the fault lines that marked historical disputes. A half dozen demonstration projects along these lines could establish design principles for personality capture and emulation in the context of community science.

References

1. http://en.wikipedia.org/wiki/Caesar_Code. Accessed 4 July 2013.
2. http://memory.loc.gov/ammem/nfhtml/nfhome.html. Accessed 21 June 2013.
3. http://mase.itc.nagoya-u.ac.jp/CARPE2006/. Accessed 21 June 2013.
4. Bush. V. (1945). As we may think. *The Atlantic*, July 1945. http://www.theatlantic.com/magazine/archive/1945/07/as-we-may-think/303881/. Accessed 21 June 2013.
5. Gemmell, J., Williams, L., Wood, K., Lueder, R., & Bell, G. (2004). Passive capture and ensuing issues for a personal lifetime store. *Proceedings of the First ACM workshop on continuous archival and retrieval of personal experiences* (pp. 48–55). New York: ACM.
6. Cherry, S. (2005). Total recall. *IEEE Spectrum, 42*(11), 24–30. (The cover introduced this article).
7. http://www.media.mit.edu/people/dkroy. Accessed 21 June 2013.
8. van den Hoven, E., Sas, C., & Whittaker, S. (2012). Designing for personal memories: Past, present and future. *Human Computer Interaction, 27*(1–2), 1–12.
9. Whittaker, S., Kalnikaite, V., Petrelli, D., Sellen, A., Villar, N., Bergman, O., Clough P., & Brockmeier, J. (2012). Socio-technical lifelogging: Deriving design principles for a future proof digital past. *Human Computer Interaction, 27*(1–2), 37–62.
10. Kalnikaite, V., & Whittaker, S. (2012). Synergistic recollection: How to design lifelogging tools that help locate the right information. In M. Zacarias & J. V. Oliveira (Ed.), *Human computer interaction: The agency perspective* (pp. 329–348). London: Springer.
11. Lofland, J., & Stark, R. (1965). Becoming a world-saver: A theory of conversion to a deviant perspective. *American Sociological Review, 39*(6), 862–875.
12. Bainbridge, W. S. (1978). *Satan's power* (p. 39). Berkeley: University of California Press.
13. Bainbridge, W. S. (1992). *Social research methods and statistics: A computer-assisted introduction*. Belmont: Wadsworth.
14. Sutherland, E. H. (1937). *The professional thief*. Chicago: University of Chicago Press.
15. Shaw, C. H. (1930). *The Jack Roller*. Philadelphia: Albert Saifer.
16. Heyl, B. (1979). *The madam as entrepreneur*. New Brunswick: Transaction.

17. Dollard, J. (1935). *Criteria for life history*. New Haven: Yale University Press.
18. Griswold, W., & Wright, N. (2004). Cowbirds, locals, and the dynamic endurance of regionalism. *American Journal of Sociology, 109*(6), 1411–1451.
19. Boswell, J. (1820). *The life of Samuel Johnson*. London: Davis.
20. http://en.wikipedia.org/wiki/James_Boswell. Accessed 4 Jul 2013.
21. Kolodner, J. L. (1983). Indexing and retrieval strategies for natural language fact retrieval. *ACM Transactions on Database Systems (TODS), 8*(3), 434–464.
22. Kolodner, J. L. (1983). Maintaining organization in a dynamic long-term memory. *Cognitive Science, 7*, 243–280.
23. Kolodner, J. L. (1983). Reconstructive memory: A computer model. *Cognitive Science, 7*, 281–328.
24. Anderson, S. J., & Conway, M. A. (1997). Representation of autobiographical memories. In M. A. Conway (Ed.), *Cognitive models of memory* (pp. 231). Cambridge: MIT Press.
25. Crevier, D. (1993). *AI: The tumultuous history of the search for artificial intelligence*. New York: Basic Books.
26. Bainbridge, W. S. (2012). Artificial intelligence. In W. S. Bainbridge (Ed.), *Leadership in science and technology* (pp. 464–471). Los Angeles: Sage.
27. McCarthy, J., Minsky, M. L., Rochester, N., & Shannon, C. E. (1955). *A proposal for the dartmouth summer research project on artificial intelligence*. http://www-formal.stanford.edu/jmc/history/dartmouth/dartmouth.html. Accessed 9 Mar 2013.
28. Newell, A. (1990). *Unified theories of cognition*. Cambridge: Harvard University Press.
29. Simon, H. A. (1996). *The sciences of the artificial*. Cambridge: MIT Press.
30. McCorduck, P. (2004). *Machines who think*. Natick: Peters.
31. Minsky, M., & Papert, S. (1969). *Perceptrons*. Cambridge: MIT Press.
32. Rumelhart, D. E., & McClelland, J. L. (1986). *Parallel distributed processing*. Cambridge: MIT Press.
33. Hampton, J. A. (1997). Psychological representation of concepts. In M. A. Conway (Ed.), *Cognitive models of memory* (pp. 81–110). Cambridge: MIT Press.
34. Shanks, D. R. (1997). Representation of categories and concepts in memory. In M. A. Conway (Ed.), *Cognitive models of memory* (pp. 111–146). Cambridge: MIT Press.
35. Radvansky, G. A., & Zacks, R. T. (1997). The retrieval of situation-specific information. In M. A. Conway (Ed.), *Cognitive models of memory* (pp. 173–213). Cambridge: MIT Press.
36. Brown, R., & Kulik, J. (1977). Flashbulb memories. *Cognition, 5*(1), 73–99.
37. Finkenauer, C., Luminet, O., Gisle, L., El-Ahmadi, A., Van Der Linden, M., & Philippot, P. (1998). Flashbulb memories and the underlying mechanisms of their formation: Toward an emotional-integrative model. *Memory and Cognition, 26*(3), 516–531.
38. Anderson, S. J. & Conway, M. A. (1997). Representation of autobiographical memories. In M. A. Conway (Ed.), *Cognitive models of memory* (pp. 217–246). Cambridge: MIT Press.
39. Bainbridge, W. S. (1989). The religious ecology of deviance. *American Sociological Review, 54*, 288–295.
40. http://sfi.usc.edu/about. Accessed 2 June 2013.
41. sfi.usc.edu/; www.glohistory.org/; www.oberlinheritage.org/; www2.cambridgema.gov/historic/oralhist_home.html; www.jsc.nasa.gov/history/oral_histories/oral_histories.htm; www.bl.uk/historyofscience. Accessed 6 July 2013.
42. Ornstein, B. (Ed.). (1981). *Tod's point: An oral history*. Greenwich: Greenwich Library.
43. http://www.oralhistory.org/about/. Accessed 6 July 2013.

Chapter 7
Text Analysis

For decades, computers have managed increasing terabytes of written text using increasingly diverse and complex methods. However, it has proven very difficult to achieve high levels of validity with any of the several techniques of natural language processing or NLP. The primary reason, which this chapter will elucidate, is that words do not themselves possess meaning, but rather we invest them with meaning, collectively and individually, and thus they remain meaningless unless embedded in our lives. Lexicographers, grammarians, and artificial intelligence scientists exaggerate the extent to which language is systematic, or rather they render it more systematic than it naturally would be through their influences in education. An alternative approach, which this book advocates, would be to connect linguistic data derived from a person with all the other kinds of data covered here, to achieve comprehensive capture as the basis for emulation.

A secondary reason is that the equivalent of market factors have shaped natural language processing, infusing it with tensions that have some tendency to distort the science. This can be described as a contest between efficiency and accuracy, as accomplishment of some practical tasks requires processing large volumes of text using rather superficial statistical methods, but therefore in the absence of any deep theoretical understanding. The villain in this drama, if there indeed is one, is the demand of military and security government agencies for quick solutions to practical problems, starting decades ago with the rather focused goal of translating text from Russian to English, and then finding terrorists' communications in a vast flood of innocuous email messages and telephone calls. More recently the villain acquired an accomplice, in industry's campaign to replace human workers with computers in telephone dialog systems.

NLP is such a vast field that this chapter cannot cover even a tiny fraction of it, but will especially focus on personality capture and emulation issues related to two of the major NLP fields: document classification and language translation. Both have immediate applications but also reveal profound issues, notably the fact that every human personality is embedded in a culture and every voice speaks words primarily coined by long-deceased strangers. We can imagine a system designed to emulate the voice and verbal constructions of a particular human being, and set it to talk about topics defined in other chapters of this book, for example reciting

W. S. Bainbridge, *Personality Capture and Emulation,* Human-Computer Interaction Series,   151
DOI 10.1007/978-1-4471-5604-8_7, © Springer-Verlag London 2014

an autobiography based on recorded episodic memories of the person, arranged in chronological order. But the words uttered by the voice, and the realities described by them, would not make any sense unless the listener shared background information with the person emulated. Additionally, full emulation requires the simulated voice to express new thoughts, which reminds us that emulation must be a dynamic process, allowing the personality to evolve beyond the state it was in when it was captured.

While natural language processing has made substantial progress in recent years, this field has progressed largely by ignoring one of its foundational traditions: embedding the text in a coherent system of meaning. For example, the *General Inquirer* system that features prominently here was originally built back in the 1960s on the basis of comprehensive theories of human meaning, but more modern systems tend to use brute statistical force rather than theory. One advantage of General Inquirer for present purposes is that it came out of the same, intellectually massive attempt to understand the meaning of human personalities at Harvard described in the first chapter of this book, and even incorporates a version of the Semantic Differential. Without dismissing more recent theory-based efforts, I must report that social science and computer science have gone their separate ways since the 1970s, and it is high time they reunited.

Ideally, the reintroduction of theories based on cognitive science could improve the ability of computerized NLP systems to extract meaning from text produced by a specific person. But which theory? One answer is the theory most compatible with that person's own thought processes. An alternative theory would be the one most compatible with the thought processes of the user, that other individual who functions as the audience for the emulation of the first individual's personality. This chapter develops principles linking text generated by selected individuals to the appropriate theories in their cases, and advocates a new synthesis between theory and methods that frankly has yet to be developed. It concludes, however, with a rather existentialist meditation on translation, that calls into question our ultimate goals, and thus renders problematic the technical means to achieve them.

The convergence of all the language-related sciences and technologies, as a major first step toward taking them all to a much higher level of sophistication, will take many years. Yet there is a form of personality capture and emulation that can already be achieved at high quality, and has already been practiced for perhaps four thousand years: writing and reading. When we read a book aloud, we become the author speaking the author's words. When we read a book silently, we make in our mind the thoughts that were the author's, to the extent that we have a good image of the person who was the author, and the goals the author had in writing that particular work. Today's NLP cannot make full sense of sentences like these: "I trust you because I know that you are not cursed with the terrible trait of absolute and unswerving truthfulness, that you could lie like one of your own Virginia gentlemen if a lie would save others from sorrow or suffering." [1] "Der Mensch is ein Seil, geknüpft zwischen Thier und Übermensch,—ein Seil über einem Abgrunde." [2] Yet a properly prepared human can understand such words, and in projects such as online blogs we are beginning to preserve the words of many people who are not professional authors.

7.1 Historical Linguistics

A vast recent literature provides the reader with both introductions and detailed explorations of contemporary computerized natural language processing. Yet some of the oldest work is most suitable as the basis for future innovations. As it happens, my uncle, Angus McIntosh, was a linguistics specialist at Bletchley Park, the British decryption center during the Second World War, where Bombe and Colossus computers cracked German codes. He later became a professor at the University of Edinburgh, working in historical linguistics, with an emphasis on Middle English and Scots. This was a team effort, and visits to Edinburgh during its heyday gave me some perspective on his group's evolving work.

Central to the rigorous methodology was conducting a linguistic survey, either through interviews of living people or through systematic perusal of written manuscripts. I remember seeing a vast card catalog of Scots—specifically several cards representing the Scots word for *spider*, as used by several different individuals. The famous fable of Robert the Bruce learning persistence for the struggle of Scottish independence from watching a spider struggle to complete its web provided this word with intellectual significance. Just now, I entered spider into an online English-Scots dictionary and got: *attercap*, *speeder*, *spinner*, *wabster*, and *weaver* [3]. Clearly, some of those five words express different conceptions of what a spider is or does, rather than being identical concepts differing only in their dialect. Looking *wabster* up in the online reference work, *A Linguistic Atlas of Older Scots*, I find that an alternative early spelling was *webster* [4]. This naturally brings to mind the spider's web, but also a pun that might be a name origin: *Webster's Dictionary*. The words used by individuals differed also in exact spelling and pronunciation, depending upon where they lived and personal variables as well. Even today, after spelling was standardized, pronunciation varies, but so, too, do associations, such as the one that evokes the image of what kind of web-based network of words would constitute an online spider dictionary.

Angus's magnum opus was *A Linguistic Atlas of Late Mediaeval English*, which took many years to create with M. L. Samuels and Michael Benskin as co-authors plus a team of junior scholars who went on to accomplish their own successes in later decades [5]. Published in 1986, this is a four-volume work, based on applying a linguistic questionnaire to a thousand English manuscripts that could be identified in terms of their geographic origin. The third volume is a set of maps, showing how a word or linguistic construction varied across England. A crucial scientific point to note is that the maps are all different, some very much so, because communication patterns vary by the sector of human life the words concern. Words relating to family relations may be determined very much by local culture, while words and word forms having to do with economic exchange could have a wider geographic distribution determined by trading patterns. Variations may also reflect sequences of historical events, that shaped different parts of language at different times in different places.

The *Atlas* documented geographic variations in the English language over the century prior to 1450, before London English set standards for the entire country, and variations were indeed rather extreme. Today, an updated version of the *Atlas* can be accessed online [6]. Item 113 in the questionnaire was *death*, as noun or adjective, and here are the many alternatives: dead, deade, ded, dedd, dede, deed, deede, deeth, deeþ, deeþe, deethe, deȝtt, deey, deght, degth, det, detȝ, deth, deþ, dethe, deþe, dethȝ, dey, deye, deyþ, deythe, and died. The questionnaire has five additional categories: for the verb *to die*, the infinitive form of that verb, and three forms of the past *died*.

The standardization of English reduced but did not eliminate regional differences, and it is still the case that language varies across geography, social groups and networks, topics of discourse, and individuals. The variations can be exceedingly complex. On the one hand, this provides much individual variation that can be used for capturing one person's style and vocabulary. On the other hand, this complexity may prevent us from developing simple methods of capture.

For example, it is a gross oversimplification to speak of *a language* or *a dialect of a language*. When Margaret Laing and Roger Lass undertook the successor project to create *A Linguistic Atlas of Early Middle English*, covering the period 1150–1325 they recognized: "There are no such things as dialects. Or rather, 'a dialect' does not exist as a discrete entity. Attempts to delimit a dialect by topographical, political or administrative boundaries ignore the obvious fact that within any such boundaries there will be variation for some features, while other variants will cross the borders" [7, 8]. Similarly, a person's use of language will vary by topic area, yet many words and constructions will cross topic boundaries.

Even the term *historical linguistics* can have different meanings. One is to study the history of language, and another is to use language variations to study other aspects of history. The classic example, and the one most relevant here, is the 1963 study by Frederick Mosteller and David Wallace, using statistical methods based on word counts to identify the author of a dozen of the 77 Federalist Papers that played such an important role in the emergence of the United States as a nation [9]. Published anonymously under the pseudonym Publius in the period 1787–1788, they are prominently discussed and published today on the Web, and Google Books offers the full text of an 1802 edition, the introduction to which struggles with the issue of attributing authorship. Alexander Hamilton was known to have written the largest number, James Madison somewhat fewer, and John Jay wrote five.

Hamilton was killed in a duel 2 years after that edition was published, so we do not have written reminiscences from him later in life, although others claimed to know what he said about authorship. Many years later, Madison asserted his own claims to authorship, and a controversy ensued for many decades about the 12 disputed papers. The general method used by Mosteller and Wallace was to count the frequency of common words in essays known to have been written by either Hamilton or Madison, and compare with the frequencies in the disputed dozen. Note that these two men would have pronounced the words somewhat differently, although we do not have recordings of their speech to allow us to know exactly how, but they used standard spelling and dictionary meanings, so historical dialectology like the atlases of Middle English are no help here. But they differed in the use of some common words, that reflected cognitive differences in the ways they organized concepts.

Mosteller and Wallace focused on words like *by*, *from*, and *to*, finding for example that Madison used *by* more often than Hamilton did, while Hamilton was more likely to use *to*. The biggest difference was for the word *upon*, used far more frequently by Hamilton. Since the goal was to identify authorship, words like these that expressed very abstract relations between concepts proved to be the best markers. Words naming concepts, such as *war*, were less useful for this purpose, because they differed according to the topic of the particular essay. Mosteller and Wallace called these *contextual* words, which may be a better term than *topical*, because the social context of the communication can be as important as the topic, and contextual implies both. The methodology employed many words as markers to provide the maximum statistical reliability, and the final verdict was that Madison had written the dozen disputed Federalist Papers.

Truth to tell, settling cases of disputed authorship is a very rare task for historians and scientists who study language. Shortly after Mosteller and Wallace published, Rokeach, Homant and Penner tried a very different method, having trained coders to judge the values expressed in anonymized essays by Hamilton and Madison, arriving at the same result [10]. The agreement between these two studies, using very different methods, suggests that it is indeed possible to distill rather fundamental aspects of personality from written texts. Exactly how remains unclear even today.

NLP research on document classification has gone in a very different direction, classifying in terms of topic not author. This is a key feature of website search engines, which use text in combination with in-coming web links to recommend pages in response to the user's search terms. A decade or two ago, it was thought that document classification could be done entirely automatically, and perhaps that will be possible in future, but currently the best methods combine human judgment with machine NLP. For example, one set of documents can be classified by humans, and then a computer can use the results of human work as the basis for classifying additional documents [11–14]. Some of the methodological developments have concerned the exact algorithms to be used in the automatic part of the work, and on rare occasions researchers even return to the Federalist Papers because they provide a standard corpus for comparison of different methods [15].

In the general period when Mosteller, Rokeach and their colleagues were working, there was great interest in theory-based analysis of language by means of computers. I do not mean to suggest that no work of that kind has been done since, but is has been overshadowed by atheoretical NLP work, for example brute-force computation of *n-grams*, word combinations of various lengths that often are treated as units, appear at various frequencies in speech or written text, and may offer more insight into meaning than individual words do [16, 17]. Thus, for present purposes it seems most fruitful to return to the theory-rich origins of NLP, half a century ago, with the hope that other authors in future can attempt to pull together all the subsequent and frankly fragmented work, and make their own contributions to personality capture and emulation via written text.

7.2   General Inquirer

When I entered graduate school at Harvard in 1971, a side room of the floor of William James Hall devoted to computation was filled with boxes of IBM cards, a computer memory storage medium of that period, punched with the rhetoric of the 1968 U.S. presidential election campaign. I soon came to know Philip Stone and was impressed by a computer program he had developed, called General Inquirer, for the theory-based analysis of written text, based on word counts [18]. One of the earliest studies was an experiment to see how well the system could classify scientific documents about computers, compared with human coders, and the entire project can be conceptualized as a pioneer form of human-centered computing [19]. Lest this seem too antique to be relevant today, I should mention that as recently as 2002, Elvin Lim published research about political rhetoric using General Inquirer in *Presidential Studies Quarterly* [20]. Furthermore, one application identified early in the history of this tool is especially relevant to this book, computer-coding of free responses to questionnaire items [21]. The methodology is timeless, counting the usage of words that fit into many different categories, according to established theories in social and behavioral science.

From the very beginning, Stone and his collaborators were aware of the problem of word-sense disambiguation, the challenge of dealing with the fact that many words have multiple meanings, *run* being the worst offender [22]. But even before the development of the huge NLP lexicons and corpora of today, they had the simple solution of using many words, which various theories placed together in a category, and developing a system that could handle very large texts such as entire books. Now, in 2013, I can use the current version of General Inquirer to analyze authors as well as texts, and begin with four texts that can illustrate the general principles: The U.S. Declaration of Independence, a snarky essay by Mark Twain about the Pilgrim Fathers, the optimistic girl's novel, *Rebecca of Sunnybrook Farm*, and Sigmund Freud's popularization of Psychoanalysis, *Dream Psychology* [23–25].

The first two of these are short, each less than 2,000 words, while the other two are long, and long documents generally do a better job of representing the author than short ones. The authorship of the first two is somewhat complex, because Jefferson was writing on behalf of a group, and "Mark Twain"was not the real name of the person. The popularity of *Rebecca* testifies to the fact it expressed the hopes of young girls a century ago, as well as the personality of the novelist. A standard conundrum for psychologists is the extent to which Freud's ideas reflect his own personality, versus the personalities of his patients, but his book was clearly intended as advertising and thus to be attractive to neurotics more generally.

A website devoted to General Inquirer is hosted by Harvard University, having a URL including "wjh" for William James Hall, and beginning with a memorial sentence: "We mourn the loss of Philip Stone who died on January 31st, 2006, and we dedicate the continuation of this site to his memory." [26] I registered as a researcher with the site, which gave me access to a complete version of General Inquirer, to which I could upload any text, and used the standard dictionary to count the number of words in fully 184 categories, some of which were subsets of others, but all of which covered a range of social psychology concepts. What follows should be considered not as deep scientific research, but as another pilot study intended to show a direction by which advances in NLP could contribute to personality capture and emulation. The eight texts considered here, plus the two additional ones in the following section, were all available online, thus emphasizing the ways in which information technologies converge to facilitate personality capture.

Table 7.1 connects General Inquirer to earlier chapters of this book, because it begins by reporting results for words assigned to the dimensions of the Semantic Differential: positive (1,045 words), negative (1,160), strong (1,902), weak (755), active (2,045), and passive (911) [27]. In Chap. 3 we used a version of the semantic differential employing just 12 pairs of words, four for each of these categories, but over the years many social scientists have used different word sets suitable for their particular research. For example, Fred Fiedler developed a new set of 24 pairs of terms for a study of relations between leaders and groups, such as: cooperative-uncooperative, energetic-tired, and practical-impractical [28].

In comparing the categories in Table 7.1, we must remember that the word lists contain different numbers of items, and they may not perfectly represent equal frequency of use in the entire corpus of the English language. Yet differences across the four documents are striking. The Declaration of Independence has both more positive and more negative words than the others. It has more strong, active words, and fewer weak, passive works. This reflects its power as a political document.

In traditional paper-based questionnaires, the semantic differential was presented as equal numbers of antonym pairs reflecting the three primary dimensions of evaluation (good versus bad), potency (strong versus weak) and activity (active versus passive). Here I calculated ratios, for example getting an evaluation score of 1.4 for the Declaration of Independence by dividing its positive score by its negative score (6.4 %/4.5 % = 1.4). This is lower than the evaluation ratios for the three other documents, not because the Declaration is unevaluative, but because it strongly contrasts good with evil. Thus we may often wish to analyze data in multiple ways, to find different but often equally valid lessons from it. Social statisticians often compare not merely averages between two populations, but variance as well. In terms of political ideology, for example, the United States may have become more polarized, quite apart from any shift in the center of the spectrum.

The 16 other word categories in Table 7.1 were selected to illustrate analytical principles. Affiliation (557 words), Hostile (833), Power (689), and Submission (284) are subsets, respectively, of Positive, Negative, Strong, and Weak. Affiliation reflects social affiliation or interpersonal supportiveness, while Hostile reflects a concern with hostility or aggressiveness—if not exactly expressing hostility on the part of the author. Similarly, Power and Submission express concerns about control or authority versus dependence, vulnerability, or withdrawal. The Active-Passive dimension of the Semantic Differential does not have vocabulary subsets.

The antonyms Virtue (719 words) and Vice (685) belong to a cluster of emotional categories, the others including words for example about pleasure and pain. The General Inquirer website separates out from emotion the Overstated (696 words)

Table 7.1 General inquirer analysis of four highly varied texts

	Declaration of independence	"Plymouth Rock and the Pilgrims"	Rebecca of Sunnybrook farm	Dream psychology
Author	Thomas Jefferson et al.	"Mark Twain" (Samuel Clemens)	Kate Douglas Wiggin	Sigmund Freud
Words	1,322	1,740	73,530	51,750
Semantic Differential				
Positive	6.4%	5.3%	4.4%	3.9%
Negative	4.5%	2.2%	2.1%	2.6%
Strong	15.4%	6.3%	5.7%	7.5%
Weak	1.6%	2.5%	2.4%	2.4%
Active	10.0%	7.5%	7.7%	8.8%
Passive	3.7%	4.0%	4.4%	8.2%
Evaluation	1.4	2.4	2.1	1.5
Potency	9.7	2.5	2.4	3.2
Activity	2.7	1.9	1.7	1.1
A Few of the Many Other Scales				
Affiliation	4.7%	2.1%	2.1%	1.8%
Hostile	3.6%	1.1%	0.7%	1.0%
Power	8.5%	1.8%	1.1%	2.0%
Submission	2.1%	1.0%	0.7%	0.9%
Virtue	3.9%	2.7%	2.2%	1.8%
Vice	1.7%	1.1%	0.9%	1.0%
Overstated	5.6%	3.9%	4.1%	4.8%
Understated	0.6%	2.5%	2.9%	2.5%
Doctrine	2.5%	0.9%	0.2%	0.4%
Economic	1.1%	0.7%	0.9%	0.5%
Legal	2.8%	0.2%	0.1%	0.2%
Political	4.8%	1.0%	0.2%	0.3%
Religious	0.4%	0.7%	0.4%	0.0%
Collectivities	4.4%	1.6%	0.4%	0.3%
Self	0.2%	4.3%	2.4%	1.8%
Time consciousness	1.9%	2.3%	3.6%	2.8%

and Understated (319) categories, representing emphasis or de-emphasis "in realms of speed, frequency, causality, inclusiveness, quantity or quasi-quantity, accuracy, validity, scope, size, clarity, exceptionality, intensity, likelihood, certainty and extremity." Three of the four publications use somewhat more overstatement than understatement, but of course authors must sell themselves to their readers, and the categories included more than twice as many overstated as understated words. As we might expect, the Declaration of Independence is much more overstated than the others, and far less understated. Looking back at Power and Submission we see the Declaration is more extreme than the others on both counts, but its references to submission words is only to reject them, which is more directly expressed by its low understatement score.

Doctrine (217 words) concerns "organized systems of belief or knowledge, including those of applied knowledge, mystical beliefs, and arts that academics study." Economic (510 words) concerns "economic, commercial, industrial, or business orientation, including roles, collectivities, acts, abstract ideas, and symbols, including references to money [and] names of common commodities in business." Legal (192 words), Political (263), and Religious (103) collect words relating to those societal institutions. The religion scores illustrate an important point. We generally think of numbers below one percent as insignificant, but even in a religious discussion many of the words will be about issues of mundane human life, and not refer to the supernatural or ecclesiastical practices. Twain was writing about Pilgrims, and Freud rejected religion, so Twain's higher religion score is meaningful, despite being a small number.

Collectivities (191 words) was one of the categories often used to disambiguate word meaning in General Inquirer research that focused on other categories, but also measured a concern with human groups. Self, with only 7 words, may seem insignificant as a category, yet these were important words like *I* and *me* that refer to the first person singular, and strongly indicate the expressive standpoint of an author. Time consciousness (273 words) describes when events take place, and how quickly. As we saw in the case of the research by Mosteller and Wallace, abstractions like time consciousness may reflect distinctive characteristics of a person, as may also a focus on groups versus oneself.

Having gained some familiarity with the category system used by General Inquirer, we can gain further insight into its personality capture potential by analyzing four books, two of which are autobiographies, and two of which are philosophical novels. The Wikipedia article on Clifford Whittingham Beers explains why his case would be interesting for personality capture: "In 1900 he was first confined to a private mental institution for depression and paranoia. He would later be confined to another private hospital as well as a state institution. During these periods he experienced and witnessed serious maltreatment at the hands of the staff. After the publication of *A Mind That Found Itself* (1908), an autobiographical account of his hospitalization and the abuses he suffered during it, he gained the support of the medical profession and others in the work to reform the treatment of the mentally ill." [29, 30] Thus, he not only had an unusual personality that might provide a benchmark for capture technology, but also criticized the conventional treatment of people like himself, thus bringing into question the traditional scheme for understanding human variation. Dave Ranney lacks a Wikipedia page, but was a prominent spokesman for the New York City Mission Society a century ago. He had been an alcoholic street bum much of his life, but restored to health and productivity by using his disreputable past as a resource for helping other people [31].

Arguably, *A Princess of Mars* by Edgar Rice Burroughs was the first really influential American science fiction novel, but it also can be conceptualized as a philosophical treatise, something that academic philosophers and literature professors have never considered doing [32]. Some key works of popular art express intellectual perspectives that are valid and interesting, but stand outside the scope of academic schools of thought, so this is one prime example of that possibility.

Furthermore, once we conceptualize *A Princess of Mars* this way, we are ready to consider the expressions of any person in philosophical terms. *Thus Spake Zarathustra* by Friedrich Nietzsche is structured like a novel, despite pretending to be a religious scripture, and although Nietzsche is recognized as a major philosopher, it is precisely because he bucked the trends in formal academic philosophy [33]. Burroughs wrote in the first person, from the standpoint of his main character, while Nietzsche wrote in the third person yet clearly identified with his character. So both novels have autobiographic qualities, so long as we understand they describe deep principles of the individual's thoughts and values, rather than external events.

In Table 7.2, we see that Ranney's inspirational book uses comparatively more positive than negative language, but less either strong or weak language, than the other three, and more religious terminology. Both Ranney and Beers emphasize self more than Burroughs and Nietzsche, given that they were writing autobiographies, but only Mark Twain in Table 7.1 does so even to the extent of Burroughs and Nietzsche. It is worth noting that Nietzsche's book was analyzed in an English translation by Thomas Common, and later we will consider issues raised by translation. The fact that Common's title uses the archaic form *spake* rather than *spoke*, reflects the fact that the book was written to some extent as a radical addition to the bible, and Common worked in a period when the archaic King James version of the bible reigned supreme in English-speaking Protestant churches. We can respect the attempt of the General Inquirer to provide solid measurement of standard social-psychological theories, but as the fluidity in the scales used by the Semantic Differential suggests, we must constantly adjust to changes in the community of discourse for which a written work was intended.

How would the General Inquirer scores for a text written by a particular person be used for personality emulation? Many complex answers may be found in future, but here is a simple one that can serve as a placeholder. Suppose we have the scores for writings by Edgar Rice Burroughs and want to create a more popular translation into American English of *Also Sprach Zarathustra*, the German original of Nietzsche's book. We first either take one of the several existing English translations, or use NLP to create a new one. We run it through General Inquirer, and get all 184 scores. Then we write a computer program that will iteratively substitute alternate words—synonyms or near matches—each time selecting a substitute that gets the scores closer to the ones derived from Burroughs. Eventually, no more substitutions are possible, given whatever algorithm we have decided to use, and we publish the result. Then human reviewers can tell us whether only the style was changed to be closer to that of Burroughs, or whether the ideas have also changed.

7.3   Other Lexicon Approaches

A recent alternative to General Inquirer is Linguistic Inquiry and Word Count, which incorporates a very different set of categories believed to have psychological significance, from pronouns to emotions [34]. Research using this system indicates

Table 7.2 General inquirer analysis of four psychological-philosophical books

	A Mind That Found Itself	Thirty Years on the Bowery	A Princess of Mars	Thus Spake Zarathustra
Author	Clifford Whitting-ham Beers	Dave Ranney	Edgar Rice Burroughs	Friedrich Nietzsche
Words	64,362	35,282	67,383	90,144
Semantic differential				
Positive	4.7%	3.8%	3.5%	5.2%
Negative	3.3%	1.9%	3.2%	3.0%
Strong	8.1%	5.5%	8.1%	6.2%
Weak	2.6%	1.8%	2.6%	2.5%
Active	9.3%	9.6%	8.6%	5.6%
Passive	5.8%	4.0%	4.7%	4.8%
Evaluation	1.4	2.0	1.1	1.7
Potency	3.1	3.1	3.1	2.5
Activity	1.6	2.4	1.8	1.2
A few of the many other scales				
Affiliation	1.7%	2.5%	1.8%	1.9%
Hostile	1.7%	0.8%	1.9%	1.5%
Power	2.1%	1.2%	1.7%	1.5%
Submission	1.6%	0.7%	0.7%	0.8%
Virtue	2.2%	1.6%	1.6%	2.4%
Vice	1.5%	0.8%	1.1%	1.5%
Overstatement	4.9%	3.3%	4.5%	5.2%
Understatement	2.8%	2.6%	2.7%	1.8%
Doctrine	0.4%	0.1%	0.2%	0.4%
Economic	1.1%	1.2%	0.5%	0.4%
Legal	0.5%	0.4%	0.3%	0.2%
Political	0.5%	0.1%	0.4%	0.3%
Religious	0.2%	1.3%	0.1%	1.2%
Collectivities	0.5%	0.4%	0.6%	0.3%
Self	7.6%	7.8%	5.6%	4.4%
Time consciousness	4.7%	4.4%	3.6%	3.4%

a significant degree of stability across text topic areas, within individual people, implying stability in personality and this method's reliability of measuring it [35]. Also, the results of this word-count approach can be integrated with concepts like the Big Five personality dimensions, as in one study that did so with respect to extraversion, or even unusual dimensions such as autism [36, 37]. However, NLP methods run into difficulty in analyzing naturally occurring language that has not been edited for grammar, clarity, and spelling, even in online communications where the language is in the form of text [38].

To explore the technical challenges in using word lists to analyze printed documents, and to suggest a direction that NLP-based personality emulation might take, I wrote a simple computer program to scan through a long text for all the occasions when one of the 1,600 adjectives from the Self program are used. Recall that this was an extension from the Semantic Differential methodology, and the adjectives belonged to 800 antonym pairs, but were presented separately to the user, who rated each one in terms of how good it was for a person to possess the given quality, and how much the user possessed that quality.

I ran the six books described in the previous section through this adjective tabulation software, plus two books I had written myself, both of which were currently available online. One, titled *Sister Ohio*, was a biography I had written about my great-grandmother, Lucy Seaman Bainbridge, who herself had written several books, all about her life experiences and one being explicitly an autobiography. She had toured Asian missions of U.S. Protestant denominations in 1879–1880 with her husband and son, and in the period 1891–1906 had been director of the Woman's Branch of the New York City Mission Society. This book was published only online, in the digital library of the Association of Religion Data Archives. The other book was a sociological study of how Harvard students conceptualized astronautics, *Goals in Space*, based on questionnaires and originally published by a university press, but when the rights were returned to me I put it on my personal website.

Adding these two online books written by myself illustrates how many people in the future may post extensive writings of their own, which NLP can then exploit for secondary purposes including capture and emulation. In developing the statistical analysis modules of the Self software I had naturally needed a set of test data, so I had answered the 3,200 questions myself, and here will use my own data in a very modest pilot study. This has the effect of emulating how one person would have read the books, reacting to the author's words in terms of the reader's values. My goal here is to identify issues and begin to frame hypotheses and analytical methods, not to come to any firm scientific conclusions, which would be the job of later research using diverse and perhaps population-representative data. Table 7.3 shows a few results.

Words on the list of 1,600 adjectives appear 3,471 times in *Rebecca of Sunnybrook Farm*, constituting about 4.7% of that text. *Sister Ohio* contains 112,018 words and uses adjectives from the list 4,548 times; the corresponding numbers for *Goals in Space* are 77,663 and 3,937. It is worth noting that the adjectives appear with about the same frequency across most of the books, even in the case of the two by Freud and Nietzsche, which are translations into English from German. If we were doing a deep comparison of these books, we would note that the people who were the topics of *30 Years on the Bowery* and *Sister Ohio* worked for the same Society, and thus their books overlap considerably as to perspective and setting, whereas Nietzsche is considered a precursor of Freud in the history of depth psychology. *Rebecca of Sunny Brook Farm* was a novel for girls, whereas *A Princess of Mars* was a novel for boys, both written a little over a century ago.

The Good and Much scores were calculated as in the following example. The word *scientific* was used fully 113 times in my book, *Goals in Space*, which after all employed the methods of social science to examine a science-based technology. In Self, I had rated *scientific* at 7 on the 8-step bad-good scale, and 8 on the little-much scale that expressed how much I believed the word applied to myself. These ratings express personal values and self-conception, not of course objective judgments. The over-all Good and Much scores were weighted on the basis of how often a word was

Table 7.3 Scan of eight books for the 1,600 self adjectives

Book	Fraction	Good	Much	Most common
Rebecca of Sunnybrook Farm	4.7%	4.97	4.77	Little (191), just (115), old (93), better (68), right (67), young (59), poor (48), white (48), even (46), certain (38), full (36), small (36)
Dream Psychology	4.7%	5.03	4.75	Unconscious (118), sexual (74), just (56), even (54), found (52), certain (47), little (44), patient (41), conscious (39), repressed (32), infantile (31), young (26)
A Mind That Found Itself	4.4%	5.00	4.72	Even (86), patient (64), certain (59), found (57), little (56), violent (43), insane (42), sane (40), able (37), best (33), right (31), just (30)
Thirty Years on the Bowery	3.3%	5.06	4.83	Little (84), old (56), right (55), just (53), young (41), better (34), hard (28), poor (27), best (24), found (24), used (21), even (18)
A Princess of Mars	4.4%	4.76	4.53	Little (120), green (103), dead (76), even (65), found (61), strange (58), red (56), behind (55), just (49), seen (48), wild (42), mighty (40)
Thus Spake Zarathustra	4.5%	4.88	4.76	Even (224), old (156), little (91), just (87), best (85), small (70), light (64), found (62), better (60), longing (50), deep (48), human (48)
Sister Ohio	4.1%	5.07	4.78	Little (132); just (99); old (80); found (73); young (71); even (62); poor (57); religious (53); small (52); right (50); large (48); dead (46)
Goals in Space	5.1%	5.56	5.06	Human (172), average (134), scientific (113), social (113), better (94), general (79), important (79), future (74), even (73), different (62), public (58), technical (52)

used: $113 \times 7 = 791$ good points and $113 \times 89 = 904$ much points. This was done for all the adjectives, and then the scores for a scale were added, and divided by the total adjective count of 3,937 to get the mean. Note in Table 7.3 that the book I not only wrote, but in which I explored the topic that had been the focus of my earlier doctoral dissertation, has the highest mean Good and Much scores of the eight books.

Two factors limit the extent to which over-all scores like this can represent the personality of an author or reader. First, as we noted in the case of the low Evaluation score for the Declaration of Independence, a writing may emphasize both ends of a semantic dimension, such that perhaps the variance would be a better measure than the mean. This is another way of saying that topics matter, as well as the ways in which authors express themselves. But it also implies that average scores represent a lowest common denominator, reflected in the fact they do not differ much across the books. Close examination of subsets of antonym pairs can be useful in dealing with this problem. For example, since one of the measurement scales in

Self is bad-good, these two words could not be included as stimuli. However, two antonym pairs related to good-bad are among the 800 pairs, the comparative better-worse and superlative best-worst, and they can be used to measure the extent to which the author or reader prefers somewhat more extreme evaluations. In *Rebecca* the word better was used fully 68 times, and best was used 35 times, so just missed being included in Table 7.3. *Better* was common in half the books, suggesting their authors tended to think in terms of comparative goodness.

The second issue is the classic problem of word sense disambiguation. The last column of Table 7.3 lists the dozen most common adjectives from the set of 1,600 in each book, with the number of times it was used in parentheses. Note that the books differ significantly in word use frequency. Freud used *unconscious* 118 times, and *sexual* 74 times. The frequent usage by Burroughs of *green* (103) and *red* (56) reflects the fact he imagined two competing races on Mars, the Green Martians and the Red Martians. But some of the words common in several books were typically not used as adjectives to describe a person: *even, just,* and *found*. Ranney's title uses *found* as a verb, and as I scan through the texts using my word processor's search function, I find many meanings, including not only *located* or *discovered*, but also *to establish* and *perceived as*. The Self software included the antonym pair *lost-found*, and the user is instructed to consider all the stimuli as adjectives describing a person, so the word meanings are disambiguated from the start.

Nietzsche was the only one of the authors to include *light* among the most-used adjectives. If we are to believe the Online Etymology Dictionary, the English word *light* is actually three quite different words that fused in their spelling and pronunciation, with three different meanings: not heavy, brilliant, and more rarely to touch down in the sense of to *alight* [39]. English is a Germanic language, and modern German clearly distinguishes *Licht* (illumination from a lamp) versus *leicht* (easy or the opposite of heavy). Scanning the German original reveals that *Licht* was used 84 times, and *leicht* was used 35 times but with a variety of meanings and in several forms. All words are metaphors, and the German blurring of easy with not heavy for *leicht* is comparable to English meanings of *ease* from the French, where comfort is invoked, more than simplicity. Granting that word sense disambiguation is a continuing problem, that contemporary NLP tends to handle it with mixed success by looking at the use of a word in context, we can imagine how we can go from whatever ever level of capture success we can achieve, to emulation at that level.

7.4   Author Emulation

Among the more intriguing ideas, that may be only a short distance outside our current technical grasp, is to write a new novel in the style of a deceased novelist, by applying automatic techniques to the existing corpus of that author's works. This can actually be used to emulate the reader, as well as the author, if we start with the words favored by a particular reader, and enlist the reader as a collaborator in the emulation process, perhaps using software like Self or other methods to be described here.

It is not uncommon for a trade book publisher to recruit a new writer to extend a profitable series, and the *Oz* books are a remarkable example. In 1900, L. Frank Baum published *The Wonderful Wizard of Oz*, and continued to write novels about this fantasy realm until his death in 1919. At that point, his publisher recruited Ruth Plumly Thompson to continue the series, followed by John R. Neill who had illustrated many of the books and thus was quite familiar with the mythos, then Jack Snow, Rachel R. Cosgrove, Eloise Jarvis McGraw and Lauren Lynn McGraw. The Wikipedia page that lists these and many other Oz-related works says: "Ruth Plumly Thompson's style was markedly different from Baum's. Her tales harked back to more traditional fairy tales. She often included a small kingdom, with a prince or princess who saves his or her kingdom and regains the throne or saves Oz from invasion. Thompson even respelled Baum's respelling 'Nome' as the more traditional 'Gnome.'" "Illustrator John R. Neill's vision of Oz is more manic than Thompson or Baum's. Houses often get up and do battle, and everything can be alive. His entries take Oz's color scheme (blue for Munchkin Country, red for Quadling Country, etc.) to an extreme, extending it to sky and skin colors." [40] Thus, Baum's successors had their own distinctive styles while adhering to many of the details of the world he created, and they wrote under their own names.

The Nancy Drew mysteries, popular among early-teen girls, were written by a woman named Carolyn Keene. Except that Carolyn Keene was herself a fictional character, and the name was a house pseudonym for a team effort, outlined in all its complexity on the Wikipedia page for the series [41]. *The Secret of the Old Clock*, the first of the series published in 1930, was outlined by Edward Stratemeyer who was also responsible for these popular series: The Rover Boys, The Bobbsey Twins, Tom Swift, and The Hardy Boys. Mildred Augustine Wirt Benson then did most of the writing for *The Secret of the Old Clock*, as she did for many others in the series. Edward Stratemeyer functioned as her editor, and his daughter, Harriet Stratemeyer Adams revised the novel years later. In the genres of popular fiction, it is not uncommon for two or more authors to contribute to a series, whether their identities are clearly separated as with the Oz books, or completely tangled up as with Nancy Drew. The division of labor between an author and an editor varies greatly, and we could cite many examples in which a second author finishes a work that a first author left unfinished at death. There are many variants of posthumous collaboration, as for example one of the most popular orchestral works is *Pictures at an Exhibition*, written for piano by Modest Mussorgsky and orchestrated by an equally fine composer, Maurice Ravel.

Recently, a number of computer scientists have been exploring techniques for assembling narrative structures semi-automatically, in what many call interactive drama [42–47]. The primary sources of this work seems to be the Georgia Institute of Technology, which has long been a center for serious research on computer games, often emphasizing role-playing. The idea is that the story would unfold as the user experiences it, and an artificial intelligence system might work out the implications of the user's decisions, in a drama that never turns out exactly the same, no matter how many times it is performed. Here I will not delve deeply into that technical literature, but merely note that some rather solid methodology already exists, if we can decide how author emulation might be used to create new works of literature.

To illustrate what issues we must deal with in emulating an author's work, and the range of resources authors may have provided for us, I will use the example of Edgar Rice Burroughs, specifically his Mars novels which were directly imitated by both *Flash Gordon* and *Star Wars*. Beginning in 1911 with *A Princess of Mars*, Burroughs wrote ten novels about an imaginary, inhabited version of the planet Mars, which he called *Barsoom* [48]. An additional story, "John Carter and the Giant of Mars," was published under his name but is believed to have been written by his son, John Coleman Burroughs. The fact that full texts of many of the novels are available online, makes this a convenient example.

One technically feasible idea would be to take a novel, such as *A Princess of Mars*, and make a list of all character names and all nouns and verbs that seemed distinctive to the cultural and physical setting. A software program could be written so that a reader could personalize the novel before reading it on a tablet computer. The fourth novel in the series, *Thuvia, Maid of Mars*, has a glossary in the back, and the computer interface could allow the reader to change each of the terms before reading the novel. For example, here are the brief entries for four characters, for which readers could substitute names of real people they actually knew, or exotic-sounding names they invented on the spot:

> Dejah Thoris. Princess of Helium.
> Sarkoja. A green Martian woman.
> Sola. A young green Martian woman.
> Zad. Tharkian warrior.

With some justice, it can be said that George Lucas renamed Barsoom to Tatooine in his *Star Wars* stories, and Princess Dejah Thoris became Princess Leia Organa. Imagine a female reader switching all the genders, replacing physical weapons with magic, and moving the setting to Oz:

> Hajed Siroht. Prince of Emerald City.
> Sarkoj. A blue Munchkin man.
> Sol. An old blue Munchkin man.
> Zada. Wicked witch of the West.

Sword might become *wand*, and *shield* could become *healing spell*. Then names, nouns and verbs would automatically switch, to create a novel 90 % identical to *A Princess of Mars* but titled *A Prince of Oz*. Since the novel is out of copyright, doing do would be legal, but artistically suspect. To be really successful, emulation of an author must be carried out on multiple levels simultaneously, from the grammar and lexicography of individual sentences, through the style and structure of distinct scenes, up to the way that chapters fit together to make the entire work. Burroughs followed a number of formulas to structure his novels, for example having some catastrophe separate the protagonists into two groups that wander thorough exotic territories in search of each other, alternating chapters between the two groups, and ending each chapter with a cliffhanger that would not be resolved until a chapter about the other group had been read. Essentially all of his novels were adventure travelogues, punctuated with many scenes in which the protagonist interacts with an animal or intelligent creature, sometimes violently, but also in a wide range of other ways.

Burroughs died in 1950, but a living author could collaborate in the capture and emulation process. Suppose you wrote an electronic detective novel called *The Tenure Track Killings*, in which assistant professors at a college were being murdered on the eve of their ascent to the "immortality" of associate professor status. Readers could select from a list of 2,000 colleges, perhaps choosing their alma maters, and the software would automatically adjust the settings and many other details, after checking the college's website and the Wikipedia article about it. The murder of a sociologist at the University of Washington would take place in Savery Hall, but the corresponding murder at Harvard would be in William James Hall. A love tryst at Oberlin College would play out in the Arboretum, and an attempt to escape George Mason University would be on the CUE Bus. We cannot now guess how far, technically or culturally, this kind of *localization* might go, for example perhaps using the names of real public figures at the college for characters who play innocent auxiliary roles, such as being an eyewitness to a crime or welcoming the detective to the campus. Localized electronic books would be a kind of intelligent agent that served as progeny for their authors.

7.5 Thus Spoke Nietzsche

The philologist and philosopher who most influentially asserted that language and wisdom must be understood in terms of transcendent poetry, was Friedrich Wilhelm Nietzsche. In many respects the opposite of a reductionist, he at times suggested that human thought could best be expressed through music, rather than words. His short poem, called "Zarathustra's Roundelay" by Wikipedia, was set to music in the *Third Symphony* by Gustav Mahler and *The Mass of Life by Frederick Delius*, but perhaps the best setting is the opening section of the Zarathustra tone poem by Richard Strauss, which has no words at all. The first two lines are a powerful challenge to anyone who aspires to know the truth:

Friedrich Nietzsche:
Oh Mensch! Gieb Acht!
Was spricht die tiefe Mitternacht?

This could be taken as the challenge that motivated Sigmund Freud, and all the subsequent depth psychologists [49]. Yes, what do these words mean? They mean that meaning is mysterious. Perhaps they trigger an infinite regress, asserting that beneath any one interpretation lurks another very different one. Wikipedia offers fully five alternative translations: [50]

Thomas Common:
O man! Take heed!
What saith deep midnight's voice indeed?

Alexander Tille:
O man! Take heed!
What saith deep midnight, indeed?
Walter Kaufmann:
O man, take care!
What does the deep midnight declare?
R. J. Hollingdale:
O man! Attend!
What does deep midnight's voice contend?
Adrian Del Caro:
Oh mankind, pray!
What does deep midnight have to say?

All the translators agree upon is *deep midnight*. However, an argument can be made for this version of the second line: "What does Deep Midnight say?" The next line is four words spoken by a person named Midnight: "ich schlief, ich schlief" (I slept, I slept). The *ch* in *ich* is softer than an English *ch*, and the line sounds like a whisper. Perhaps that is why Midnight *spricht* rather than *sagt*, *speaks* rather than *says*, to approximate the sound of whispering winds, rather than to convey an explicit concept. German capitalizes common nouns as well as proper nouns, so Mitternacht could be the name of a person, were it not for *die tiefe* (the deep) before it. Yet the third line personifies midnight, so it might be legitimate to move that personification into the second line. Nietzsche was a poet, as well as philologist and philosopher, so we could ask "Was spricht tiefer Nietzsche," using the voice of howling winds, and recognizing in the adjective that Nietzsche was masculine, while the German language makes midnight grammatically feminine.

Freud would have said, this Midnight represents the subconscious mind, that sleeps within and may be very different from our outward appearance, yet provides the fundamental basis for meaning. Perhaps each translator invested his own meaning into the poem, just as Nietzsche himself did. The English-language version of Wikipedia includes this summary in its page for Nietzsche:

…a German philosopher, poet, composer, cultural critic, and classical philologist. He wrote critical texts on religion, morality, contemporary culture, philosophy, and science, displaying a fondness for metaphor, irony, and aphorism. Nietzsche's key ideas include the "death of God", the Übermensch, the eternal recurrence, the Apollonian and Dionysian dichotomy, perspectivism, and the will to power. Central to his philosophy is the idea of "life-affirmation", which involves questioning of all doctrines that drain life's expansive energies, however socially prevalent and radical those views might be. His influence remains substantial within philosophy, notably in existentialism, post-modernism, and post-structuralism, as well as outside it. His radical questioning of the value and objectivity of truth has been the focus of extensive commentary, especially in the continental tradition. [51]

Given that Nietzsche wrote in German, it seems reasonable to give slightly greater emphasis to the German-language Wikipedia page for him, which includes this summary of his orientation:

Den jungen Nietzsche beeindruckte besonders die Philosophie Schopenhauers. Später wandte er sich von dessen Pessimismus ab und stellte eine radikale Lebensbejahung in den Mittelpunkt seiner Philosophie. Sein Werk enthält scharfe Kritiken an Moral, Religion, Philosophie, Wissenschaft und Formen der Kunst. Die zeitgenössische Kultur war in seinen Augen lebensschwächer als die des antiken Griechenland. Wiederkehrendes Ziel von Nietzsches Angriffen ist vor allem die christliche Moral sowie die christliche und platonistische Metaphysik. Er stellte den Wert der Wahrheit überhaupt in Frage und wurde damit Wegbereiter postmoderner philosophischer Ansätze. Auch Nietzsches Konzepte des „Übermenschen", des „Willens zur Macht" oder der „ewigen Wiederkunft" geben bis heute Anlass zu Deutungen und Diskussionen. [52].

These two paragraphs say very different things, for three reasons. First, and most obviously, they are written in different languages. Second, they were written from the standpoint of different cultures, most obvious in the first sentence of the German paragraph, which mentions the earlier German philosopher, Arthur Schopenhauer, who appears in the English-language page, but in a section on Nietzsche's early life, rather than highlighted in the initial summary. Third, the two Nietzsche pages were clearly written by different groups of people, because their organization is different and the text in one is not a translation of the text in the other. Accessing the German-language page in the Chrome browser, only a single click of the computer mouse is required to make Google Translate render the following English-language version of the above paragraph:

> The young Nietzsche was particularly impressed by the philosophy of Schopenhauer. Later he turned from his pessimism and turned from a radical affirmation of life in the center of his philosophy. His work contains sharp criticism of morality, religion, philosophy, science, and forms of art. The contemporary culture in his eyes live weaker than that of ancient Greece. Recurring target of Nietzsche's attack is especially Christian morality and the Christian and Platonic metaphysics. He put the value of the truth at all in question and became a pioneer of postmodern philosophical approaches. Nietzsche's concept of the "superman", the "will to power" or the "eternal return" to this day give rise to interpretations and discussions.

At the present time, no automatic translation of text is perfectly accurate. For example, in the second sentence, *turned from* is an odd translation of *stellte* which would better be rendered as *placed*. However much automatic translation advances, Nietzsche himself would have predicted that complete success would never be achieved. One reason was that he was a philologist, and thus understood very well the complex subtleties of human language. A second reason, stated in both Wikipedia quotations, is that he did not believe in the existence of truth and was a precursor of philosophical postmodernism.

"All men are liars." Well, if that is true, then perhaps this statement itself is a lie and not true. Is it true that Nietzsche did not believe in the existence of truth? Does a true statement expressed in one language become less than true when translated into another language? Does a true statement spoken by one person become less true when quoted exactly in the same words by another person? A statistician, of course, might propose a different theory of truth, in terms of measurable probabilities of error, and the confidence interval around an estimate. In mathematics, the controversial school of thought known as fuzzy logic claims to be very different from statistical thinking, yet blurs the concept of truth which was hard-and-fast in traditional symbolic logic [53]. The Polish linguistic philosopher Alfred Korzybski used to say, "The word is not the thing. The map is not the territory." [54] Yet in retrospect, both Nietzsche and Korzybski can be viewed as mystics, even in Korzybski's case founding a movement called General Semantics, which like Psychoanalysis could with equal justice be called a science or a cult.

7.6 Problematic Transcendence

In 1889, Nietzsche suffered a complete mental breakdown, from which he never recovered, and the possible causes continue to be debated, although one common theory attributes it to syphilis, thus a brain condition rather than something that might have had psychoanalytic or philosophical roots. Having lost his own mind, Nietzsche eventually became the puppet of his sister, Elizabeth, who was a proto-Nazi and edited some of his late works as a vehicle for her own anti-Semitic propaganda. The translation of *Zarathustra* by Common includes an essay by her, but I did not include it in my word analysis. For decades, readers did not realize that Nietzsche's identity had been hijacked by his sister, and it remained for Walter Kaufmann and others to rescue him long after his death.

One factor that facilitated confusing Nietzsche with the Nazis is that he had developed but perhaps not fully communicated a doctrine of *Übermensch*. As the English-language Wikipedia page for this German word explains, "There is no overall consensus regarding the precise meaning of the Übermensch, nor on the importance of the concept in Nietzsche's thought" [55]. Thus it was easy around 1940 to assume it was the same concept as the Nazi notion that Germans could become Supermen—the Master Race. By 2010, a more common analogy was with the international and relatively benign Transhumanist movement that believed advanced technologies could give any of us superhuman abilities [56].

Poor Nietzsche! Rich Nietzsche! Never has a modern philosopher been so abused and used as he. I have done it myself, taking the title and the 11 chapter epigrams of my 2007 book, *Across the Secular Abyss*, from him [57]. Stefan Lorenz Sorgner of the Department of Philosophy of the University of Erfurt in Germany argues that Nietzsche was indeed a precursor of Transhumanism, which raises the issue of whether the technologies described in this book might be used not merely to capture and emulate but also to augment a human being's personality—achieving apotheosis [58]. This links immediately back to Nietzsche's primary definition of Übermensch, in his poetic and semi-biblical masterwork, *Also Sprach Zarathustra*:

> Der Mensch is ein Seil, geknüpft zwischen Thier und Übermensch,—ein Seil über einem Abgrunde. [59]

Zarathustra is Zoroaster, the Moses of the Zoroastrian religion, who has gone into meditative exile, and now returns to humanity with a new revelation. Here are three standard but different translations of the sentence:

> Alexander Tille:
> Man is a rope connecting animal and beyond-man,—a rope over a precipice [60].
> Thomas Common:

Man is a rope stretched between the animal and the Superman—a rope over an abyss [61].
Walter Kaufmann:
Man is a rope, tied between beast and overman—a rope over an abyss [62].

All three agree that *Seil* means *rope*, and there are different majorities for *Thier* meaning *animal* rather than *beast*, and "Abgrund" meaning "abyss" rather than "precipice." There is no agreement about "Übermensch," nor for that matter about the more common word "geknüpft," which Google Translate gives as "linked" when only that one word is entered into it. Here is how three different online translation services render the entire sentence:

Google Translate:
The man is one rope, tied between beast and overman—a rope over an abyss [63].
Babelfish:
Man is a rope, tied between beast and Overman,—a rope over a precipice [64]
Free Translation:
The person is a rope, attached between Thier and superman,—a rope over an abyss [65].

I assume the presence of *rope* in the sentence told Google Translate to render "geknüpft," as "tied" rather than "linked." The last of these automatic translation systems balked on Thier, and gave neither "beast" or "animal," because this is an archaic spelling of "Tier," and only the modern form must be in its dictionary. I believe "beast" is a better translation than *animal* in this specific context, although for a reason the automatic systems could not have comprehended. Nietzsche imagines humanity is a transitional form, comparable to a stage in biological evolution but not encoded in physical genes, with beastly pre-humans behind us, and superior superhumans ahead. The metaphor of the rope over a chasm implies we cannot safely stay where we are, but must have the courage to move forward, even though we cannot comprehend our destination—the new form of being we can become. The particular scene in *Also Sprach Zarathustra* includes a tight-rope walking performer, that gives Zarathustra his metaphor, even though he says humanity *is* a rope rather than *walks on* a rope. Sorgner prefers to translate "Übermensch" as "overhuman," to avoid any implication that an overman must be male, but other Transhumanists like to use the word "posthuman" for the ultimate goal of human enhancement.

With a few notable exceptions, leading Transhumanists are not scientists or engineers, but philosophers, ethicists, even artists [66]. Their goal seems to be to establish the cultural preconditions for human transformation, not to accomplish the needed technical innovations themselves. Thus in their actual practice, many contemporary Transhumanists are not that very different from Nietzsche, working in the humanities more than the sciences. At the risk of oversimplification, we can say that the sciences offer four potential routes across the abyss: biological, computational, psychotherapeutic, and utopian. The first two are most often discussed today in Transhumanist publications, the third is closer to Nietzsche's approach, and the fourth deserves more attention than it currently receives.

Biological transformation assumes that new biomedical technologies will be able to extend human life indefinitely and augment our physical and mental abilities. A serious challenge for this perspective is the apparent deceleration in the progress of medical technologies in recent years, as reflected in the declining increase in the average life span, and the serious negative side effects of some drugs that appear to enhance abilities. In science fiction, nanites are invented that can enter the human body and change it at the cellular level, but this notion has no connection to real nanotechnology as it exists today [67–70]. A more technically reasonable approach, engineering viruses to do this nanoscale repair work, is fraught with hazard—notably the problem of preventing the viruses from evolving to serve their own needs rather than ours—and seems unlikely on political and public health grounds quite apart from technical feasibility.

This is not the place to evaluate the biotechnology approach, so I merely note that its success is uncertain. Whatever progress is possible will be achieved with the help of advanced computer technology, as we already see in gene sequencing and charting the structure of proteins.

Computational transformation assumes that computers will soon achieve the capabilities of the human brain, and that one or another method will be found for transferring human memories or personalities into information systems, perhaps continuing to act within the material world via teleoperation of robots [71, 72]. This is a long-term goal for the research presented in this book, although personality capture and emulation are scientifically interesting topics with potential technological applications, even if they fall far short of this vision.

The constant advance in computing capabilities, so-called Moore's Law, seems to have slowed, and the long-prophesied new molecular computing techniques are not developing at all fast [73, 74]. Progress in artificial intelligence remains frustratingly slow, and the field of AI remains fragmented. Computational techniques available today can emulate human personalities with low fidelity that undoubtedly can be improved, but many people would say that nothing short of perfect transfer from meat to machine would constitute success.

Psychotherapeutic transformation involves the use of training, interaction, or mental discipline techniques to improve the human mind, and these were very popular throughout the twentieth century. Clearly, such techniques can be valuable, if one counts education in the sciences among them, but the ability of methods like Psychoanalysis, mind control, behavior modification, or Scientology to reshape human personalities is dubious [75, 76]. It can even be argued that higher education in the humanities sold itself as one of these character-building techniques, but the idea that reading novels or poetry can improve a person is at best unproven. This approach is especially salient here, because it is the one that Nietzsche himself chose and through which his work had significant impact.

Utopian transformation involves revolutionary reconstruction of society, on the assumption that the best way to make better people is to place them in a better social system. The most vigorous variant of this approach was Marxism, but the failure of the New Soviet Man to be any better than anybody else put the lie to its hopes. However, there is a certain logic to the utopian approach, in that humans are at least greatly the product of their social environments, and human behavior is largely oriented toward serving social demands. Most key dimensions of human action would be meaningless without social structures: economic exchange requires a market; communication requires a shared language; artistic creation takes place in relation to a particular culture even when it diverges from existing standards; erotic and reproductive behavior express themselves through families; even philosophy cannot survive without schools. Changing the nature of these institutions, therefore, should change the nature of the people inside them.

Could any conceivable technology resurrect Nietzsche? First we must note the ambiguity concerning when he well and truly died. His mind ended in 1889, but his body survived until 1900. One of Zarathustra's doctrines was that a philosophically aware person should "die at the right time," yet Nietzsche did not live up to that standard [77]. After his death he experienced a remarkable adventure, being held captive by the Nazis until he was rescued, a quarter-century after their deaths, by Walter Kaufmann.

Arthur Schopenhauer, whom Nietzsche originally admired, considered reality to be "Wille und Vorstellung," which cannot be translated precisely and is usually given either as "will and idea" or "will and representation" [78–80]. Schopenhauer also described the world as "embodied music," yet the music Nietzsche composed struck me as quite bland when I encountered a book of his songs. However, that defect was remedied by Richard Strauss who composed the familiar tone poem, *Also Sprach Zarathustra*, in the period when Nietzsche's body still lived, but his mind had died. Thus it is uncertain whether we can claim that when Nietzsche's words died, his melody lingered on.

Yet we can say, he still lives. Of course the truth of this sentence depends upon what the pronoun "he" indicates, and he, meaning Nietzsche the man, argued against the notion of absolute truth. Entering "Nietzsche" into the Google search engine results in an estimated 25,600,000 hits, although some small fraction must be references to other people with that same name. All the writers who have argued for well over a century about what Nietzsche really meant must have expended far more brain power than he ever exercised during his normal lifetime. Their very diversity of views was quite compatible with his own profound ambiguities. Now that Google Translate and its competitors are beginning to translate the world's literature, machine intelligence is beginning—just beginning—to emulate the mind of Friedrich Nietzsche.

7.7 Conclusion

Just as we cannot today capture a personality with perfect accuracy using natural language processing, we cannot capture the potential of NLP in a single chapter. Yet four words suggest the potential: fidelity, extension, affiliation, and transcendence. Today, we can capture the linguistic style of an individual only at low fidelity, like Edison with his first phonograph, yet gradually increasing fidelity seems likely. However, we seek not merely to reproduce a person's verbal expressions, but to extend them into new topics, new times, and new experiences. Language is a social product, as well as the primary tool of social communication, so it embeds the individual in a specific group, anchoring a person through subcultural affiliation. Communication takes place between people, and thus goes beyond the limits of each individual, providing a potential route for transcendence of the human condition.

References

1. Burroughs, E. R. (1917). *A princess of Mars* (p. 169). New York: Grosset and Dunlap.
2. Nietzsche, F. (1895). *Also Sprach Zarathustra* (p. 16). Leipzig: Naumann.
3. http://www.scots-online.org/dictionary/engscots.htm. Accessed 11 May 2013.
4. http://www.lel.ed.ac.uk/ihd/laos1/laos1_frames.html. Accessed 18 May 2013.
5. McIntosh, A., Samuels, M. L., & Benskin, M. (1986). *A linguistic atlas of Late Mediaeval English*. Aberdeen, Scotland: Aberdeen University Press.
6. http://www.lel.ed.ac.uk/ihd/elalme/elalme.html. Accessed 11 May 2013.
7. Laing, M., & Lass, R. (2006). Early middle English dialectology: Problems and prospects. In A. van Kemenade & B. Los (Eds.), *Handbook of the history of English* (p. 417). Oxford: Blackwell.
8. www.lel.ed.ac.uk/ihd/laeme1/laeme1_frames.html. Accessed 11 May 2013.
9. Mosteller, F., & Wallace, D. L. (1963). Inference in an authorship problem. *Journal of the American Statistical Association, 58,* 275–309.
10. Rokeach, M., Homant, R., & Penner, L. (1970). A value analysis of the disputed *Federalist papers. Journal of Personality and Social Psychology, 16*(2), 245–250.
11. Liu, R.-L., & Lu, Y.-L. (2002). Incremental context mining for adaptive document classification. Proceedings of the eighth ACM SIGKDD International Conference on Knowledge Discovery and Data Mining (pp. 599–604). New York: ACM.
12. Deng, S., & Peng, H. (2006). Document classification based on support vector machine using a concept based vector model. Proceedings of the 2006 IEEE/WIC/ACM International Conference on Web Intelligence. Washington: IEEE.
13. Mourão, F., Rocha, L., Araújo, R., Couto, T., Gonçalves, M., & Meira, W. Jr. (2008). Understanding temporal aspects in document classification. Proceedings of the 2008 International Conference on Web Search and Data Mining (pp. 159–170). New York: ACM.
14. Salles, T., Rocha, L., Pappa, G. L., Mourão, F., Meira, W. Jr., & Gonçalves, M. (2010). Temporally-aware algorithms for document classification. Proceedings of the 33rd International ACM SIGIR Conference on Research and Development in Information Retrieval (pp. 307–314). New York: ACM.
15. Bosch, R. A., & Smith, J. A. (1998). Hyperplanes and the authorship of the disputed Federalist papers. The American Mathematical Monthly, 105(7), 601–608.
16. Martin, J. H. (2004). Natural language processing. In W. S. Bainbridge (Ed.), Berkshire encyclopedia of human-computer interaction. Great Barrington: Berkshire.
17. Jurafsky, D., & Martin, J. H. (2009). Speech and language processing: An introduction to natural language processing. Upper Saddle River: Pearson Prentice Hall.
18. Stone, P. J., Dunphy, D. C., Smith, M. S., & Ogilvie, D. M. (1966). The general inquirer: A computer approach to content analysis. Cambridge: MIT Press.
19. Borko, H., & Bernick, M. (1963). Automatic document classification. Journal of the ACM, 10(2), 151–162.
20. Lim, E. T. (2002). Five trends in presidential rhetoric: An analysis of rhetoric from George Washington to Bill Clinton. Presidential Studies Quarterly, 32(2), 328–366.
21. Frisbie, B., & Sudman, S. (1968). The use of computers in coding free responses. The Public Opinion Quarterly, 32(2), 216–232.
22. Kelly, E. F., & Stone, P. J. (1975). Computer recognition of English word senses. Amsterdam: North-Holland.
23. Twain, M. (1910). Plymouth rock and the pilgrims. In Mark Twain's speeches (pp. 17–24). New York: Harper.
24. Wiggin, K. D. (1903). Rebecca of sunnybrook *farm*. Boston: Houghton Mifflin.

25. Freud, S. (1920). *Dream psychology*. New York: James A. Mccann.
26. http://www.wjh.harvard.edu/~inquirer/. Accessed 19 May 2013.
27. http://www.wjh.harvard.edu/~inquirer/homecat.htm. Accessed 12 May 2013.
28. Fiedler, F. E. (1958). *Leader attitudes and group effectiveness*. Urbana, Illinois: University of Illinois Press.
29. http://en.wikipedia.org/wiki/Clifford_Whittingham_Beers. Accessed 19 May 2013.
30. Beers, C. W. (1908). *A mind that found itself*. New York: Longmans.
31. Ranney, D. (1910). *Dave Ranney: Or, thirty years on the Bowery*. New York: American Tract Society.
32. Burroughs, E. R. (1917). *A princess of Mars*. Chicago: McClurg.
33. Nietzsche, F. (1909). *Thus Spake Zarathustra*. Edinburgh: Foulis.
34. Tausczik, Y. R., & Pennebaker, J. W. (2010). The psychological meaning of words: LIWC and computerized text analysis methods. *Journal of Language and Social Psychology, 29*(1), 24–54.
35. Pennebaker, J. W., & King, L. A. (1999). Linguistic styles: Language use as an individual difference. *Journal of Personality and Social Psychology, 77*(6), 1296–1312.
36. Mehl, M. R., Gosling, S. D., & Pennebaker, J. W. (2006). Personality in Its natural habitat: Manifestations and implicit folk theories of personality in daily life. *Journal of Personality and Social Psychology, 90*(5), 862–877.
37. Newton, A. T., Kramer, A. D. I., & McIntosh, D. N. (2009). Autism online: A comparison of word usage in bloggers with and without autism spectrum disorder. In *Proceedings of the SIG-CHI Conference on Human Factors in Computing Systems* (pp. 463–466). New York: ACM.
38. Crowston, K., Allen, E. E., & Heckman, R. (2011). Using Natural language processing technology for qualitative data analysis. *International Journal of Social Research Methodology*, 1–21.
39. http://www.etymonline.com/index.php. Accessed 20 May 2013.
40. http://en.wikipedia.org/wiki/List_of_Oz_books. Accessed 18 Feb 2013.
41. http://en.wikipedia.org/wiki/Nancy_Drew_Mystery_Stories. Accessed 29 Oct 2013.
42. Bogost, I., Mateas, M., Murray, J., & Nitsche, M. (2005). Asking what is possible: The Georgia tech approach to Games Research and Education. *International Digital Media and Arts Association Journal, 2*(1), 59–68.
43. Skorupski, J., Jayapalan, L., Marquez, S., & Mateas, M. (2007). Wide ruled: A friendly interface to author-goal based story generation. In *Proceedings of the 4th International Conference on Virtual Storytelling* (ICVS 2007), Saint Malo, France. December 5–7, 2007.
44. Dow, S., MacIntyre, B., & Mateas, M. (2008). Styles of play in immersive and interactive story: Case studies from a Gallery Installation of AR Façade. In *Proceedings of the 2008 International Conference on Advances in Computer Entertainment Technology* (pp. 373–380). New York: ACM.
45. Magerko, B., Fiesler, C., Baumer, A., & Fuller, D. (2010). Bottoms up: Improvisational micro-agents. In *Proceedings of the Intelligent Narrative Technologies III Workshop* (Article 8). New York: ACM.
46. Porteous, J., Cavazza, M., & Charles, F. (2010). Applying planning to interactive storytelling: Narrative control using state constraints. *ACM Transactions on Intelligent Systems and Technology, 1*(2), article 10.
47. Sullivan, A., Grow, A. l., Mateas, M., & Wardrip-Fruin, N. (2012). The design of Mismanor: Creating a playable quest-based story game. In *Proceedings of the International Conference on the Foundations of Digital Games* (pp. 180–187). New York: ACM.
48. Lupoff, R. A. (1976) *Barsoom: Edgar Rice Burroughs and the Martian Vision*. Markham: Mirage.
49. Chapman, A. H., & Chapman-Santana, M. (1995). The influence of Nietzsche on Freud's ideas. *The British Journal of Psychiatry, 166*, 251–253.
50. http://en.wikipedia.org/wiki/Zarathustra%27s_roundelay. Accessed 11 May 2013.
51. http://en.wikipedia.org/wiki/Nietzsche. Accessed 20 Jan 2013.
52. http://de.wikipedia.org/wiki/Nietzsche. Accessed 20 Jan 2013.
53. Lin, T.-D. (2012). Fuzzy logic. In W. S. Bainbridge (Ed.), *Leadership in science and technology* (pp. 488–495). Los Angeles: Sage.

54. Korzybski, A. (1933). *Science and sanity: An introduction to non-Aristotelian systems and general semantics*. Lancaster: International Non-Aristotelian Library.
55. http://en.wikipedia.org/wiki/%C3 %9Cbermensch. Accessed 20 Jan 2013.
56. Bainbidge, W. S. (2010). Burglarizing Nietzsche's Tomb. *Journal of Evolution and Technology, 21*(1), 37–54.
57. Bainbidge, W. S. (2007). *Across the secular Abyss*. Lanham: Lexington.
58. Sorgner, S. L. (2009). Nietzsche, the overhuman, and transhumanism. *Journal of Evolution and Technology, 20*(1), 29–42.
59. Nietzsche, F. (1895). *Also Sprach Zarathustra* (p. 16). Liepzig: Naumann.
60. Nietzsche, F. (1896). *Thus Spake Zarathustra* (p. 8). London: Macmillan.
61. K. Francke, W. G. Howard & I. Singer (Eds.). (1914). *The German classics, vol. 15* (p. 277). New York: German Publication Society.
62. Nietzsche, F. (1954). *The Portable Nietzsche* (p. 126). New York: Penguin.
63. http://translate.google.com/. Accessed 20 Jan 2013.
64. http://www.babelfish.com/. Accessed 20 Jan 2013.
65. http://www.freetranslation.com/. Accessed 20 Jan 2013.
66. M. More & N. Vita-More (Eds.). (2013). *The Transhumanist Reader*. Chichester: Wiley.
67. M. C. Roco & W. S. Bainbridge (Eds.). (2001). *Societal implications of nanoscience and nanotechnology*. Dordrecht: Kluwer.
68. M. C. Roco & W. S. Bainbridge (Eds.). (2006). *Nanotechnology: Societal implications—Individual perspectives*. Berlin: Springer.
69. M. C. Roco & W. S. Bainbridge (Eds.). (2006). *Nanotechnology: Societal implications—Maximizing benefit for humanity*. Berlin: Springer.
70. Bainbridge, W. S. (2007). *Nanoconvergence*. Upper Saddle River: Prentice-Hall.
71. Kurzweil, R. (1999). *The age of spiritual machines*. New York: Penguin.
72. Moravec, H. P. (1988). *Mind children: The future of robot and human intelligence*. Cambridge: Harvard University Press.
73. Cong, J., Nagaraj, N. S., Puri, R., Joyner, W., Burns, J., Gavrielov, M., Radojcic, R., Rickert, P., & Stork, H. (2009). Moore's law: Another casualty of the financial meltdown? In *Proceedings of the Design Automation Conference*. New York: ACM.
74. Palem, K. V., Chakrapani, L. N. B., Kedem, Z. M., Lingamneni, A., & Krishna Muntimadugu, K. (2009). Sustaining Moore's Law in Embedded Computing through probabilistic and approximate design: Retrospects and Prospects. In *Proceedings of the 2009 International Conference on Compilers, Architecture, and Synthesis for Embedded Systems*. New York: ACM.
75. Salter, A. (1952). *The case against psychoanalysis*. New York: Holt.
76. Rachman, S. (1971). *The effects of psychotherapy*. New York: Pergamon.
77. Rempel, M. (2009). Dying at the right time. *Philosophy Now, 76*(November/December), 23–25.
78. Schopenhauer, A. (1859). *Die Welt als Wille und Vorstellung*. Leipzig: Brockhaus.
79. Schopenhauer, A. (1983–1986). *The world as will and idea*. London: Trübner.
80. Schopenhauer, A. (1966). *The world as will and representation*. New York: Dover Publications.

Chapter 8
Virtual Worlds

Online virtual worlds, in which the user is represented by an avatar interacting with other avatars within a somewhat realistic visual environment, are an excellent laboratory for developing both capture and emulation, often in a highly integrated manner. Two kinds of virtual worlds will be examined here, primarily gameworlds like *World of Warcraft* (WoW) that naturally generate elaborate statistics about the behavior of each of millions of avatars, but also a non-game world called *Second Life* where the most interesting results of human action are the objects, environments, and expressions that users create. In addition, we explore how these worlds are larger than they might seem, because the social life they support extends to wikis and other forms of online communication and memory. This chapter brings the book to a logical conclusion, by examining not how people can be understood through their reaction to stimuli, as covered by the early chapters, but how they freely express their individuality within a complex world.

In their popular book *Infinite Reality*, Jim Blascovich and Jeremy Bailenson argue that the human mind responds to computer-generated virtual realities as if they were the physical world, seeking to achieve personal goals inside them. We might express this in the following words: Virtual realities are both real and ideal. As leading researchers on the psychology and computer science of avatars and virtual reality systems, Blascovich and Bailenson confidently state:

> ...the brain doesn't much care if an experience is real or virtual. In fact, many people prefer the digital aspects of their lives to physical ones. Imagine you never aged, could shed pounds of cellulite, or put on muscle mass at the touch of a button. Think about never having a bad-hair day, expressing an involuntary grimace, or getting caught staring. Think also about a world with no putrid smells but plenty of delightful ones, when it rains only when you are inside, and where global warming is actually just a myth. In this world, your great-grandfather is still around and can play catch with your six-year-old daughter. There is no dental drill or swine flu in this place. [1]

To the extent that virtual worlds are realistic, they can be laboratories for capturing human behavior, including human interaction. For example, in *World of Warcraft*, teams of five players often send their characters into instanced locations where they must cooperate for 2 or 3 h in battling enemies and achieving goals, communicating by voice or typed text that can be compared with what their virtual representations actually do. Because WoW is a role-playing game, these representations are called

W. S. Bainbridge, *Personality Capture and Emulation*, Human-Computer Interaction Series,   177
DOI 10.1007/978-1-4471-5604-8_8, © Springer-Verlag London 2014

characters rather than *avatars*, because like characters in a drama they have some degree of personality separate from that of the actor. In my own WoW research, I ran 23 distinct characters, with different names, appearances and histories, for a total of about 2,700 h, yet all of them contained significant aspects of myself. Thus one of the methodological challenges that is also a research opportunity, is how to distinguish a person's natural personality from the roles that person plays under different conditions. This is not a flaw of virtual worlds, but an issue about human nature in general. It takes time and effort to learn to play any significant role, yet there always remains a degree of *role distance* that separates the person from it [2–4].

As befits the final chapter of this book, the topic integrates personality capture with emulation. In addition to avatars and characters, there is a third related concept, *agents*. There are at least two cases in *World of Warcraft* where a non-player character, operated by frankly rather simple computer programming, represents an actual deceased person who had been a player [5]. At a bridge in the Mulgore region of WoW, stands a character named Ahab Wheathoof who asks the player to find and feed his lost dog, Kyle. This mission was designed, and the character was voiced, by a boy named Ezra Chatterton, who was struggling with a fatal disease and died October 20, 2008 [6]. Another mission ends by meeting an Elf named Caylee Dak in Shattrath City, and meditating while she recites a poem about transcendence of death. She is an automated version of the character a young man named Dak Krause operated before his death on August 22, 2007 [7]. Ultimately, we can imagine using advanced artificial intelligence methods to emulate a deceased person realistically, but in the meantime it is also possible for a living human being to operate an avatar based on a deceased person, as a form of veneration but also to learn more about the meaning of life by trying to experience it from the perspective of another person [8].

Most immediately, virtual worlds capture a vast amount of information about the behavior of anyone who operates a character or avatar, although much research will be required before we can build highly realistic emulation agents. Happily, a very large number of excellent researchers are working on pieces of this puzzle [9, 10]. Some, like Blascovich and Bailenson, are quite aware of the radical possibilities that could utterly transform our culture. Others are more modestly focused on difficult scientific or technical problems they personally find interesting. The fact that multiplayer games are a major industry worldwide implies that an excellent practical basis exists for significant progress.

For example, many contemporary researchers in computer vision, graphics, and avatar design have been developing methods to capture and emulate the physical motions of a person, such as gestures, facial expressions, and postures. As it happens, my colleague Alex Schwarzkopf has been the demonstration subject for one of the most prominent efforts of this kind, Project LifeLike [11–13]. We have a standing joke that only if I meet him in the public restroom can I really be sure it is the man rather than his avatar, because the avatar does not need to deal with bodily functions. His avatar's job was to communicate with human visitors to the National Science Foundation's information system, on a temporary experimental basis, not to undertake more action-oriented missions, so we shall not examine Ask Alex here. Rather, we will begin with a man named Sean who died before reaching half of the age of Alex.

8.1 An Electronic Obituary

On September 11, 2012, Sean Smith met his death under circumstances that were highly unusual, continue to be hotly debated, and had a surprising connection to the Internet virtual worlds often called *massively multiplayer online games* (MMOs). Along with Ambassador J. Christopher Stevens and two other men, Smith was killed in the attack on the American diplomatic mission at Benghazi, in Libya, during what CNN called, "4 hours of fire and chaos." According to early reports, the proximal cause of death was either fire, or the fact that help was delayed: "For Smith, the rescue came too late. He had already succumbed to smoke inhalation by the time they arrived." [14] Had this been a virtual reality, the avatar representing Smith would have returned to life, perhaps beating back the terrorists in a replay of the battle, but the harsh reality of the material world does not offer postmortem second chances. This observation is not frivolous or irrelevant, because Smith was a leading player and even a diplomat in the gameworld *EVE Online*, as evidenced by the torrent of praise-filled memorials that washed across Internet as soon as the grim news was reported.

Smith's Wikipedia page indicated he played compatible roles in two realities. In the material world, he was an "information management officer" for the United States Foreign Service. His private online existence reflected similar personality traits and responsibilities:

Smith was known as a leading player and former member of the Council of Stellar Management in the EVE Online gaming community (under the username "Vile Rat") and was a moderator on the Something Awful forums. On the day of his death, Smith typed a message to the director of his online gaming corporation that read, "Assuming we don't die tonight. We saw one of our 'police' that guard the compound taking pictures." EVE Online's Council of Stellar Management published a tribute to Smith two days after Smith's death. Spontaneous reactions from the player base included a mass renaming of outposts throughout the game world. [15]

Clearly, several references in the paragraph will be obscure to most readers, so a few explanations are required. *EVE Online* is one of the most sophisticated online virtual worlds, marketed as a game because that is how the marketplace defines many online environments today where people may create very real communities. In 2009, and then again in 2013, I studied *EVE* by running multiple avatars through it, not getting anywhere near as far into the environment as Smith did, but learning its general characteristics [16]. To offer a concrete description, I am now launching *EVE* and will run it simultaneously with the word processor in which I am writing these words.

At the present, I have three avatars, Theo Logian, Cogni Tion, and Gala Xy. Theo belongs to the highly religious Amarr Empire, Cogni to their technological rivals the Minmatar, and Gala to the Caldari who are somewhat aloof from the historic conflict between Amarr and Minmatar. I am logging in as Theo now, and I see him, lean, sinister, and standing inside his computer-filled office in a space station orbiting the planet Ashab VII, which he happens to be visiting. He is not in a mood to undertake a mission, or engage in a battle in one of the wars raging in the EVE gal-

axy, so he decides to earn money mining one of the asteroid belts in the Ashab solar
system. He walks out onto a balcony overlooking the spaceship he uses for mining,
which he named Uranus. His main warship, named Neptune, is currently parked in
the adjacent Amarr system. At this point in his career, he owns several space ships,
and Uranus belongs to the Bestower class, officially described thus:

> The Bestower has for decades been used by the Empire as a slave transport, shipping human
> labor between cultivated planets in Imperial space. As a proof to how reliable this class
> has been through the years, the Emperor himself has used an upgraded version of this very
> same class as transports for the Imperial Treasury. The Bestower has very thick armor and
> large cargo space.

At this point, the Uranus has only one mining laser, to extract minerals from asteroids at any distance less than 10 km, but the ship has room for a second. Therefore,
Theo checks the online marketplace to see if he can buy another mining laser. There
is a Civilian Miner for sale at only 569 Interstellar Kredits (ISK) right where he is,
but it is much inferior to the Miner I he already owns. In the nearest solar system,
Amarr itself, many Miner I and even Miner II systems are for sale, with the lowest price for a Miner II being 1,220,000 ISK. He currently has 1,287,697, but he
does not want to let his cash on hand get much below 1,000,000 ISK. He decides
to mine 1,000,000 ISK worth of ore, and decide later whether to buy a Miner II, or
obtain the schematic required to manufacture his own from the raw materials he is
collecting.

So, Theo enters his ship and commands it to undock from the space station. In
most virtual worlds, the user is represented by an avatar that looks more or less like
a human being, but in EVE, one is primarily represented by the ship one pilots. EVE
offers a very sophisticated yet easy-to-use navigation system, and Theo checks to
see what options there are for mining. The gas giant planet Ashab VIII, somewhat
larger than our own Jupiter, has fully seven asteroid belts, so Theo selects the first
one and tells his ship to warp there, which takes only a minute.

Arriving at Ashab VIII-1 Asteroid Belt, he sees that another player named LadySarah is already mining. Checking the database for this avatar gives a worrisome
result. LadySarah is a wanted criminal with a 100,000 ISK bounty on her head, and
Theo's mining ship completely lacks weaponry. Despite the fact that they are in
High Security Space where piracy is practically impossible, he quickly warps to the
second asteroid belt. He finds nobody else at that location and goes into a 5 km orbit
of one of the asteroids, switching on the mining laser and drawing out concentrated
veldspar, among the most common minerals but still worth harvesting.

If Theo were on a special mission, or part of a team battling other players, he
would need my full attention. But while he mines that asteroid in High Security
Space, I can return to the word processor, to clarify some other points about *EVE
Online*. The abbreviation for the money, ISK, is also the abbreviation for the Ice-
landic króna, and *EVE* was created by a team of game designers in Reykjavík, Ice-
land. Launching back in 2003, it has been constantly improved and expanded. The
premise is that humanity had begun to colonize a distant galaxy through a natural
wormhole called EVE, when the wormhole collapsed, leaving half-built colonies on

several worlds. Civilization collapsed, but has been rebuilding for many years, from at least four of the colony planets.

A player performs a number of pre-defined missions in early weeks of visiting EVE, primarily as training exercises in regions of High Security Space where a truce between competing interstellar societies provides a degree of safety for new players. After gaining experience, each avatar is expected to join a player-created group called a *corporation*. When Sean Smith sent an electronic message to "the director of his online gaming corporation," that was the kind of group identified. The name of the particular player corporation is GoonSwarm, among the most aggressive, innovative and controversial groups. Its leader, The_Mittani, was a close friend of Vile Rat, in both the virtual and material worlds. A day after Smith's death, The_Mittani posted a memorial outlining how intensely Smith integrated these two realities:

> We knew that Vile Rat was in Benghazi; he told us. He commented on how they use guns to celebrate weddings and how there was a constant susurrus of weaponry in the background. He was in situ to provide IT services for the consulate, which meant he was on the net all the time, hanging out with us on Jabber as usual and talking about internet spaceship games. The last time he did something like this, he was in Baghdad in 2007 or 2008. He would be on jabber, then say something like 'incoming' and vanish for a while as the Kayatushas [Katyushas] came down from Sadr City—State had been in the former Saddam Hussein palace on the Tigris before they built that $ 2bn fortress-embassy later. He got out from his Baghdad post physically unscathed and had some more relaxing postings after that.
>
> I'm clearly in shock as I write this as everything is buzzing around my head funnily and I feel kind of dead inside. I'm not sure if this is how I'm supposed to react to my friend being killed by a mob in a post-revolutionary Libya, but it's pretty awful and Sean was a great guy and he was a goddamned master at this game we all play, even though a lot of people may not realize how significant an influence he had. It seems kind of trivial to praise a husband, father, and overall badass for his skills in an internet spaceship game but that's how most of us know him, so there you go. [17]

The Council of Stellar Management (CSM) is an advisory panel of players, periodically elected by the players, and Vile Rat joined it in April 2011, one of the 14 members of the Sixth Council. Two days after Smith's death, Mark "Seleene" Heard, the chairman of the Seventh Council who had served with Smith on the Sixth, wrote a memorial blog:

> If I had to name Sean's greatest contribution to EVE I would sum it up in one word: CONTENT. EVE doesn't rely on pre-written story lines to give color and richness to the universe. EVE's story is a narrative birthed and dragged forward kicking and screaming by the players. The player-driven saga of EVE has seen time and time again how the fortunes of tens of thousands of people can turn on the words of a few, or even just a single player. Sean was one such player and over the years he directly or indirectly touched and influenced the lives of countless people.
>
> EVE's community is well known for being a dark and cut throat place but as a whole, I believe everyone realizes that real life takes priority over anything in the virtual world. I have seen very few negative or disrespectful comments in the wake of Sean's passing. It's impossible for us to not relate to this tragedy. Even to those that did not know him personally, Sean was "one of us".

Sean made the world we all play in much more dangerous while simultaneously making
the world we all live in that much safer. I already fear the real world ramifications that may
come as a result of Sean's death.

People who play EVE all too often confuse the in-game actions and personalities of the
characters played with their real life counterparts. If this senseless tragedy accomplishes
anything positive in the tiny corner of the world that is the EVE community, I hope it helps
people remember that even the most "Vile Rat" can be, in reality, a warm and funny guy
with friends and family that care about him. [18]

In the context of personality capture, Heard's comments make two contradictory
points: (1) Someone who behaves in an "evil" manner inside a game may be "good"
in the real world. (2) The skills and abilities required to negotiate the real and virtual worlds may be very much the same. But these points are contradictory only if
we have a naive view of human nature. While Psychoanalysis may have gotten the
details wrong, it may indeed be the case that each good person has a hidden dark
side. Or rather, in a real world marked by conflict the question is not good versus
evil, but loyalty to one's group, which may at times mean violating abstract norms
in dealing with outsiders, while remaining true to the norms for insiders. Thus the
contradiction may really be between reality—whether manifested in the physical
place, Libya, or the virtual place, *EVE*—and our illusions about human nature.

In the same blog, another player named Two Step wrote: "I think the best way
to talk about Sean is to use his own words. Here are some things he said to me recently: 'You are as powerful as you want to be. I hope good things. I want the CSM
to succeed. I'll do what I can to help.' I think that last one especially sums up what
we all loved about Sean—he was always willing to help others." Most formal obituaries praise the deceased person, but most deceased persons are not the subject of
formal obituaries. The Wikipedia page for the September 11, 2012, Benghazi attack
lists all four American victims: J. Christopher Stevens, Sean Smith, Glen Doherty,
and Tyrone S. Woods. Yet most news reports focused on Ambassador Stevens, and
we here have focused on Smith. Obituaries thus tend to be elitist, in the apotheosis
tradition.

One role of an obituary is to present a role model that living people may follow,
and if others do even in slight degree imitate the behavior of a deceased person
in their own lives, then a very real form of emulation has taken place. On a more
abstract level, elitist obituaries serve to remind readers of the values of the culture,
as reflected in a mythologized version of the life of a prominent member, simultaneously constructing the official history of the community. As Smith's example
shows, subcultures in society may revere and thus emulate different deceased persons—an information officer versus an ambassador—so a larger fraction of the total
population may survive through emulation, the more differentiated into subcultures
the society may be.

Hours later, after I finished writing the first draft of this section, I returned to
Theo Logian, found that his ship held 8,977 m^3 of concentrated feldspar, about
1,000 below its maximum capacity. He warped to a distant jumpgate, went to a
space station orbiting Amarr VIII, refined the ore, and sold the resultant 238,811
units of tritanium [sic], and bought a Miner II. However, his ship had a limited turret

capacity, so he replaced his old mining laser with this new and better one, but was not yet able to operate two at once. That would require further engineering work.

One engineering point is prominently missing in the story of Sean Smith; Vile Rat also has died, yet this may not have been necessary. Suppose *EVE Online* had a contest, the winner of which could take over the Vile Rat avatar, with the criterion for winning being adhering most closely to Vile Rat's traditional behavior. Suppose *EVE Online* took the ships operated by Vile Rat, and made them non-player ships in an arc of missions, operated by artificial intelligence following the tactics Vile Rat tended to use during battles. Both of these feasible memorializations would require having a good deal of data about how Vile Rat behaved inside *EVE*, yet all this behavior was at least briefly housed on the *EVE* Internet server, because that is the real environment where everything happens, and thus was available for capture. This point can be explored through consideration of two very different massively multiplayer online role-playing games.

8.2   Avatar Statistics

Already, gamelike virtual worlds collect a tremendous amount of data about an individual's behavior, as illustrated by the web-based character databases of *World of Warcraft* and *Battleground Europe* (*World War II Online*). Every movement of a character, and every in-game action of the player, is sent over Internet to the game's central server and is stored at least temporarily on that computer. Some of the data are kept a very long time, for example a record of whether or not a WoW character has visited places like Auberdine, Astranaar or Sentinel Hill. Table 8.1 shows crude exploration data for two of my own characters, as of late 2008, when the maximum experience level cap was 80. Maxrohn (Max) a level 75 Human priest who belonged to the Alliance faction, and Catullus (Cat) a level 80 Blood Elf priest who belonged to the opposing Horde faction.

Near the upper right corner of the table, we see that Darkshore is an Alliance zone recommended for characters level 10 or above, having 9 subzones. Of these, Max visited 7, but Cat did not visit any. My book about *World of Warcraft* includes a picture of Max flying over Auberdine, the Night Elf town in Darkshore, and most players save screenshot pictures that could supplement the official travel data in documenting their characters' experiences [19]. Astranaar is in Ashenvale, a contested area with 18 subzones, 4 of which were visited by Max, and 11 by Cat. Like Darkshore, Westfall is an Alliance zone, but dominated by Humans rather than Night Elves. The table reveals that Max visited all 14 subzones in Westfall, whereas Cat had seen only 4. The top of the table confirms that Horde characters like Cat explore more of the Horde territory reserved for low-level characters, whereas Alliance characters like Max visit more of the Alliance areas. Cat explored absolutely all of the Outland and Northrend subzones, while Max did little in the most advanced Northrend subzones, a reflection of the fact that he did not reach level 80. The data for this table came from the online Armory database that offered

Table 8.1 Exploration achievements of two *World of Warcraft* characters, Cat and Max

	Level	Areas	Cat	Max
Horde:				
Durotar	1	11	6	4
Eversong	1	25	24	0
Mulgore	1	14	5	0
Tirisfal	1	16	8	4
Barrens	10	25	21	5
Ghostlands	10	16	16	1
Silverpine	10	15	14	3
Contested:				
Redridge	15	11	3	11
Stonetalon	15	11	7	0
Ashenvale	18	18	11	4
Duskwood	18	13	4	12
Hillsbrad	20	12	11	11
Wetlands	20	15	7	12
Thousand Needles	25	9	9	4
Alterac	30	15	15	14
Arathi	30	16	16	16
Desolace	30	15	12	6
Stranglethorn	31	27	23	25
Badlands	35	14	14	1
Dustwallow	35	7	4	5
Swamp of Sorrows	35	11	11	8
Feralas	40	16	14	12
Hinterlands	40	14	13	13
Tanaris	40	20	20	14
Azshara	45	19	16	15
Blasted Lands	45	9	3	6
Searing Gorge	45	7	7	4
Felwood	48	12	8	12
Un'goro Crater	48	7	6	6
Burning Steppes	50	10	10	7
West Plaguelands	50	13	13	13
East Plaguelands	53	23	22	22
Winterspring	53	13	9	11
Silithus	55	7	2	6
Alliance:				
Azuremyst	1	17	0	2
Dun Morogh	1	18	2	11
Elwynn	1	12	7	12
Teldrassil	1	11	2	11
Bloodmyst	10	28	0	0
Darkshore	10	9	0	7
Loch Modan	10	11	3	11
Westfall	10	14	8	14
Outland:				
Hellfire	58	18	18	15
Zangarmarsh	60	18	18	18

Table 8.1 (continued)

	Level	Areas	Cat	Max
Terokkar	62	21	21	17
Nagrand	64	21	21	19
Blade's Edge	65	26	26	20
Netherstorm	67	22	22	15
Shadowmoon	67	13	13	10
Northrend:				
Borean Tundra	68	13	13	12
Howling Fjord	68	21	21	15
Dragonblight	71	18	18	10
Grizzly Hills	73	14	14	12
Zul'Drak	74	14	14	8
Sholazar	76	12	12	3
Storm Peaks	76	16	16	3
Crystalsong	77	8	8	7
Icecrown	77	15	15	1
Miscellaneous:				
Moonglade	1	1	1	1
Deadwind Pass	55	3	1	1
Quel'Danas	65	1	1	0
TOTAL		881	679	542

data about as many as a thousand variables for every one of the millions of North American characters level 10 or higher.

World of Warcraft is notable for placing much personal data online, but *Ever-Quest II, Lord of the Rings Online, and Dungeons and Dragons Online* have comparable if more modest public databases. Here is another example of very extensive data about the behavior of online game players. On November 19, 2009, Captain Swoop67 took off in a Royal Air Force Spitfire MkIIB from Courcy Airfield just north of Reims, France, on an area defense mission. Forty-four minutes later, he was shot down by Major General Ramse888 of the Luftwaffe, flying a Bf109F1, better known as a Messerschmitt 109. A few minutes later, the two tangled again, and this time Captain Swoop67 was the victor. We know these facts because they were available for anyone to see in the online database of the multiplayer game, *Battleground Europe* [20]. In fact, Swoop was the highest rated fighter pilot, in this virtual reenactment of the war after the war to end all wars, having experienced a total of 2,348 kills and 1,011 deaths since he joined the RAF on October 1, 2002, giving him a glorious career kill-to-death (K/D) ratio of 2.32. Swoop67 also briefly served in the French army and air force, but primarily flew Spitfires for Britain.

Table 8.2 hints at the vast data collected during Swoop's seven-year career, listing the opponents Swoop faced in his nine most recent winning and losing flights, so Ramse888 appears twice, but so does Tinky123 who was defeated by Swoop when flying a clumsy ground-attack Junkers 87 "Stuka," but who trounced Swoop when flying a Messerschmitt 109 fighter. To get the information about each opponent I had to enter his name manually into the database's search engine, but of

Table 8.2 Opponents of an RAF pilot in eighteen recent sorties

Player	Aircraft	Sorties	K/D Ratio	Enlisted
Last 9 Victims:				
Maj Gen Ramse888	Bf109E4	61	1.05	Jan 06 2006
Lnc Corp Ra66it	Bf109F1	109	1.00	Sep 02 2009
Lt Col Tinky123	Stuka	626	2.77	Nov 12 2006
Maj Gen Heehop	Bf110c	39	0.96	Apr 20 2007
QM Sgt Coopes	Bf109F1	55	1.28	Nov 22 2005
Lnc Corp Ra66it	Bf109F1	109	1.00	Sep 02 2009
2nd Lt Vongotti	Bf109E4	78	1.48	Jun 21 2007
Lt Col Peck27	Bf109E4	57	2.20	Jan 23 2002
Sgt Maj Acegacek	Bf109F1	74	2.78	Oct 27 2006
Last 9 Killers:				
Maj Gen Ramse888	Bf109F1	61	1.05	Jan 06 2006
Sgt Maj Levarris	Bf110c	112	3.09	Jan 01 2007
Corp Goeth27	Heinkel	224	1.40	Mar 05 2003
Lt Solution	Bf109E4	92	2.53	Feb 14 2009
Col Sgt Angle25	Bf109E4	22	3.08	Feb 15 2008
Sgt Maj Weisse8	Bf109E4	122	1.51	Apr 11 2008
Lt Col Sirkkeli	Bf109E4	94	3.93	Apr 27 2005
Sgt Tass	Bf109F1	11	0.88	Sep 16 2001
Lt Col Tinky123	Bf109E4	626	2.77	Nov 12 2006

course the company that hosts the game has much more direct access to all this information. Players of this game can also serve in the armies of the three nations, operating armored vehicles or serving as foot soldiers, and in the navies. Thus, an individual has a great range of decisions to make prior to undertaking any particular mission, and the mission itself will test versatility, skill, reaction time, and personality characteristics like patience and aggressiveness. As a series of duels, the game tests a player in comparison with many different opponents, thus calibrating measurements of the individual in terms of a large population.

In the most significant MMO, *World of Warcraft*, it is quite common for a user to operate a particular avatar for 500 or even 1000 h, which could easily take the data for that avatar far into the gigabyte range. To illustrate the current situation and future possibilities, we shall consider Gonzorina, the avatar of John Bohannon, the journalist who created the Gonzo Scientist online feature for *Science* and who inspired the conference I organized in *World of Warcraft* in May 2008, and Kvinesdal, the avatar of Wayne Lutters, an academic with expertise in social computing who was one of the leading conference participants [21]. I know both men personally, but their avatar and real-world names were connected on several web pages, so the following does not violate their privacy.

Gonzorina is a female Troll huntress, so right away we know she belonged to the Darkspear tribe and entered the world in the Valley of Trials in Durotar, a zone of the Kalimdor continent on the planet Azeroth, because this is how all Trolls begin. Standing immediately before her was Kaltunk, a male Orc, whose approximate location in the Durotar coordinate system is 43,68. He tells every newcomer to talk with another Orc named Gornek, who is nearby at 42,68, just west of Kaltunk and inside a den. Thus, we infer that Gonzorina walked one coordinate unit westward, after talking with Kaltunk. However, the exact route she took, wandering northward perhaps to look around the area, was transmitted to and from the game server, and could have been recorded with a precision of about one virtual meter, which is much smaller than a coordinate unit. Gornek undoubtedly sent Gonzorina north a short distance to kill ten mottled boars, then back to collect ten scorpion tails by killing these huge insects, but the exact speed, locations, and style with which she accomplished this were transmitted across Internet before being erased. New Trolls complete a number of training quests in the Valley of Trials, before exploring Durotar, notably the Troll village called Sen'jin, a central fortification named Razor Hill, and the great city Orgrimmar to the north.

At the end of July, 2010, I looked Gonzorina up in WoW's online database, seeing she had reached the top level 80 of experience and was a member of a guild named Science. A picture showed her wearing a tabard with an infinity symbol, which marks her as a member in good standing of this guild. She is holding a powerful crossbow called the Felglacier Bolter, an heroic weapon that could be obtained only in the Pit of Saron in Icecrown Citadel on the Northrend continent of Azeroth. She also carries an axe named Nighttime that can be obtained only in the Forge of Souls, also in Icecrown Citadel. No player with experience below level 80 can use any of these weapons, and the two heroic ones became available only on December 8, 2009. Thus, one way in which virtual worlds define personalities is in terms of their possessions, something that is true in the world at large, and understanding the things a person owns helps us understand the person.

The Achievements tab of Gonzorina's database page includes a section called Exploration that reports which subareas she has ever visited in the four main territories WoW then had: Kalimdor, the Eastern Kingdoms, Northrend, and Outland which is a broken fragment of a planet separate from Azeroth. Of the seven zones in Outland, Gonzorina had completed exploration of only one, Zangarmarsh on April 11, 2009. She has never even entered another, Shadowmoon Valley, and visited only three of the 22 areas in Netherstorm, the two highest levels in Outland. Apparently, instead of exploring these zones, she jumped ahead to Northrend, as soon as she reached the level of experience needed to go there, where she could advance more rapidly. In terms of areas, she has entered 93 % of those in Northrend, and 61 % of those in Outland.

In contrast, my own most advanced WoW avatar, Catullus, has visited 100 % of the areas in both Outland and Northrend, but has not fought inside Icecrown Citadel. This suggests that Gonzorina and Catullus, or their players, have very different goals, values, or personalities, Gonzorina being more oriented toward rapid upward mobility and high-level achievement, and Catullus, more oriented toward exploration. A good way to consider a few of the hundreds of other variables describing characters in the Armory is to compare Gonzorina with Kvinesdal, who is very different, in Table 8.3. We see data describing Kvinesdal at two points in time, but Gonzorina had become inactive by 2013, so is represented only with 2010 data.

Table 8.3 Selected statistics about two characters from the online WoW database

Characteristic	Gonzorina, July 2010	Kvinesdal, July 2010	Kvinesdal, January 2013
Race	Troll	Blood Elf	Blood Elf
Gender	Female	Male	Male
Class	Hunter	Warlock	Warlock
Rank in Science Guild	0 (Master)	3 (Member)	3 (Member)
Experience level	80	80	81
Achievement points	1545	1080	1915
Exploration achievements	11	12	56
Dungeon and raid achievements	83	2	9
Profession achievements	6	42	51
Quests completed	1405	1683	2151
Daily quests completed	17	479	>500
Total deaths	247	146	158
Total raid and dungeon deaths	138	3	3
Resurrected by another player	73	0	0
Total 5-player dungeons entered	171	7	7
Greed rolls made on loot	1392	7	7
Emblems acquired	458	8	8
Total cheers	50	0	0
Total waves	52	34	34
Cooking skill	0	450	525
First aid skill	0	450	490
Fishing skill	0	366	396
Herbalism skill	410	0	525
Skinning skill	450	450	470
Tailoring skill	0	390	511

The first three variables are selected when the character is created, and cannot be changed later: race, gender, and class.

Recognizing that their data relate to a particular point in history, we can compare the personalities of Gonzorina and Kvinesdal. Achievement points are a pure measure of status, earned by accomplishing a variety of feats, but not translatable into increased power or possessions. They were introduced into WoW about 6 months after the conference as one of a number of enhancements intended to encourage players to keep striving through their characters, even after they had reached the experience ceiling. Exploring every area in a zone earns 10 achievement points, for example, and every zone on a continent earns 25. Gonzorina had completed 11 exploration achievements, which means she visited all areas within 11 of the 61 zones, and Kvinesdal had done the same for 12 zones by July 2010, and fully 56 by January 2013.

Gonzorina, however, had completed far more achievements in dungeons by July 2010 than Kvinesdal, 83 versus 2, and Kvinesdal added only about one every 4 months thereafter. These are separate virtual environments, such as a castle or a cavern, where teams of typically five players battle against the enemies who hold the place. Apparently Gonzorina is much more of a team player, earning social status by cooperating with others in group adventures. A suggestion of what motivates Kvinesdal is that he scores much higher on professional achievements, completing 42 versus 6 for Gonzorina. We see that Kvinesdal has completed somewhat more quests than Gonzorina, especially the variety called daily quests. These are usually simple missions—not chained together into long strings of quests with an important story line—that can be repeated each day and usually earn virtual gold and goods as well as experience, but not much social status. Daily quests are usually done solo.

WoW characters often "die" and then are "resurrected," and the table shows that Gonzorina died more often than Kvinesdal, because dungeons are dangerous. A character who dies may be resurrected by a team-mate who has the requisite ability, or will naturally resurrect at a nearby graveyard. She was often resurrected by a comrade, while he never was.

When members of a team kill an enemy, there may arise a question about who gets to loot a valuable weapon or other thing from the corpse. If a player desperately needs the thing, to complete a collection or because it suits their character's function, the communication interface lets them select "need," in which case that player gets the thing unless somebody else also said "need." More often, players select "greed" meaning they want the thing just because it is valuable, and all the "greed" players roll virtual dice to see who gets it. Thus the fact that Gonzorina participated in 1392 greed rolls made on loot, compared with only 7 greed rolls for Kvinesdal, indicates that she is playing in teams, while he is playing solo most of the time. Similarly, emblems are earned in top-level team dungeons, where team members may cheer each other when they win. In the wider WoW world, passing strangers sometimes wave at each other, so Kvinesdal has received waves but not cheers.

Near the bottom of the table we see why Kvinesdal has achieved so much more professionally than Gonzorina. Any character may practice three secondary professions—cooking, first aid, and fishing—plus selecting two out of a list of primary professions. Kvinesdal has excelled at all three of the optional professions, while Gonzorina has not even started any of them. Between 2010 and 2013, Kvinesdal must have dropped one of his original major skills, either skinning or tailoring, to take up herbalism. Professions in WoW do not contribute to overall experience, so the fact that Kvinesdal's level went only from 80 to 81 over 3 years does not mean he is lazy, but that he prefers creating things to killing enemies. Furthermore, the WoW level cap on experience was not raised from 80 to 85 until December 7, 2010. Coincidentally, on that very day Kvinesdal achieved the exalted status, Illustrious Grand Master Cook.

8.3 Virtual World Wikis

Everybody is familiar with Wikipedia, but many are not fully aware how many thousands of specialized wikis exist, and how they can be media for expressing and preserving the personalities of the contributors. Wikis vary greatly in how the work

Table 8.4 A selection of MMO game wikis

Topic	Name	URL	Articles
World of Warcraft	WoWWiki	www.wowwiki.com/	97,963
World of Warcraft	Wowpedia	www.wowpedia.org/	110,644
World of Warcraft	Wowhead	www.wowhead.com/	
EverQuest II	EQ2i	eq2.wikia.com/wiki/	62,993
Lord of the Rings Online	LOTRO-Wiki	lotro-wiki.com/	50,228
Fallen Earth	Fallen Earth	fallenearth.wikia.com/wiki/	12,440
The Secret World	The Secret World Wiki	wiki.crygaia.com/view/	3,585
The Secret World	The Secret World	www.ign.com/wikis/the-secret-world/	
The Secret World	The Secret World	unfair.co/	602
Pirates of the Burning Sea	PotBS Wiki	potbs.wikia.com/wiki/	5,484
Pirates of the Caribbean Online	Pirates of the Caribbean Online Wiki	piratesonline.wikia.com/wiki	2,505
EVE Online	EVElopedia	wiki.eveonline.com/en/wiki/	13,754
EVE Online	EVE Wiki	eve.wikia.com/wiki/	1,754
Final Fantasy XIV	FFXIVCore	wiki.ffxivcore.com/	
City of Heroes	Paragon Wiki	paragonwiki.com/wiki/	
The Matrix Online	Matrix Wiki	matrix.wikia.com/wiki/	1,165
Star Wars Galaxies	SWG Wiki	swg.wikia.com/wiki/	9,573
Star Wars: The Old Republic	WIKI SWTOR	www.wikiswtor.com/	4,773
Star Wars	Wookieepedia	starwars.wikia.com/wiki/	100,600
Star Trek Online	STO Wiki	www.stowiki.org/	6,195
Star Trek	Memory Alpha	en.memory-alpha.org/wiki/	35,474
Star Trek	Memory Beta	memory-beta.wikia.com/wiki/	41,460
Neverwinter Nights	NWN Wiki	nwn.wikia.com/wiki/	3,540
Neverwinter	Neverwinter Wiki	neverwintergame.wikia.com/wiki/	25
Second Life	Second Life Wiki	wiki.secondlife.com/wiki/	9,288

is organized, and the mix of principles has evolved over the years, both within long-lasting wikis and across the field as a whole. All major English-language online role-playing games I have checked indeed have wikis, sometimes more than one. Today, when a significant new game launches, wikis are already in place, presumably based on information the game company provided or even created by that company. The general assumption is that players will update and add articles after a wiki's early days, but often a small number of professionals do a significant fraction of the work. Like some other forms of online social media, independent wikis that do not belong to the game company are typically small businesses supported by advertising. Table 8.4 provides an anchor for an introductory discussion, listing some of the many game-related wikis I have used extensively in studying the listed games, with data from January 22, 2013, about the number of articles, in cases where the wiki reported that statistic.

Table 8.4 lists only a small subset of the game-related information communities currently online, but it provides a good basis for understanding the current variety of the genre. WoWWiki and Wowpedia are direct competitors, but it just happens I relied upon WoWWiki during my 2007–2008 research on *World of Warcraft*, as well as Wowhead, which is not set up in wiki format but serves similar functions. Wowhead is an information system in which each page is set up by the organizers, one for each quest, location, object, and non-player character, then players post information, for example about how they completed each mission.

An example is the mission "When Death is Not Enough" in the Western Plaguelands area of *World of Warcraft*. This quest is offered by a female non-player character named Lindsay Ravensun, who is one of the Forsaken who belong to the Horde. In the WoW mythos, the Forsaken are undead, half-corpse characters lead by the Banshee Queen, Sylvanas Windrunner, a break-away faction of the Lich King's Scourge, who defied his death knight champion, Arthras. When a player accepts this quest, she automatically inserts the character's name into her reply: "If we're to win this war for Andorhal, we need to use our newest, most versatile weapon: Val'kyr. Take my enthralled Val'kyr with you, [name of player's character], and kill the simpering Alliance scum that remain on Felstone. Once they are dead, she will bring them back to this world... as one of us. The Forsaken shall not die out!" [22]

Some of the comments posted on Wowhead concerned technical matters, and in so doing expressed the knowledge and skill of their authors. For example, in "When Death is Not Enough," walking away from the farm would cause the Val'kyr to disappear, but she would reappear again as the farm was approached. The related mission "Combat Training" caused many problems for players, as the Val'kyr was controlled through a "pet bar" of special icons, some players had little prior experience with pets, and often the bar did not appear or could not be used. On November 26, 2010, a Wowhead contributor named Wolfjr reported: "Currently the quest is bugged and the Val'kyr will have no pet bar. To get around this make the macro: '/ cast Call to Arms' and use it while targeting Forsaken Troopers." On December 5, 2010, Lazaro398 reminded readers that the pet could not be operated in conjunction with another one. On June 29, 2011, Ulzimate added "Don't make the same mistake I did. I wanted to watch my newfound slaves beat up an Abomination, so I just sicced my Valkyr and five Forsaken babbies on the Abom and, as all pet owners know, if only your pets kill a monster, you don't get credit for it. I had to wait for the stupid Abomination to respawn to finish the quest." [23]

However, the postings on these sites are not limited to brute facts, or puzzle-solving strategies, and often serve to express the personalities of the posters as well as their skills. Seven Wowhead contributors debated the deeper meaning of "When Death is Not Enough," in terms of their own personal values as well as their interpretation of the mythos:

Kaskie: "I feel a bit weird doing this quest. Are we the Forsaken that embittered/desperate that we need to stoop to Arthas' level to bolster our ranks?"
Fojar38:   "They're no more invaders than the Argent Crusaders are. Simply being opposed to the Forsaken doesn't make any given group invaders; especially considering that the Forsaken never controlled any parts of the Western Plaguelands until they take over in Cataclysm, while the Alliance controlled

the region since the Second War up until the Third War. Furthermore, in the Vanilla questchain, Alliance players can deliver the pendent to Ol' Emma, also known as Emma Felstone. She has just as much claim to the region as Jeremiah does, and it seems that the Argent Crusade agrees on account of the fact th [sic]"

Witteafval: "Totally out of character for my blood elf paladin. If I wasn't going for the zone quest achievement, I would have skipped this whole chain. It's just one more item on my growing list of reasons why I dislike the Forsaken."

ladlegard: "But if you step into the lore a little more, you can see that it's justified. Sylvanas is not....balanced. She's desperately altered, heartbroken and embittered for life because of what Arthas did to her. It's like the school bully. He/she bullies because they've been bullied before, it's a vicious circle. I was a bit disgusted (as a Forsaken char) as well when I experienced this quest chain, but I completely understood its motivation. In the end....Sylvanas needs love. From someone or other."

Fojar38:   "http://www.wowhead.com/npc=3520" [the page for Ol' Emma, whom Fojar38 mentioned earlier]

Neritha: "I wouldn't consider laborers (read: farmers) to be 'armed and trained soldiers' Also, you speak of invasion and thievery? Jeremiah Felstone, to which the farm belongs, isn't the only owner of it. But I guess you've never heard of Ol' Emma (better known as Emma Felstone) who currently resides in Stormwind."

Lifebaine: "I understood it to be thus: the forsaken ARE dead, and thus cannot create new life (no progeny) It Is Sylvanas' only way to bolster not only her ranks, but now her own unique culture, granted it is a very grim one. She also did not make slaves of the forsaken-they choose to serve and worship her for a second chance at something resembling life. As the newly risen are not slaves, if they chose to forgo undeath, i believe they have that choice."

Takata: "The only thing I hate about this quest is that you don't have enough time to loot the corpse before the Val'kyr changes the dead Alliance Laborer's corpse into an undead. I even had auto loot on and still couldn't target a corpse and my character got stuck in an awkward position after trying to loot a corpse." [24]

The wikis that follow the WoW trio in Table 8.4 are highly varied. *EverQuest II* is a direct competitor of WoW, although neither can be said to imitate the other, and both possess very well developed fictional cultures. *Lord of the Rings Online* is closely based on the books by J. R. R. Tolkien, rather closer in fact than the popular movies are. *Fallen Earth* and *The Secret World* are remarkably creative virtual worlds representing our Earth facing one or another apocalypse, technological in the case of *Fallen Earth*, and supernatural in the case of *The Sacred World*. The IGN and Unfair sites for *The Secret World* are more like walkthrough guides than conventional wikis, produced by a small number of contributors, and offering complex pages including videos that recorded their own avatar's actions. *Pirates of the Burning Sea* and *Pirates of the Caribbean Online* depict the Caribbean around the year 1700, the first with a fair degree of historical accuracy, and the second based upon the Disney horror comedy movies. While *EVE Online* is set in outer space, in many respects it is highly realistic, because the gameplay emphasized creation of virtual technologies and social organizations. Search engines display this description of EVElopedia: "Official wiki hosted by the game makers and contributed to by players. Includes an item database and game guides." The description of EVE Wiki is quite different: "EVE Wiki is a community site that anyone can contribute to.

Discover, share and add your knowledge!" Given the great variety of virtual worlds currently available, the first way a related wiki describes a poster is simply that the person felt enough harmony with its subculture to join the community.

The striking fact about the next four—*Final Fantasy XIV, City of Heroes, The Matrix Online,* and *Star Wars Galaxies* is that the wiki existed as of January 22, 2013, but the game did not. *Final Fantasy XIV* was in hiatus as a new version was being prepared, but the others have apparently vanished forever. The death of worlds must be kept in mind, if we plan to use them for personality emulation. *Star Wars: The Old Republic* essentially killed off *Star Wars Galaxies*, as Lucas Arts, the company holding the copyrights, worked with a different company to create a newer gameworld. Wookieepedia is a general *Star Wars* wiki, with some references to the game, and of course wikis of all kinds can record aspects of contributors' personalities. Similarly, there is a small wiki for *Star Trek Online,* but two large ones for the general *Star Trek* subculture, Memory Alpha being true to "canon" lore deemed to be authentic, and Memory Beta permitting material that does not adhere closely to the future as presented in the television programs. *Neverwinter Nights* is primarily a solo player computer game in the *Dungeons and Dragons* tradition, but with multi-player online components, while *Neverwinter* is an MMO that had not yet launched at the time the data were collected. *Second Life* is the non-game virtual world to be discussed in the following section.

To understand better how contributors express themselves in a wiki, we can look more closely at WoWWiki. Its statistics page reported it has a total of 254,718 pages, including 97,963 that it calls *content pages*, each being like a blog or short encyclopedia page. The others include talk pages, pages for the contributors, redirects, and other miscellaneous pages. The content pages include 61,111 uploaded graphic images, generally screenshots taken inside *World of Warcraft.* Pages are not merely written by an individual then posted, but edited—which often means expanded—and many pages were created with hardly any content as place holders prior to expansion. WoWWiki says there had been a total of 2,630,560 page edits by January 22, 2013, an average of 10.33 per page. Since WoWWiki is one of the biggest and most often visited of game wikis, one might imagine that large numbers of people are constantly editing, but in fact just 227 people had performed an action on the wiki in the past 30 days. In part, this seemingly low number reflects the maturity of *World of Warcraft,* about 4 months after the most recent expansion of the game during which there undoubtedly was a brief period of furious wiki-expansion activity. But it also reflects a fact that human-centered computing researchers have seen in other information volunteer communities, such as open-source software networks, namely that a few people do most of the work.

A contributor named Fandyllic has made fully 73,248 edits, Raylan13 made 32,528, and Kirkburn made 28,319, although both Raylan13 are Kirkburn are members of WoWWiki's staff, while Fandyllic describes himself as a bureaucrat, administrator, and crazy person. For purposes of understanding how a dedicated but non-professional contributor might express a personal orientation through a wiki, I shall focus on RyanPT. Note: All the information that follows is public, and we do not know this person's real-world identity, so we are not violating the individual's privacy here.

RyanPT says he is a Canadian living in Winnipeg: "I'm a University student with a love of computers and an obsession with World of Warcraft. If you have a question or need some help feel free to leave a message on my talk page. I'm usually on in the mornings and evenings. I am currently studying for an exam, so I will be on less often for a little while. For The Horde!" One area of his expertise is the riding profession and mounts. RyanPT has 15 characters, including a level 88 Blood Elf Frost Death Knight. He made his first contribution to WoWWiki on December 7, 2012, editing the article about the Death Knight class of avatars to update a sentence that had become obsolete when the Mists of Pandaria expansion occurred, September 25, 2012, and the experience level cap was raised to 90. The old sentence read, "There are no racial limitations for creating your death knight." RyanPT's new sentence reads: "Currently the Pandaren cannot become death knights."

The information available about a wiki contributor's behavior is quite remarkably detailed, especially if one logs in as a fellow contributor so one can dig deeper into the history of each page. Each contributor has a WoWWiki page, not counted among the content pages, that includes a list of every edit that contributor ever made, arranged in chronological order. I told the wiki to display the maximum number of contributions on a single page, which is 500, and copied the source code for each of RyanPT's contributions on the three pages that resulted. The oldest one, first as it appears to the user, then complete with the HTML, reads:

04:38, December 7, 2012 (diff | hist).. (-12).. Death Knight
<li class=""><a href="/Death_Knight?oldid=2626824" title="Death Knight">04:38, December 7, 2012 </a> (<a href = "/Death_Knight?diff = prev&oldid = 2626824" title = "Death Knight" > diff </a> | <a href = "/Death_Knight?action = history" title = "Death Knight" > hist </a>).. < span dir = "ltr" class = "mw-plus-minus-neg" title = "32,655 bytes after change" > (-12) </span> .. < a href = "/Death_Knight" title = "Death Knight" > Death Knight </a></li>

The number − 12 near the end merely reports that his new version is 12 bytes smaller than the original page, now exactly 32,655 bytes. The "diff" refers to the difference between the old and new versions, and clicking on it opens the Death Knight history page with the original passage and the changed passage clearly displayed at the top. During the 6 weeks of his involvement, RyanPT added 188 new pages to the wiki, taking a total of 1,400 actions altogether. In 85 of these edits, RyanPT uploaded a file, usually screenshot illustrations. Just 16 edits were forum postings, 31 were on talk pages associated with one or another of the wiki's content pages, and 178 were on user talk pages associated with pages belonging to contributors. Of these, 21 were on RyanPT's own user page, and 37 were on Fandyllic's user page. Clearly, WoWWiki contains a great deal of information about RyanPT's behavior during the 6 week span of his life examined here.

Perhaps easiest to analyze is the topical focus of many of RyanPT's contributions. His profile claimed expertise on mount riding, and indeed, he did a lot of work in this area, including 131 edits on the main Mount page, adding a total of 8,169 bytes. Another 31 edits were on the page for a particular kind, Cloud Serpent

Mounts, and he also paid attention to Dragon Turtle Mounts and Gryphon Mounts. What he was mainly doing was adding links to new pages he was posting about new mounts. At appropriate levels of skill, any player may acquire mounts for his or her avatar, from conventional horses to giant birds and even more unlikely species, by purchasing reins for the beast. Over time, *World of Warcraft* has added many, and 152 of RyanPT's edits, including many of his new pages, concerned one or another kind of reins, each really being a description of the particular mount.

We can identify other interests this particular individual possesses, by noting other kinds of pages that received many edits. RyanPT did 59 edits on the Herbs by Area page, indicating that one of his main professions was herbalism, and he was telling other players where particular herbs could be harvested. He also did 71 edits on the List of Ore by Zone page, and 27 on the List of Mining Nodes, indicating that another gathering profession, mining, was also one of his favorites. Especially interesting are his 25 posts on the Violations page of the wiki, where spammers, trolls, and gold farmers who misuse the wiki are identified so their posts can be blocked. During the period, RyanPT was one of just three people serving as the police force for WoWWiki, the others being Fandyllic and Raylan13 on whose user page RyanPT had posted 64 times.

8.4   Second Life Gesture

An entire book could be written about the current state of information technology designed to capture and emulate physical human movements, including dance and gesture, and indeed a vast library on this topic exists. Here, we will explore several issues in simplified form, within the virtual environment *Second Life,* where many forms of behavioral capture and emulation are relatively easy. The technical methods are simple but that very fact makes a crucial point. Movies that make extensive use of motion capture, like *Avatar,* require actors to go through the exact motions required by the script and desired by the director, to be reproduced as relatively long sequences on the screen. This achieves precision and expressiveness at the cost of flexibility.

We have defined emulation not in terms of precise duplication of past actions by the person, but as creation of a system able to undertake new actions in the style and with the skills of the person. *Second Life* can display short episodes of motion capture, and repeat complex sequences of programmed movements, but its flexibility lies in the fact that it can concatenate many short animations into a sequence, like letters in a word and words in a sentence. This fine-grained modularity harmonizes with the emphasis this book has given to questionnaire methodologies, because each separate motion is analogous to a separate question, and questions can be assembled into factors and scales.

This exploration will be carried out from the standpoint of an avatar intentionally based on a deceased person, who lived a very brief life, never had the opportunity to do the things the avatar will do in *Second Life,* and left precious little information on which to base any emulation. Her name was Cleora Emily Bainbridge, my grandfather's sister, and lived from November 8, 1868, until April 14, 1870. One damaged tintype photograph exists, plus a few descriptions by her parents, notably in a novel her father published in 1883, where one of the two heroines was clearly a fantasy of the life she might have enjoyed, had she lived [25]. I used her as the avatar to explore the influential gameworld, *EverQuest II*, in my book *eGods*, which was a critique of religion from the perspective of modern culture [26]. I then created other avatars based on her in other virtual worlds, to explore other features of a life that ended so prematurely, and here report on her quest for physical mobility in *Second Life*.

Dying before reaching the age of one and a half, the original Cleora must not have learned to dance, and may not even have walked. Her cause of death was recorded as "water on the brain," but we do not know whether symptoms like paralysis began long before her demise, although the one surviving photo of her depicts an apparently normal little girl. The Cleora in *Second Life* is a young adult, possessing the red hair the records suggest the original Cleora may have had, but initially lacking possessions other than one set of casual clothing, and with no memory of experiences. Every *Second Life* avatar begins with the ability to perform movement, not merely to walk, and indeed to fly, but also to gesture. The goal of this last pilot study in this book is quite simple, to explore Cleora's ability to gesture, and go on a quest to add to the range and complexity of gestures she possesses. Each single gesture will belong to other avatars as well, but her particular collection defines her personality in terms of the movements she has chosen to learn.

Every avatar has a collection of standard gestures, accessible from a pull-down menu called Communicate. When I entered *Second Life* as Cleora, using a Windows operating system, ten of them could be invoked through function keys, as listed in Table 8.5, and by a slash command entered into text chat. Each was a fairly complex series of avatar movements, accompanied by a sound. Two of them, /getlost and /please used the same animation unit, which inside the gesture macro system was called Disdain, so /please was not a polite request for help, but an expression of contempt. The system allows the user to assign any gesture to any key, and combine them to some extent, but other tools are used to create the movements from scratch, generally outside *Second Life*.

In addition, eight dance segments could also be activated by means of function keys. For example, pressing F9 caused Cleora to throw both arms straight out to her left and right sides, take a wide side-step right, cross her left leg behind the right, and then cross the right leg behind the left while pulling the arms back then pushing them out again, followed by spinning around once clockwise while holding her hands up near her face. Somehow I imagined this vigorous but awkward movement is not the kind of dance she would want to do, so I looked for a more suitable alternative that would be easy to implement immediately. If Cleora had been a real person, early in her explorations of *Second Life*, here is how she could assemble more suitable choreography.

One of the available but unassigned movements was /hula. She slowly extended her left arm straight to the side, gracefully moving her right arm in the same direc-

Table 8.5 Ten starting gestures for cleora, in *Second Life*

Keyboard	Text Chat	Movements	Sounds
F2	/clap	Claps hands a half dozen times in front of waist, with arms bent at elbows, toothy smile and blinking	Clapping sound
F4	/hey	Waves with right hand, slight smile, eyes close very slightly	"Hey!"
F5	/wow	Mouth opens wide for a moment, no other movements	"Wow!"
F6	/getlost	Eyes briefly close as mouth sneers, raising upper lip only on left side to show teeth	"Get lost."
F8	/laugh	Mouth opens wide, eyes close, hands hold belly, bends first far back at waist then forward, as body jerks up and down	Female laughter
Shift + F8	/cry	Mouth open in a frown, eyes close, hands cover face while heads jerks backward and forward four times, then body straightens as right arm wipes across face	Female weeping sounds
Ctrl + F4	/please	Same as /getlost	"Please!"
Ctrl + F6	/lookinggood	Big smile, showing teeth, eyes close slightly	"Looking good!"
Ctrl + F8	/bored	Left forearm moves horizontal with hand supporting right elbow, right arm supports chin, head slumps, fingers of right hand tap head	Female sigh
Ctrl + F10	/embarrassed	Mouth opens showing teeth, eyes open, right hand with fingers open touches upper chest, body wiggles, head drops and hand goes toward forehead hiding face	Female breathy giggle

tion across her chest, turning her face in the same direction and slightly waving the arms, then slowly reversed direction toward the right and performed the exact same movements in a symmetrical manner, followed by facing forward and slowly moving her arms in that direction, before opening her arms and returning them to their rest position. Another gesture that seemed right for Cleora was /blowkiss, slowly extending her right hand palm upward and blowing across it. In the gesture assignment window I set F9 so it was no longer connected to the violent Dance 1 moves, but to /hula, adding /blowkiss and the text "Cleora loves you!" to the /hula animation. It was also necessary to include a line, "Wait: until animations are done," to hold the second animation until the first one was finished, and in the result the two animations very smoothly blended together. Now, pressing F9 would cause her to say in the local text chat, "Cleora loves you," do a brief hula dance, and blow a kiss, as shown in Fig. 8.1.

The capture and emulation logic here is very simple. Were Cleora actually alive, perhaps age 15 as she would have been when her father published his novel, she could explore *Second Life*, collecting and creating gestures that suited her own,

Fig. 8.1 Cleora performing two selected animations, combined in one gesture routine

special personality. Each one could be described as a procedure in a computing language, recorded and thus preserved indefinitely, and transferrable to other avatars. Indeed, the gesture assembly window we just used to modify /hula is a very simple programming environment, where we assembled three actions in a particular order. If a different user operated the Cleora avatar, the collection of available gestures would still express her personality, or an amalgam of her and the user. An artificial intelligence script could make her walk around one of the public areas of *Second Life*, performing her little ritual toward each other avatar she meets, emulating the original Cleora.

The first example, in Fig. 8.1, combines two animations, each of which was separately appropriate for Cleora, but make an especially appropriate combination. Thus, the capture and emulation involves not only collecting suitable animations, but using them under correct circumstances, which requires combining them as the spoken syllables of speech combine to make words and sentences, that express the experience of the specific person under the given conditions. A more complete picture of the possibilities was achieved by having Cleora explore widely.

Her first step was to use the search facility to seek advertisements posted by vendors in *Second Life* who sell gestures or animations, after which she teleported to their establishments. The first store listed, Careless Gestures, consisted of four somewhat disreputable looking two-story buildings, walls covered with posters advertising many different kinds of gesture, often erotic in nature, allowing a customer to buy single gestures or entire sets. Cleora was looking for gestures that might reflect her own personality, and wondered if she might have affinities with the fictional fantasy adventuress, Buffy the Vampire Slayer. With no idea what she was getting, except the hint provided by the name, she bought a Buffy gesture named "Take Charge" for L$ 40–40 Linden dollars, the currency inside *Second Life*, worth about 15 cents in US currency. She added the gesture to her active list, assigning it to the key F10, and tried it out. The gesture was great, but forced Cleora to say words into the text chat she strongly disliked: "I JuST LoVE iT WhEn YOu TaKe ChARgE, YoU MaN YOu!" It was a simple matter to remove that text from the macro in the gesture system, and this became the first purchased gesture in Cleora's new kinesics set, listed at the top of Table 8.6

The six examples in Table 8.6 can be compared in several ways, but only some of them can actually be combined. The last one in the list does not appear to be an animation, but a piece of clothing. However, clothing adapts to the movements of the avatar, and this dress has several long pieces that flow around rather actively in reaction to walking or falling, so it really is a form of animation. The act of buying clothing is equivalent to answering a preference question, and in *Second Life* one is selecting movements as well as attire. The Midnight Rose dress was purchased in a store projecting the style of the 1890s, the decade in which the real Cleora would have been in early adulthood, had she lived, and it seemed very appropriate for her. Figure 8.2 shows Cleora going through the actions of fainting, while wearing the dress, and it actively participates in the faint, adding movement and drama.

Technically, fainting could be combined with other actions, such as the two shown in Fig. 8.1. It is an animation, which means it is a movement procedure that includes multiple steps but is handled as a unit, and it is marked so that the user has full permissions to modify and copy it. The terms are slightly confusing, but a *gesture* is a short program that may contain animations, but could instead just contain sounds or text. However, a feature of the faint animation prevents using it as one word in an action sentence. At the end, Cleora is lying on the ground some distance away from the spot she was standing, but the animation automatically returns her to a standing position at that original spot, making her jump unrealistically. If one added an animation that made her lie on the ground for a while, she would suddenly stand at the end of fainting, and drop again into the second animation. The sleeping child animation would be a very nice conclusion for fainting, but the purchaser does not get permission to modify it, so it cannot be combined with other animations through the gesture programming system.

The FSTand_04 animation, provided by A&M MOCAP Animations Workshop, is a motion capture sequence of a real woman moving in a way that is not exactly dancing but sashaying over a small area, and returning to the starting point, such that it can repeat endlessly without any jerk at the end. The movements are graceful and expressive, but would have duplicated the behavior of whatever real person was captured at the workshop. Indeed, anyone may hire A&M to do a motion capture session of their own movements, and upload the result to *Second Life* or to many other game or virtual environment platforms [27]. FSTand_04 did not come with

Table 8.6 Animations and gestures collected in several second life places

Source	Advertisement	Gesture or Animation	Cost
Careless Gestures	SL's #1 Gesture Store since 2007! 99% of our gestures are animated. 5000+ Gestures. Top Quality and absolutely the Best	Buffy the Vampire Slayer gesture "Take Charge"—a knowing smile, nodding vigorously, then moving the hands as if confidently shooting revolvers	L$ 40
Animations by loufa Shilova	Animations & Poses, poses and animations shop all animations and poses you need!	Faint3 animation: turning, throwing head back, left arm reaching out, right arm behind head, falls to the left onto the ground	L$ 199
Sheena Kamala	KAMALA ANIMATIONS— Builders and Personal Use	Sleeping child animation: lying on right side, slowly moving arms and legs as if in a dream or adjusting for comfortable slumber	L$ 750
A&M MOCAP Animations Workshop	Motion capture dances and dance animations. New dances release each day	FSTand_04: female cycle of graceful walking movements from and to the starting point, first with left hand on hip and right hand waved with bent elbow, then both hands on hips, waving hips and walking around in two forward and backward phases, but always looking forward	L$ 120
Anglican Cathedral of Second Life	A distinctively Anglican church within SL for those who are Anglicans or who share the Anglican heritage, and for those of other denominations who value what we provide. We also welcome those who are exploring the Christian faith	Cross gesture: Leaning forward slightly, makes the sign of the cross, raising the right hand to the head, moving it straight down to the waist, then to the left and across the chest, ending with the hand over the heart	L$ 0
Candace Hudson Thrift Shop	Visit HUDSON's Clothing for Quality Womans Fashion—Dress, Gowns and Jewelry. Find Role Play costumes from Peasant, Gypsy, Bohemian and Pirate to Eyes, Steampunk, Boots & Shoes, Mens wear, Antique, Fireplace, Furniture	Midnight Rose dress: includes pants, corset, lace stockings, and flex skirt that moves while she walks as if blowing in the wind	L$ 49 marked down from L$ 175

Fig. 8.2 Cleora fainting while wearing the midnight rose dress

permissions required to assemble it with other components into a larger program, but of course customers of A&M could specify whatever permissions they wanted.

At the entrance to the Anglican Cathedral in *Second Life*, many free things are provided, including a cross necklace which Cleora immediately wore. It fit beautifully just above the bodice of her dress, and expressed her Christian faith, given that the real Cleora's father was a Baptist minister and her mother was a leader of interfaith Protestant organizations. Perhaps as an expression of her solid faith, the cross remained firmly in its proper place, rather than animating like her dress, even when she fainted. The Cathedral offered both gestures, which could not be modified, and 15 freely modifiable animations. In addition to the cross gesture, she concatenated three different cross animations, one in the western style, one in the eastern style—which differed in which direction the cross-bar was drawn, and a relaxed version of the western style that was less vigorous than the one in the table. Thus, animations can be collected from different cultures, that Cleora might find expressed her own preferences, or were interesting to try on occasion precisely because they were not one of her own habitual behaviors.

Human cognition and behavior can be modeled as the meaningful assembly of units at various levels of aggregation, like atoms assembled into molecules into living cells into the entire organism, if the modularity of language is an overused metaphor. What Cleora would do depends upon her circumstances, as well as her wishes. Had she lived, she would have played different roles at different stages of her life. The challenge in assembling actions, illustrated by the fact there was no easy way for her to recover from a faint, can be solved partly in the selection of sequences of actions that are logical successors of each other, and in providing the emulation system with the ability to interpolate in realtime a smooth transition from one pose to another. Already, much is known about how to accomplish this, because avatar animation of American Sign Language for the benefit of deaf people has been the focus of good research, and the prosody of how to connect gestures is a key challenge [28, 29]. On the highest level, the challenge is integrating across all the topics covered in this book.

8.5 Conclusion

Progress in personality capture and emulation is bound to take place, because both cognitive science and information technology continue to advance, and researchers will undertake many projects that will contribute, whether they intended to do so or not. However, we may have reached two take-off thresholds, at which concerted efforts may both feasible and rewarding. First, some fields may be ready to converge, achieving more than either could alone, not merely in capture and emulation but in many other worthwhile endeavors related to them, providing new career opportunities for people who naturally enjoy spanning disciplines. Second, it is possible that new industries and attractive non-profit activities may now be feasible, whether a much more pleasant alternative to grim and expensive cemeteries for the deceased, or collective community history projects to render their memories active participants in the world of tomorrow. More modestly, the methods outlined in this book can be used to design personalized information systems and semi-autonomous artificial intelligence assistants, and perhaps even to develop new forms of education and psychotherapy that help a person evolve through improved self-emulation. Oh, if I could only see the path that you, yourself, will choose to explore!

References

1. Blascovich, J., & Bailenson, J. (2011). *Infinite reality: The hidden blueprint of our virtual lives* (p. 3). New York: William Morrow.
2. Becker, H. S., Geer, B., Hughes, E. C., & Strauss, A. L. (1961). *Boys in white: Student culture in medical school.* Chicago: University of Chicago Press.
3. Goffman, E. (1961). *Encounters: Two studies in the sociology of interaction.* Indianapolis: Bobbs-Merrill.
4. Coser, R. L. (1966). Role distance, sociological ambivalence, and transitional status systems. *American Journal of Sociology, 72*(2), 173–187.
5. Gibbs, M., Mori, J., Arnold, M., & Kohn, T. (2012) Tombstones, uncanny monuments and epic quests: Memorials in World of Warcraft. *Game Studies, 12*(1).
6. http://www.ezrachatterton.org/. Accessed 6 June 2013.
7. http://www.wowwiki.com/Caylee_Dak. Accessed 6 June 2013.
8. Bainbridge, W. S. (2013). *eGods.* New York: Oxford University Press.
9. Yang, K., Marsh, T., Mun, M., & Shahabi, C. (2005). Continuous archival and analysis of user data in virtual and immersive game environments. In *Proceedings of the 2nd ACM workshop on continuous archival and retrieval of personal experiences* (pp. 13–22). New York: ACM.

10. Normoyle, A., Drake, J., Likhachev, M., & Safonova, A. (2012). Game-based data capture for player metrics. In *Proceedings of the eighth AAAI conference on artificial intelligence and interactive digital entertainment* (pp. 44–50). Menlo Park: AAAI.

11. Lee, S., Carlson, G., Jones, S., Johnson, A., Leigh, J., & Renambot, L. (2010). Designing an expressive avatar of a real person. In *Proceedings of the 10th international conference on intelligent virtual agents* (pp. 64–76). Berlin: Springer.

12. Puklavage, C., Pirela, A., Gonzalez, A. J., & Georgiopoulos, M. (May 19–21, 2010). Imitating personalized expressions through an avatar using machine learning. *Proceedings of the twenty-third international florida artificial intelligence research society conference*. Daytona Beach, Florida.

13. Mejia, R, (2012). Posthuman, postrights? *Explorations in Media Ecology, 11*(1), 27–44.

14. Aarthun, S. (2012). *4 Hours of Fire and Chaos: How the Benghazi Attack Unfolded. CNN*. www.cnn.com/2012/09/12/world/africa/libya-consulate-attack-scene/index.html. Accessed 13 Sept 2012.

15. http://en.wikipedia.org/wiki/Sean_Smith_(diplomat). Accessed 9 Feb 2013.

16. Bainbridge, W. S. (2011). *The virtual future: Science-fiction gameworlds*. London: Springer.

17. http://themittani.com/news/rip-vile-rat. Accessed 23 July 2013.

18. http://wiki.eveonline.com/en/wiki/Dev_Blog:2012.09.13_A_Tribute_to_Sean_%27Vile_Rat%27_Smith. Accessed 23 July 2013.

19. Bainbridge, W. S. (2010). *The warcraft civilization* (p. 150). Massachusetts: MIT Press.

20. http://csr.wwiionline.com/scripts/services/persona/service.jsp?pid=236339. No longer available as of 23 July 2013.

21. Bainbridge, W. S. (Ed.). (2010). *Online worlds: Convergence of the real and the virtual*. London: Springer.

22. http://www.wowhead.com/quest=26937. Accessed 23 July 2013.

23. http://www.wowhead.com/quest=26938#comments. Accessed 23 July 2013.

24. http://www.wowhead.com/quest=26937#comments. Accessed 23 July 2013.

25. Bainbridge, W. F. (1883). *Self-giving: A story of christian missions*. Boston: D. Lothrop.

26. Bainbridge, W. S. (2013). *eGods: Faith versus fantasy in computer gaming* (p. 59). New York: Oxford University Press.

27. http://www.mocap-dancer.com/about.html. Accessed 1 June 2013.

28. Huenerfauth, M. (2009). A linguistically motivated model for speed and pausing in animations of american sign language. *ACM transactions on accessible computing, 2*.

29. Huenerfauth, M., & Lu, P. (2012). Effect of spatial reference and verb infection on the usability of american sign language animations. *Universal Access in the Information Society, 11*, 169–184.

Appendix

Ten Personality Capture and Analysis Programs

Developed near the middle of this extensive research project, these user-friendly programs were written for the Windows XP operating system, and work on some of the more recent versions. They can be found at Springer Extras (http://extras.springer.com) by searching for the book's ISBN (978-1-4471-5603-1).

Together, these programs allow the user to evaluate 20,000 stimuli, each in terms of two measurement scales, for a total of 40,000 personality capture measurements. Each of the ten programs incorporates analysis modules that summarize the user's responses in interesting ways, thus providing secondary benefit beyond mere personality capture, and the beginnings of theory-based personality emulation. Each program offers output options, which may be used to transfer the items into different software or databases for use in other research projects. Or, the programs themselves may be used as research tools.

Action: 2,400 verbs, assembled from standard reference works, covering a wide range of human activities including most of the verbs commonly employed by speakers of standard English. Scales: dislike-like and passive-active. A system for recording your preferences for things you might do and your conceptualizations of them. The results may help you plan future activities.

Association: 2,000 pairs of words, of which 1,000 were paired off in terms of standard relations such as synonym or antonym, while the other 1,000 were paired randomly. Scales: weak-strong and unimportant-important. A software tool for tracing some of the mental connections in your mind. In a sense, you are the dynamic pattern of associations in your brain's neural network.

Beliefs: 2,000 statements drawn from a range of prior studies and standard opinion poll sources. Scales: false-true and unimportant-important. A software system for exploring your fundamental beliefs. The results may help you clarify why you believe or feel in particular ways.

Beliefs II: 2,000 statements, 1,500 of which were derived from the responses of about 4,000 people to a series of 11 open-ended items that had been included in an online questionnaire. Scales: false-true and unimportant-important. The goals are the same as those of the original Beliefs program, but the scope of topics was expanded.

W. S. Bainbridge, *Personality Capture and Emulation,* Human-Computer Interaction Series, 205
DOI 10.1007/978-1-4471-5604-8, © Springer-Verlag London 2014

Emotions: 2,000 stimuli categorized in terms of 20 emotions, of which 1,000 came from a pair of questionnaires administered through The Question Factory, a website created to develop survey items, and 1,000 were derived came from searches of the World Wide Web to find texts describing situations that elicited each of the emotions. Scales: bad-good and little-much. An exploration of your typical feelings, moods, and motivations. It clarifies your desires and worries, and it can help you seek or avoid various situations, actions, people or other things that stimulate 20 primary emotions in you.

Experience: 2,000 brief descriptions of personal experiences, most of which came from open-ended questions in a major survey of 1,025 members of a worldwide missionary group, people who have a very wide range of personal experiences as they travel widely and live under a variety of conditions. Scales: bad-good and never-recently. A system for exploring your memories and desires. It clarifies your satisfactions and frustrations, dreams and nightmares, and it can help you plan what experiences to have next.

Self: 1,600 qualities a person might have, selected in 800 antonym pairs but separated in the questionnaire, constituting an extension of the classical Semantic Differential technique. Scales: bad-good and little-much. A tool for sketching the image you have of yourself. It helps you follow the ancient maxim, "know thyself," and it provides a record of your values, habits, interactive style, and personality.

Taste: 2,000 foods, most derived from an open-ended question in the youth version of a major online survey, augmented from cookbooks and catalogues with items that adults might have mentioned. Scales: dislike-like and unhealthy-healthy. A record of your food preferences and nutritional beliefs. The results may help you guide future diet selections.

Wisdom: 2,000 statements adapted from all 120 episodes of the original *Babylon 5* science fiction television series, plus all the early related books, usually paraphrased or edited significantly so they express general moral, tactical, or existential ideas. Scales: false-true and unimportant-important. Patterned after the Beliefs and Beliefs II modules, this program shows how it is possible to assemble the total set of perspectives that characterize any subculture, including artistic genres and mythologies.

Year 2100: 2,000 predictions of what might happen in many spheres of human life in the year 2100, derived from responses by thousands of people to an open-ended item included in one of the first really large online social science questionnaires. Scales: bad-good and unlikely-likely. A time machine for the imagination that helps you develop your own personal picture of how the world might be a century from now. In so doing, it measures and records your values, beliefs, hopes, and goals.

Glossary

Acquiescence: The tendency of a respondent to agree with whatever a questionnaire or interview item says, regardless of its content.

Activity: The active-passive dimension of the Semantic Differential.

Agent: A computer-based system that functions somewhat autonomously as the representative of the user, and which may be conceptualized as a virtual person based on artificial intelligence.

Agreeableness: One of the Big Five personality dimensions, marked by trust, straightforwardness, and altruism.

Apotheosis: Creation of an idealized version of a person.

Avatar: The virtual representation of a person, as in a computer-generated environment, derived from the tradition in Indo-European religions for the gods to manifest themselves on Earth through limited aspects of their divine natures.

Big Five: A standard theory that there exist primarily five dimensions of human personality; in the OCEAN version: Openness to experience, Conscientiousness, Extraversion, Agreeableness, and Neuroticism.

Biological transformation: Improving human health and longevity by the use of advanced biochemical and medical methods.

Boswell: An intelligent agent that serves as the interface to an information system about the life of an individual person, ideally able to interview that person, write a biography, and speak for that person in dialogues with other people.

Case-based reasoning: An artificial intelligence approach similar to rule-based reasoning, but in which the concepts and the relations between them are derived from real-world situations.

Chunking: A process in artificial intelligence, assumed also to take place in the human brain, in which complex data are represented more simply by connecting them or encapsulating them in concepts.

Cluster analysis: A set of statistical methods for finding groups of related items in a matrix of correlations or similar coefficients.

Codebook: A guide for entering and analyzing data from a questionnaire, usually consisting of an edition of the questionnaire to which code numbers have been added for each response, often along with the distribution of responses and metadata.

W. S. Bainbridge, *Personality Capture and Emulation,* Human-Computer Interaction Series,   207
DOI 10.1007/978-1-4471-5604-8, © Springer-Verlag London 2014

Collaborative filtering: An earlier conception of what is now called *recommender systems*, information retrieval based on input from multiple users.

Computational transformation: Offloading many human cognitive function to machines, such as using calculators instead of making humans solve arithmetic problems, and employing a database to augment memory, at the extreme transferring personality itself to a robot or artificial agent.

Conditional validity: The tendency of a measure, such as a battery of questionnaire items, to represent a phenomenon accurately under some circumstances but not others, for example with some respondents but not all.

Conscientiousness: One of the Big Five personality dimensions, marked by competence, dutifulness, and a preference for orderliness.

Consciousness: The subjective experience of thought and action, often glorified in traditional cultures as a transcendent entity, but possibly nothing more than the procedure-monitoring aspect of working memory.

Confirmatory analysis: Any one of a number of rigorous methodologies that determines the extent to which a dataset supports a specified theory or hypothesis.

Concordance: In linked-respondent surveys, the correlation between the response of one person in a linked pair to a given question and the response of the other person to the same question.

Confounding factor: A variable that confuses analysis of other variables because of its strong but complex relations with them, causing problems such as suppression or spuriousness.

Correlation coefficient: A number between -1.00 and $+1.00$ that expresses the strength of the relationship between two variables.

Cultural science: By analogy with cognitive science, a new and more rigorous social science based on the convergence of those portions of traditional disciplines that concern beliefs, norms, values, symbols, and patterns of communication.

Depth psychology: Forms of theory and research on the human personality based on the premise that many factors are subconscious or otherwise hidden from view.

Dialect: A subculture within a language, reflecting regional, ethnic or class differences, typically having vague boundaries but reflecting real communication patterns.

Durability: The principle that information captured about a person must be preserved indefinitely, but emulated flexibly so that it can harmonize with changing world conditions.

Eidetic memory: A supposedly rare but possibly nonexistent ability to remember brief perceptions in fine detail without any process of rehearsing or conscious memorization.

Emotion extraction: The process of identifying the emotions expressed by a person's facial expressions and physical movements, for example using computer vision and machine learning.

Episodic memory: Recollection of a specific life event, hypothetically stored as connections between tokens representing components such as who, what, when and where.

Ethnographer: A trained, professional documenter of the culture of a group, typically a cultural anthropologist or a sociologist.

Ethnographic questionnaire: A methodology for collecting information via questions asked to respondents, in which the questions were originally derived from the same culture to which the respondent belongs.

Euhemerism: Traditionally, this word means the belief that ancient legends are exaggerations of real events, but it now can mean emulating a personality based more on the ideals the person held, than on mundane facts about the person's life.

Evaluation: The good-bad dimension of the Semantic Differential.

Exemplar model: A cognitive science theory that asserts every concept in the human mind is an abstraction based on specific instances, perhaps as few as one example.

Existentialism: A human-centered philosophical school of thought that became prominent in Europe under the disillusioned cultural conditions immediately after World War II, often viewing the world as meaningless or absurd.

Expert system: A database providing rule-based instructions for the accomplishment of complex practical tasks, conceptualized as a form of artificial intelligence but based on the archived expertise of human beings.

Exploratory analysis: The use of rigorous methods, such as factor analysis or data mining, to find simple patterns in a complex dataset, ideally deriving hypotheses that can be tested by other methods later.

Extraversion: One of the Big Five personality dimensions, marked by gregariousness and assertiveness; often spelled *extroversion* outside psychology.

Factor analysis: A statistical procedure to find underlying dimensions hidden in a correlation matrix.

Fidelity: The principle that emulation must be true to the essence of the original person, but there are multiple ways of defining that essence.

Fixed-choice items: Questionnaire items that require the respondent to select from a set of listed choices, for example by checking one of several boxes on a printed questionnaire, or pressing one key in a computer-administered questionnaire.

Flashbulb memory: An influential but outdated psychological concept, asserting that under conditions of unusual emotional arousal a person can acquire a detailed and long-lasting memory of the event.

Futurology: A general term for the serious consideration of the human future, using such methods as trend extrapolation and scenario development.

Gamma: A correlation coefficient designed primarily for use with ordinal data, in which the data scale arranges points in a set order, but not necessarily following a real-number metric.

Geolocation: The use of information technology to specify the geographic location of a fact or event, typically based on a comprehensive coordinate system.

Grounded theory: Development of a theoretical system derived from the concepts that ordinary people use in the situation under study.

Historical linguistics: The scholarly study of the history of a language, often focused on its changing vocabulary but also sometimes on grammatical shifts, or the use of linguistic studies to understand better an historical period.

Incorporation: The capture and emulation of a personality by building it into a larger socio-cultural structure.

Informant: Participant in an interview or survey who provides objective information.

Integrity: The principle that an emulated personality must be internally unified and integrated into a wider community.

Intelligence quotient: Measure of intelligence, usually test-based, defined for children in terms of mental age expressed as a percentage of chronological age, or more generally in terms of a normal curve distribution with a mean of 100 and a standard deviation of 15.

Latency of response: The delay, often measured in milliseconds, between when a stimulus is presented to a person and that person initiates a response.

Linked-respondent survey: A study in which the unit of analysis is pairs of respondents.

Localization: Modification of a technology or set of information to suit conditions at a particular place, adjusting it with respect to language, climate, or the prevalent infrastructure.

Machiavellianism: A philosophy or personality type that manipulates other people, using guile and deceit.

Machine learning: A very general term for artificial intelligence methods that over time develop a model of data, often using a subset of the data to create the model, and another subset to test it.

Metadata: Documentation associated with a dataset, such as a questionnaire codebook, that states its provenance and the meaning of the variables.

Motion capture: Entering the movements of a human being into a computer, usually by some kind of machine vision system, so they can be used to program realistic images of people in movies and videogames.

Multi-dimensional scaling: An iterative statistical analysis technique, similar to factor analysis, that begins with a matrix of distance measures ideally between all possible pairs of items, and ends with a map of the items in a limited number of dimensions, optimized to reduce the net error.

Natural language processing: A general term, often given as NLP, for a variety of computer techniques for processing human language, such as speech recognition, language translation, and text mining.

Native informant: A member of a culture enlisted by an anthropologist or other social scientist to take a more active role than a mere respondent in documenting the culture, comparable to a research assistant.

Nay-saying: A form of response bias in which the respondent tends to disagree with agree-disagree items, regardless of their content.

Negative correlation: An association between two variables in which one variable tends to increase when the other decreases.

Neural network: A general approach to artificial intelligence, based on the metaphor of the human nervous systems but not really duplicating it, in which the machine learning takes place in weights between nodes, analogous to synapses and neurons.

Neuroticism: One of the Big Five personality dimensions, marked by anxiety, hostility, and depression.

Open-ended item: Questionnaire item that gives the respondent the freedom to provide an individualized response, for example by writing text in response to a question.

Openness to experience: One of the Big Five personality dimensions, marked by exploration and fantasy; controversial because some psychologists conceptualize it as having intellectual interests and thus overlapping the concept of intelligence.

Oral history: An account of past events based primarily on material obtained through interviews with multiple informants.

Personality: A persistent predisposition to feel and behave in ways characteristic for the individual.

Personality capture: The process of entering substantial information about a person's mental and emotional functioning into a computer or information system, in principle sufficiently detailed to permit a somewhat realistic simulation.

Personalization: The fine-tuning of an information system or other technology that serves individual users, to suite the style and needs of one individual, thereby emulating some of that person's characteristics.

Personology: The multidisciplinary and hopefully rigorous science devoted to documenting and understanding the cognitive, emotional, and behavioral patterns of specific individual human beings.

Positive correlation: An association between two variables in which one variable tends to increase when the other also increases.

Potency: The strong-weak dimension of the Semantic Differential.

Preference questions: Items from a questionnaire that ask, explicitly or implicitly, how much the respondent likes or dislikes a series of stimuli.

Progeny: The creation of artificial intelligence agents or comparable technologies, as extensions of a person and thus incorporating some of that individual's characteristics.

Proverb memory: A person's recollection of a real event that has become simplified over time to reflect an abstract idea.

Psychobiography: The process of writing an account of the psychohistory of a person, often through the use of interviews.

Psychohistory: A scholarly account of the development of a person or society, usually emphasizing a series of stages of increasing psychological sophistication, each having typical emotional challenges.

Psychotherapeutic transformation: The use of training, interaction, or mental discipline techniques to improve the human mind.

Questionnaire: A standardized list of questions designed to obtain information from one or more respondents, whether administered on paper, via interview, or through a computer.

Recommender system: A commercial information system that compiles preference or behavioral data from customers in order to personalize its advertising.

Reliability: The quality of an item or index, such as a question in a questionnaire, that gives consistent results.

Respondent: Participant in an interview or survey who expresses personal opinions, feelings, and attitudes.

Rule-based reasoning: A classic approach to artificial intelligence that organizes information in terms of a hierarchy of if-then propositions.

Sattva: The virtual representation of a person other than the user, as in a computer-generated environment, derived from the Hindu concept of transcendent purity and thus expressing an idealized conception of the person represented.

Self-esteem: A sense of worthiness, often discussed as a global quality, but significant variations exist across different personal qualities and domains of life, for any normal individual.

Semantic Differential: A set of items in the paired-opposites format that measures the basic dimensions of meaning a particular concept possesses.

Short-term memory: The set of functions in the human brain that temporarily holds a small number of concepts or images, typically describing the person's current situation, as the basis for decisions about action.

Social desirability bias: The tendency of respondents to give socially acceptable answers to questions, putting themselves in a good light at the cost of providing inaccurate information.

Soul: The essence of a person, assumed by traditional religions to be indestructible and independent of the material world.

Spirit: A pre-scientific concept denoting the essence of a person's thought and action, better conceptualized today as a dynamic system of information.

Spuriousness: Invalidity with respect to correlations rather than to individual variables; the correlation between X and Y is spurious if it is really the result of a third variable Z.

Statistical significance: The probability that a correlation or other statistic represents a real difference rather than being the result of chance.

Subculture: A relatively small and delimited set of socially-constructed norms, beliefs, and symbols, usually sustained by a specific social group or network.

Suppressor variable: A variable in a dataset that has the effect of hiding a real relationship between phenomena that are measured by other variables with which it correlates.

Survey research: Social scientific data collection using questionnaires, interviews, or observations of a sample of the population, thus achieving results that can be generalized to the population.

Token: An hypothesized memory unit in the human brain similar to a word that represents a concept or encapsulates a connected set of memories, thus rendering complex neural traces more readily accessible for cognition.

Topic-specific self-esteem: A measure of how much people consider their personal qualities to be good in different areas of life, recognizing that global measures of self-esteem miss considerable individual variations.

Trading agent: A semi-autonomous artificial intelligence system that represents the user's economic interests in commerce or investment.

Transmigration: The movement of a human personality from one infrastructure to another, whether from one body to another, or from a biological body into a machine.

Transubstantiation: The shifting of a human personality from one kind of infrastructure to another, as from a biological body into a machine.

Utility: The principle that emulation must serve valuable purposes for other people, not only to justify its existence but also as a criterion to evaluate its quality.

Utopian transformation: Improving human behavior by establishing a greatly improved social environment that provides powerful beneficial influences.

Validity: The quality of an item or index that really does measure the phenomenon it purports to measure.

Virtual world: A computer simulated environment that resembles the real world to some degree, in which a person may be represented by an avatar.

Working memory: The system in the human brain that directs major verbal and nonverbal tasks, dynamically combining a small number of pieces of information, and probably the basis for the perception of consciousness.

Yea-saying bias: A form of response bias in which the respondent tends to agree with agree-disagree items, regardless of their content.

Printed in the United States
By Bookmasters